Greg A[...]

D[...] ♡ S0-ADM-759

please Return
after you have
Read. please
Try To get Through
This Book in
2 weeks or less
← Thanks

CONTEMPORARY ISSUES SHAPING CHINA'S CIVIL AVIATION POLICY

Contemporary Issues Shaping China's Civil Aviation Policy

Balancing International with Domestic Priorities

ALAN WILLIAMS
Massey University, New Zealand,
Cambridge University, UK
and Shanghai Jiao Tong University, China

ASHGATE

Published by
Ashgate Publishing Limited
Wey Court East
Union Road
Farnham
Surrey, GU9 7PT
England

Ashgate Publishing Company
Suite 420
101 Cherry Street
Burlington
VT 05401-4405
USA

www.ashgate.com

British Library Cataloguing in Publication Data
Williams, Alan.
  Contemporary issues shaping China's civil aviation policy :
  balancing international with domestic priorities.
  1. Aeronautics, Commercial--Economic aspects--China.
  2. Aeronautics, Commercial--Political aspects--China.
  I. Title
  387.7'095-dc22

  ISBN: 978-0-7546-7140-4 (hbk)
  ISBN: 978-0-7546-9183-9 (ebk)

Library of Congress Cataloging-in-Publication Data
Williams, Alan, 1934-
  Contemporary issues shaping China's civil aviation policy : balancing international with domestic priorities / by Alan Williams.
    p. cm.
  Includes bibliographical references and index.
  ISBN 978-0-7546-7140-4. Aeronautics, Commercial--China. 2. Airlines--China. 3. Aeronautics--Government policy--China. 4. Aeronautics and state--China. I. Title.
  HE9878.A4W55 2009
  387.70951--dc22

                                                                    2009014981

Mixed Sources
Product group from well-managed
forests and other controlled sources
www.fsc.org Cert no. SA-COC-1565
© 1996 Forest Stewardship Council

Printed and bound in Great Britain by
MPG Books Group, UK

Contents

List of Figures

List of Tables

Acknowledgements

Grateful thanks are due to Professor Peter Nolan at the Judge School of Business at Cambridge University for his generous permission to access his seminal works on modern Chinese business practice and to my colleague, Professor Malcolm Warner, at the same institution, who has done so much to advance our knowledge of human resource management and labour market practice in the People's Republic.

I am also grateful to my Chinese colleagues Professor K.Y. Fung, Dr Meiji Fong and Professor Jin Wei, whose knowledge of the dynamics of the Chinese economy has been an invaluable source of help over a number of years. I have also materially benefited from discussions with my New Zealand colleagues, Professors David Duval and Robert Yaansah, as well as graduate students in the School of Aviation at Massey University.

Acknowledgement must also be made with regard to the strong support throughout the project that has come from Guy Loft and his team at Ashgate, their patience, forbearance and many kindnesses is deeply appreciated. Finally I must thank my wife, Beverley, whose knowledge and understanding of China experienced over many years far exceeds mine. In addition her professional skills in information technology, as always, have been an essential element in bringing this work to its final form.

Alan Williams
31 January 2009

Preface

The decision to attempt a formal study of the civil aviation industry of the People's Republic of China emerged initially from my earlier work on the strategic development of international airports in East Asia. While doing the research for that project my awareness of the growing role of China as one of the major countries now shaping the international world of civil aviation began to take on a more discrete form and substance. Two other important factors then came into play.

The first involved my long time academic interest as a macro-economist in the dynamics of the interaction between economics and politics within developing countries. I was very fortunate at various times in my career to be active in the practical sense through seconded professional employment on a number of international agency projects in Africa, Southeast Asia and the Pacific. This experience was to be given a strong Chinese emphasis later, when I carried out a series of graduate teaching assignments over several years, as a visiting professor in the business schools of two major Chinese universities, Shanghai Jiao Tong and Sun Yat Sen, Guangzhou, which incidentally allowed me to formally gain access to the excellent English language archival sources of major bodies such as the Chinese Academy of Social Sciences.

In the early stages of planning a possible book on the modern development of Chinese aviation since the seminal year of 1949 I gave considerable thought to the possibility that the key stress might be given exclusively to the purely technical and operational aspects of the changes that were taking place in China, especially since 1978. After due consideration, however, I became aware that the operational dynamics driving market reform and the economic growth and development of all Chinese industries are deeply embedded within the much larger political process. This led me to the view that in order to understand the development processes driving the development of civil aviation in China, I would need to investigate the parallel evolution of the political as well as the economic drivers shaping the change process. The result is now before you for your professional consideration.

Abbreviations

AAPA	Association of Asia Pacific Airlines
ADB	Asia Development Bank
ASA	Air Service Agreement
ASEAN	Association of South East Asian Nations
ATM	Air Traffic Management
AVIC (1-2)	Aviation Industry Corporation
BCIA	Beijing Capital International Airport
BIAP	Baiyun International Airport, Guangzhou
CAAC	Civil Aviation Administration of China
CAB	Civil Aviation Bureau
CACC	Civil Aviation Corporation of China
CAIC	China Aviation Industry Corporation Group
CANSO	Civil Aviation Navigation Management Sources Organization
CAOC	China Aviation Oil Corporation
CAPA	Centre for Asia Pacific Aviation
CATA	China Air Transport Association
CCP	Communist Party of China
CEPA	Closer Economic Partnership Arrangement
CAB	Civil Aviation Bureau
CMI	Civil–Military Integration
COSCO	China Overseas Shipping Corporation
COSTIND	Commission of Science, Technology, Industry and National Defence
CNAC	China National Aviation Corporation
CPPCC	Committee of the Chinese Peoples Political Consultative Conference
DOT	Department of Transportation (United States)
EUAC	European Union Aviation Commission
FAA	Federal Aviation Authority (United States)
FDI	Foreign Direct Investment
FYP	Five-Year Plan
GCA	Grand China Airlines
GWDS	Great Western Development Strategy
HKIA	Hong Kong International Airport
IATA	International Air Transport Association
ICAO	International Civil Aviation Organization
LCCs	Low Cost Carriers
MLRNP	Mid and Long-Term Railway National Plan

MOC	Ministry of Communications
MOFTEC	Ministry of Foreign Trade and Economic Cooperation
MOR	Ministry of Railways
MOT	Ministry of Transport
MRO	Maintenance, Repair, Overhaul
NAHC	National Aviation Holding Company
NDRC	National Development Research Commission
ODI	Overseas Direct Investment
PLA	People's Liberation Army
PLAAF	People's Liberation Army Air Force
PRC	People's Republic of China
PRD	Pearl River Delta
PIAP	Pudong International Airport (Shanghai)
RMB	Renmimbi (Yuan)
SAR	Strategic Autonomous Region
SASAC	State-Owned Assets Supervision and Administration Commission
SC	State Council
SCIO	State Commission Information Office
SCP	Standing Committee of the Politbureau
SEZ	Special Economic Zone
SRE	State-Run Enterprise
SOE	State-Owned Enterprise
TAB	Technical Advisory Bureau
TVE	Town and Village Enterprises
USTDA	United States Trade and Development Agency
WTO	World Trade Organization
XAC	X'ian Aviation Corporation
YRD	Yangtze River Delta

Introduction

The Contextual Issues Shaping the Focus of the Book

The development of the civil aviation industry of the People's Republic of China as both a domestic and international transportation service in its own right has been an important item on the country's market liberalization and modernization agenda since 1978. At the same time the industry is not really an entirely new form of transportation in China. In fact from an historical perspective, it is possible to trace the introduction of some regional airline services virtually back to the origins of civil aviation itself in the early twentieth century.

In China's long experience of economic development there appears to have existed until the Communist revolution of 1949, a tendency for the frequent political tremors that afflicted the history of this vast and complex country especially in the twentieth century, to be reflected from an industrial perspective in various and complex forms of political, ideological, managerial and organizational turbulence.

With the accession to power of the Chinese Communist Party (CCP) in 1949, the civil aviation industry entered a period of stability in which its role as an important mode of transport was subsumed, within the larger ideological and political issues that shaped Mao Zedong's perceptions of what might constitute China's economic, political and administrative future. With regard to the very important question of transportation development, in a country that had experienced, intermittent conflict and later all out war since the 1900s, civil aviation was to find itself linked in a multimodal developmental relationship with roads, railways, waterways and maritime services all dedicated to the role of agencies whose first obligation was to ensure the advancement of the new political order.

It is a persistent obligation that has continued to a very large extent to this very day. For while the world has seen China make giant strides in the reform, liberalization and modernization of its national economy, coupled to an expansion outward into the growing world of international business and trade, the ultimate control and authority that has sanctioned these changes since 1978 remains vested within the operational context of a single-party government as exemplified in the dominant presence of the Chinese Communist Party (CCP). In other words while the active conceptualization of economic and social reforms have changed markedly from a command economy to an increasingly mixed market format, the official location and continuity in office of the CCP as the ultimate power in the state has not really changed since 1949.

It was my original intention to focus exclusively on the technical and managerial changes that had shaped the growth and development of the various sub-sectors of the civil aviation sector since the introduction of market reform based on the process of gradualism that began historically in 1978, two years after the death of Mao Zedong. The realization that this was too narrow a perspective emerged as I began to study the larger motivational and political forces that have underpinned the reform process since Deng Xiaoping sent the CCP on the continuing search for socialism with Chinese characteristics after his appointment as a key office holder in the party leadership.

Political leadership in China has passed through four generations since 1949 and will by the end of this decade, be about to transfer the leadership of the CCP to the fifth in the series. From an ideological perspective, the government holds to the firm belief that the motivation for reform has been an essentially a continuous process from 1949 to 2008. In other words the changes that began with Deng did not signal a sharp break with the immediate past and an attempt to return to the capitalist road. His real concern was rather to change the direction, pace and policy content of economic reform set in place by Mao, while retaining at the same time the role of the CCP as the primary focus of political and economic power in perpetuity.

This led me after due consideration to the view that the study of civil aviation in China, from an exclusively operational and technical perspective, really misses some essential and large problematics that are found in what can best be called the underlying political aspects of the industry's total role. These may be found as working examples, in the intensely vertical and hierarchical nature of the central planning and decision-making process as reflected in the evolving and often controversial range of duties and tasks undertaken by the civil aviation ministry commonly known as the CAAC.

The managerial confusion that has surrounded the structural shifts from airline market consolidation to deregulation and back again, offers a set of rich examples of the failure of good intentions. In addition some serious limitations on market growth have been caused by the authority granted by the national aviation law to the military, which allows the air force to maintain a significant control over aircraft entry into domestic air space.

This has often been detrimental at times in all matters relating to the operational efficiency of the commercial airline services.

In sum the continuing need to balance the study of the industry within a constant duality that shapes the subsequent interactions between its industrial and its political dimensions, will actively shape this particular study of the ongoing reform process in Chinese civil aviation.

The book comprises a series of 12 chapters which attempt to bring into perspective a selected number of important themes and issues. These have been developed and written from an overarching contemporary perspective which is based on a range of multidisciplinary viewpoints. It is also important to bear in mind that the study attempts to identify a selected number of issues, and does not claim to be a total and comprehensive analysis.

This is because the range and complexity of the issues underlying the reform movement is the product of a constant developmental intensity in the market, which is often subject to rapid changes of policy direction in the very short run. With this in mind and to paraphrase a distinguished colleague, a week can be an extended period of time in Chinese politics.

A second-order problem arises from the fact that the range and quality of available data on the aviation industry is often quite limited in its content, age, frequency and value in terms of any attempt to develop a valid and consistent longitudinal analysis. In other words the researcher is sometimes dominated in the search for evidence by the sheer size, complexity, scale and ambiguous validity of some data sources. In addition the predictive power of a given attempt at analysis, may often be offset by a sudden change of policy direction on the part of a particular agency.

As a direct consequence the primary stress throughout this work is largely focused upon strategic policy issues that are constantly evolving and frequently multifunctional in their operational range and purpose. It is also concerned with the question of the balance of priorities between the demands of the market and the larger geopolitical objectives of central government. These are more complex than is generally realized, given the fact that the state also possesses a significant financial stake in the equity bases of all of the institutional activities that take place in the aviation industry.

The Themes and Issues to be Addressed in the Chapter Sequence

The Evolutionary Pathway of Chinese Market Reform

The book will open with an attempt to trace the evolutionary path of market reform in China. It will do so by adopting, for the purpose of analysis, the conventional ideological assumption held in the external world that the reforms in 1978 took a radical change of direction from a path that began in 1949, as originally defined by the Chinese Communist Party.

The route will take us through the introduction of gradualism in reform, introduced in the second generation, then on to the shift toward the Three Represents in the third generation, before turning to the Scientific Development approach adopted by the current leadership.

The chapter will then review these ideological approaches in sequence before examining their effects on the administrative and managerial aspects of the reform process. It will conclude with an introductory examination of the ways and means in which civil aviation's key administrative agency, the CAAC, was shaped and reshaped by changing regulations and rules.

The Dimensional Roles of Civil Aviation in China

Chapters 2 and 3 will then address the ways in which civil aviation was required to respond, first to its role within the larger context of the national plan for a multimodal transportation system. This will then be followed by a review of the change in strategic and operational direction that has required the aviation industry to actively contribute toward the current development of those central and western provinces that have yet to enjoy the full benefits of economic development through market reform.

Chapter 4 returns the thematic focus in more precise detail to the consequential effects of the massive administrative reforms required by the fundamental change of managerial direction that replaced all the state-run enterprises with the introduction of state ownership. The discussion will pay specific and detailed attention to the civil aviation industry. It will also act as a gateway point leading into a sequence of chapters that will then address specific sectoral activities within aviation.

The Consequences of Administrative Reform for Aviation Operations

The extremely turbulent history of the domestic reform of airline industry will be featured in some detail, ranging from the initial introduction of liberalization to the major consolidation that has shaped the present administrative system that now covers private as well as stated-owned carriers. Chapter 5 will also cover the very important role played by foreign direct investment in civil aviation, after its general introduction across industry. It will also examine the dominant role of the three major state-owned carriers since the government introduced a return to market consolidation earlier in the current decade.

Attention will be turned in Chapter 6 to the decision by Chinese carriers to enter the international passenger market. It will consider their strategic intentions in detail, especially in relation to the decisions by three airlines to obtain membership in two of the leading global airline alliances. Discussion will also cover the expansion of external services by Chinese carriers which have been based on a wide ranging increase in the number of bilateral market entry agreements. These have been completed with the United States and the European Union, the largest and busiest aviation markets in the world, and with over 100 other sovereign states.

The role of air cargo services becomes the primary theme of Chapter 7. Its strategic importance for both the domestic and international sectors of China's industries has been recognized by the launch of several new and specialized carriers, both by the major airlines as well as new private and joint venture companies. There has also been an expansion in the number and range of international express carriers who are in the process of setting up their own dedicated facilities at key hub airports.

The actual distribution of airline services in China is heavily skewed, with the bulk of routes to be found within a virtual triangle that encompasses the core hubs located in Beijing in the northeast, Shanghai to the south east and Guangzhou in the southwest. While Beijing is landlocked, both the other sites are strategically placed on two of China's primary river systems, the Yangtze and the Pearl. Together they constitute the leading edge of the domestic aviation industry in all of its operational aspects. Chapter 7 will examine both their current domestic as well as their international roles as aviation centres located within what are continually expanding urban conurbations. These all contain a number of major international airports, as well as important aerospace firms. In the case of Beijing the focus will be directly on the important city of Tianjin, which serves as an entrepot for Beijing in Bohai Bay, and which is building an integrated aviation city which will house in future a multifunctional series of activities.

The Quest for Operational Viability in Other Aerospace Sectors

The reform process in China's aviation industry has expanded its range of activities to include plans to design and operate a range of operational activities that will include aircraft manufacturing and the targeted production of an indigenous wide-bodied jet passenger aircraft by the year 2020. The current game plan incorporates a wide range of activities including joint ventures with foreign contractors, a closer integration between civil and military production and the structural reform of major domestic firms in order to accommodate the development programme.

Chapter 9 will commence with a review of the macro-strategy which underpins the significant range of structural changes proposed in the previous discussion. It will also examine the detailed commitments that are currently being made to prepare and locate the necessary production sites that will be brought on line.

Chapter 10 will then, in turn, consider the many and various organizational problems that confront the government's future plans, as China attempts to enter an international market driven by high technology firms within what has become a highly integrated and cross-border management system. It will also examine in some detail the significant ambiguities that are currently to be found in current Chinese expectations that their already scheduled goals can actually be met.

Chapter 11 will approach China's international ambitions from another dimension. It will examine a range of topics commencing with the growing relationship between China's negotiations with the ASEAN member states with regard to a free trade agreement. This has expanded to some degree to include the possibility of a further role within the proposed 'open skies' agreement covering the member states that is planned to come on line by 2015. Discussion will also include the potential strategic advantages that might emerge within the larger context of China's future role as a leading player within the region.

The final chapter that rounds out the book will consider and review the direction now being taken by China with regard to the future of its civil aviation policies. It will take into consideration the current uncertainties that confront the industry on a global basis, and their consequences for current growth expectations, which in China as elsewhere have already led to the call for and release of considerable subsidies to the major state carriers. The chapter will also come full circle with a brief and necessarily speculative commentary on the emergent fifth generation of CPC leadership, whose tasks after entry into office, will include the future strategic guidance of the civil aviation industry.

Chapter 1
The Evolutionary Path of Market Reform in China 1949–2008

Any attempt to analyse and measure the organizational and operational impact of the fundamental changes taking place in the civil aviation industry of China, must first take into account the fact that the country has been undergoing consistent periods of political and economic reform since the Communist revolution of 1949. What the world has seen in more recent times, after China opened up to foreign direct investment and increasing degrees of market privatization, is the progressive shaping of an emergent economic entity with the potential to become a global economic power. From a domestic perspective this goal has been locked within a consistent political quest for national economic and social stability under a single-party government, which is not subject to any direct political or revolutionary challenges by alternative groups seeking administrative control over the state.

From a more specific industrial perspective, that will inform the various aspects of this study, the various state agencies charged with the task of industrial development appear to be seeking a dual outcome. The creation of a strong, efficient and competitive domestic and international aviation industry, able to enter and compete successfully in both the domestic and the growing international market as a leading player, may be perceived as the central reformist objective. At the same time government also sees the industry as a valuable tool serving the broader aims of national economic development increasingly on a multiple regional basis. The dynamic interaction between these dimensions, political stability, comprehensive market reform on a national basis, and a larger role in the global economy tends to create a strategic interaction which will both underpin and influence the themes and issues that shape this book.

Having emerged as a major economic force both regionally and internationally, China now faces a second-order need to develop what can be called a coherent national economy as a response to the fact that its economic geography comprises what has been called by Meyer (2008) one country with many markets. The policy also has a geopolitical aspect which aims to assist in the enhancement of China's conscious role and identity as a growing super-economy with an eventual global outreach.

In a overt real sense China shares a degree of communality with other countries in the East Asian region, notably Vietnam, that have been consistently seeking over the last 30 years to liberalize their traditional roles as command economies, both internally and in the external perceptions of other national states. In the Chinese case the sheer magnitude of physical geography, demography and resource availability does require that the People's Republic (PRC) be treated as a unique and special case. This is because the civil aviation industry is seen by the national government, not only as a transportation service, but also as a major instrument for advancing larger strategic objectives within both the national and the international economy.

Returning to the domestic perspective, the government has been well aware for some time that there is currently a chronic geographical imbalance in the flow on to the people at large of the material benefits that have been obtained from some 30 years of active market liberalization and deregulation. This is particularly apparent when levels of economic growth are assessed, which compare the eastern and southern coastal provinces on the one hand and the western and northern provinces on the other.

As the current Chinese government is acutely aware, the material benefits flowing from such market liberalization and some degree of corporate privatization, have been very largely enjoyed by the populations of the eastern and southern provinces, especially in the special enterprise zones and their key cities that are found in the physical parameters of the Beijing–Guangzhou–Shanghai geographical triangle. Popular estimates of the material gains made by other regional populations have suggested that up to 700 million citizens are yet to share fully in the fruits of economic growth, in a population whose official size is 1.3 billion.

It is also difficult to identify the basic motivation that has shaped the reforms that have taken place in China over the last 30 years, without taking into consideration, as already noted earlier, the fact that the Chinese Communist Party (CCP) still remains in control of the overall management of the reform process, both politically and economically. In fact the power to decide the current directions being taken by that process is now vested in the fourth generation of CCP leadership to take office since the death of Mao Zedong in 1976.

This chapter will attempt, as a prelude to the more detailed and technical study of the impact of various reforms on the civil aviation industry, to conduct a review of the ideological and policy dynamics that have shaped the growth of the Chinese economy since the CCP came to power in 1949. The purpose in doing so is to identify the earlier political and economic imperatives which have done much to shape both the strategic direction and the required components of managerial control in the civil aviation industry over the last 30 or so years.

Cognizance will also be taken during further discussion of the significant shifts in traditional communist ideology that have done so much to shape what has become popularly known as the search for socialism with Chinese characteristics. This is largely because the changes in ideological direction that have marked the post-Maoist era in China would simply not have been strategically possible in the years between 1949 and 1976, now recognized as the age of total power vested in Mao as the ultimate leader.

In order to give the reform process a chronological context over time, the discussion that follows will address a number of themes in a linked sequence. After an initial series of comments on the very long history of the search for political stability and economic growth in China, the first set of themes will address the period 1949 to 1976, in which what can be termed Maoist concepts of market reform were the dominant influence on government strategy.

This will be followed by a consideration of the various processes instigated post-1978 by Deng Xiaoping, as the ideologically creative leader of the second generation of reformers. The focus of discussion will then consider the changes associated with the third generation of CCP leadership and exemplified by the Three Represents introduced by Jiang Zemin and Zhu Rongii. It will then conclude with a consideration of the shift toward the Scientific Concept of Development introduced and led in the fourth generation by Hu Jintao and Wen Jiabao who will in turn be superseded by the fifth generation in 2012–13.

Some Preliminary Comments on the Search for Market Reform with Chinese Characteristics

Commencing in 1978, the People's Republic of China began a new process of market liberalization and structural reform that has been marked in one sense by an ideological break with its revolutionary past, as well as a somewhat unique approach to the structural modification of what had been a conventional command economy. What has popularly been referred to as the privatization of the market system, has been reflective of considerable success when GDP as well as FDI growth in China is compared with Russia and the numerous other Eastern European countries which have undertaken structural market and political reforms over the last 30 years.

From a political perspective comparisons with China's ideological *alter ego*, Russia, reveal an important distinction that helps highlight fundamental differences in strategy between what were the two largest Communist states in the world. In Russia's case the search for structural economic and social reform ended with the literal abandonment as the dominant national ideology of Marxism–Leninism. As a consequence Russia's chosen strategy tended to follow the 'big-bang' approach proposed by the World Bank and IMF, which was reflective of both the abandonment of the Keynesian tradition of market management and the rise and influence of neo-classical theory as the basis of government policy. In the language of the professional economist, the intellectual centre of gravity was shifted from Cambridge to Chicago.

This led in turn to the momentous decision in 1991, with Boris Yeltsin as leader, to virtually abandon after more than 70 years the USSR as a formal and federally unified political entity. The consequence has seen the development of a federation of independent sovereign states, the constitutional legality of which according to Asland (2007) and Service (2002) remains very controversial to this day. In the event the consequences were to result in confusion and instability. This has led in more recent times to a return to an increasing degree of political centralism exemplified during the term of Presidential office enjoyed by Vladimir Putin, whose influence now continues albeit in the role of Prime Minister.

By contrast, the official Chinese approach to economic and social reform claims to reflect a high degree of ideological continuity in the CCP's use of that term. The strategies that have been adopted in what is now described as the age of post-Maoism exhibit a high degree of gradualism, though some commentators would suggest that a pragmatic willingness to try anything once has prevailed on numerous occasions. Indeed there is evidence that gradualism has been virtually abandoned where manifest failure of a given initiative becomes apparent, as some of the matters to be discussed below will attest.

It follows logically that the ideological inputs that underlie Chinese reform strategies as they have evolved since 1978, are really reflective of the traditional balance of factional powers that exists within the CCP and which shape the relationships that exist between the various members of the Central Committee of the Politburo, the State Council and the military (PLA), all with their various perspectives and often factional claims for control of the reform process. With this important assumption in mind, we can now move the focus of discussion toward the history of the reform movement in modern China, beginning with the attempts made in the Maoist era to give a Marxist–Leninist form and substantive substance to both economic growth and political stability.

China's Market Reform under Mao Zedong: 1949–76

The success of the CCP in gaining absolute power in 1949, after the Kuomintang's defeat and the departure of Chiang Kai Shek to Taiwan was, in the reformist sense as many historians will attest, simply another opening chapter in the history of a very ancient civilization. We should therefore begin discussion with an acknowledgement of the fact that the political history of China from earliest times can be described as a consistent search for some sort of dynamic balance between political, economic and administrative power in a very large and complex country. For several thousand years beginning before the advent of Christianity its has been observed by Gray (1990) and Chow (2007) that successive generations of leaders located at some nominal political centre have tried to bring peace, prosperity and effective managerial control to a country with a very complex natural geography, and a significant number of cultural minorities who stand physically and socially apart from the dominant majority that comprises the Han people.

In turn the physical geography of the state requires that China attempt to protect its many international borders, after a long history of successive invasions. Like India, China was often subject in its long history to military incursions across its many frontiers, one of the most powerful of which was led by Genghis Khan, whose advent was to lead to the creation of the Manchu imperial dynasty. Attempts in the long age of the Middle Kingdom to manage so diverse a country as China from a national capital, first in X'ian and later in Beijing, were also subject to considerable modification at the remote periphery according to the balance of power in regional locations that was held by various clans and warlords. In other words it was the authority and control of events by such actors in specific and often rural localities and remote communities that decided whether, for example, a government edict in the name of the Emperor should be obeyed or simply ignored, in the absence of the imperial power to impose compliance.

Dynastic rule was to be actively superseded in the nineteenth century by the physical entry of the major Western powers who post-1850, took a high degree of economic and political control over the economy. It is an irony of history that this happened, suggests Quah (2002) and Chow (2007), at a time when China had developed the economic potential, had it been allowed to remain an autonomous and sovereign state, to become a major part of the international industrial revolution then underway in Britain, Europe and later the United States. It is now generally acknowledged that this period of political domination became increasingly strong after the arrival of the expatriate businessmen bringing investment capital into China. The period of foreign economic domination symbolically reinforced by the international military response to the Boxer rebellion at the turn of the twentieth century, tends to remain a major source of psychological embarrassment within the Chinese culture, down to the present time.

The twentieth century in turn was a period that simply increased the range and complexity of confusion and political chaos. With the abdication of the Qing dynasty's Dowager Empress in 1911, China was to undergo a further period of considerable instability, as the initial attempts at Republican reform directed by Sun Yat-Sen failed to gain real political traction throughout China. In the absence of a consensual and viable political system, the country was to experience further uncertainties exacerbated rurally by the localized control of various warlords over the more remote regions. Tensions and hostilities deepened in the 1930s with the Japanese invasion of Manchuria and its military expansion into China, events which subsequently brought China into World War II.

The end of international hostilities in 1945 did not restore political calm to China. In fact the second half of the decade was to see open civil war between the CCP and the Kuomintang. Finally and after the collapse of the Chang Kai Shek's government and the successful Communist takeover in 1949, a new and structural attempt to reform China both politically and economically, got underway. So dawned the age of Marxist–Leninism, with an ideological model of economic and social progress based on the experience of the Soviet Union, which had nurtured the political education of a number of future Asian revolutionaries including a number of future Chinese leaders.

The party cadres that supported Mao in the period from 1949 to his death in 1976, constituted the first generation of the post-revolutionary reform movement in China. They were to share suggests Gelber (2007) with the second generation which is now symbolized ideologically by Deng Xiaoping's thought, a common heritage and experience as natives of Shanghai and the central Yangtze valley. As a result they tended, with the notable exception of Zhou Enlai, to present something of a common viewpoint and perspective on economic and social change based mainly on their own personal and hard won practical experiences of the revolution.

Mao's own perception of economic reform was, in the 1950s, to be grounded in a strong belief in the growth of heavy industry as the core agent of change. The successful strategy of industrialization as he perceived it required a dynamic balance to be struck between the heavy industry core, with steel as its primary output and the agricultural industry, with an attendant spin-off growth of light industry offering material support. In his view this would allow both the latter sectors to act as supportive producers of equity for further investment in heavy industry.

The government also passed the controlling authority over the development programme observes Saich (2001) to bureaucrats and managers in the designated state-run enterprises (SREs). The implementation of these strategic objectives, following the Soviet model was to be carried out through three five-year plans (FYPs) commencing in 1953. The production targets set were expected to have an important political outcome, through the gradual socialization of the processes of industrialization and the successful raising of the general level of living standards for the entire population.

With considerable hindsight, there appeared to be a general consensus in later official publications according to Guogang and Wensen (1987) that a logical and consistent strategy required that a gradualist path would need to be followed if the policy was to be successful. This would have allowed the second five-year plan, beginning in 1959, to build sequentially on the gains made by the first plan in order to further advance the building of a socialist market infrastructure. It seems that no attempt was made to plan for the medium to long term, as the first FYP inevitably began to lose its sense of economic direction

What happened next was not an evaluation of current progress and a search for solutions to apparent problems, but rather the literal abandonment of any potential for economic growth through gradualism, beginning with Mao's famous edict in 1956, 'let a hundred flowers blossom, let a hundred schools of thought contend'. Symbolically he was calling for artists, writers and academic researchers to critically debate the concepts and ideas driving their work. But his real intention was to both raise and retain the dominant ideological and grass roots consciousness perhaps best described as revolutionary zeal, that he believed might be overshadowed by the introduction of the second five-year plan (FYP). His call in fact was to bring about a major change of strategic direction that in the event, was to herald a long period of increasingly ideological and economic instability.

Under the Great Leap Forward (GLF), gradualism was virtually abandoned in favour of a speeding up the rate of industrial production. Using the motto, surpass Britain and catch up with America, Mao called for China's economic development to concentrate totally on the growth of heavy industry. This directive also required that the work efforts of the entire population of the PRC should be focussed on the production of steel, with an ordained target to be set for the growth of steel production. In the absence of any real understanding of the sheer technological difficulties involved in building an industry which required such a highly integrated production system, what followed was little short of an industrial disaster.

The call actually produced the age of the backyard furnace and a fragmented and confused working population. It also led to further social reorganization of the work process as described by Ma Hong (1990) with the rise of the commune movement and the introduction of work brigades (Danwei), together with the abandonment of piece-rate wage systems and the return of private peasant land holdings to the state.

Unfortunately the timeframe set for the GLF – 1959 to 1961 – was to see the Chinese economy experience an extremely lean period of growth, as the gap between planning perceptions and output realities started to grow. Massive shortages of even basic items such as paper were accompanied by very serious famine in the countryside. The deaths of some eight million people during this period were officially admitted, while unofficial estimates ran from 12–20 million and even much higher.

It was not until 1962, that market supplies and industrial production in general actually reached pre-GLF levels. In addition, from a geopolitical perspective, China's departure from the strategic parameters set by the previous reform experiences of the Soviet Union, also led to a major and negative shift in the two countries diplomatic alignment. This signalled in turn, Moscow's fundamental ideological disagreement with Mao's aims and policy directions, which attempted to actually by-pass the bureaucracy by appealing directly to the revolutionary zeal of the mass of peasant society. It was in a very real and symbolic sense to be a dress rehearsal for the Cultural Revolution.

The Replacement of High Risk Strategies with a More Cautious Pragmatism

The importance of the breakdown in the Beijing–Moscow relationship spelled possible disaster for China. The Russians had, since 1949, been active in influencing the development of China's growth strategies, supporting their presence in the country, with both the requisite technology and specialist expertise. In 1959, however, Moscow placed a restriction on any further information being passed to Beijing and, in 1960, all expatriate Russian personnel were withdrawn from China. The subsequent period as already noted was to see increasing and often open hostility between the world's two largest Communist states.

At the same time the departure of the Russians inspired those planners with a more pragmatic view of China's developmental needs to propose a strategy based on readjustment, consolidation, filling out and raising standards. What became known as the Four Modernizations focussed upon a comprehensive need to develop industry, agriculture, defence and science and technology. While this strategy gained important support from Zhou Enlai at the Third National People's

Congress in 1964, it failed to be fully taken up at party level until 14 years later. In the meantime the CCP faced increasing periods of ideological confrontation between left and right and a growing factionalism on and into the 1970s.

The balance of Mao's life also coincided with a time of increasing tension and conflict within the actual leadership of the CCP. Matters worsened as the division between the ideologically correct 'leftists' and the more pragmatic 'rightists' began to become increasingly subject to destabilization with the growth of identifiable political factions, each one driving specific and different political agendas.

Attempts have been made to explain from a macro-theoretical perspective the underlying historical and cultural factors that informed political activity during Mao Zedong's term as a virtually unchallenged leader. It has been suggested by one contemporary scholar of Chinese politics (Baum, 1994) that when governments in China over the centuries have decided on political and economic modernization as a major policy goal, historical experience has traditionally produced a growing tension between stability and order followed by confusion and chaos. He goes on to further suggest that reform has a paradoxical dynamic which operates over four stages: flexibility–disorder–control–rigidity. As a cycle of events, flexibility is followed by disorder, which then brings about greater control. This in turn produces rigidity over time, which then begins the cycle again as it signals the need to return to flexibility.

The model gained some degree of empirical credence with the beginning of the Cultural Revolution in August 1966, ostensibly under the direction of Mao but driven by his wife Jiang Qing and the Gang of Four. The call to action later symbolized by the primary role to be played by the Red Guards, was based on what Mao perceived to be a need for the ideological purification of the party. His further exhortation that the masses should learn from the peasants and begin to denounce capitalist roaders, found its trigger in the symbolic call to tertiary students to rebel. Unfortunately, as often happens in such circumstances, the behaviours that followed made it very difficult to establish any coherent and common purpose that could be formulated into a much needed shift toward more constructive action.

Debate also continues over Mao's ultimate strategic motives and his apparent determination to by-pass the conventional bureaucratic institutions of the state in favour of a return to more grass roots form of political organization. Further confusion and internecine conflict continued until the death of Mao in 1976. There followed the election to the leadership of Mao's reputed nominee Hua Guofeng. His term of office was to be relatively brief and he is now largely remembered for the fact that during his time as leader, sustained with the material assistance of the PLA, he saw the Gang of Four finally brought to trial in November 1980.

During his relatively short period in office, Hua attempted to increase economic growth using a return to foreign trade as the strategic element. The result that followed saw a surge in the import of capital goods. This led the leadership to abandon ideological resistance to foreign borrowing, but the results, largely compounded by waste and poor management, did much to bring about the replacement of Hua Guofeng by Deng Xiaoping.

The Political Re-emergence of Deng Xiaoping

A first generation cadre and native of Sichuan, Deng literally survived the major troubles of the 1960s in the physical sense of the term. He suffered dismissal and torture during the Cultural Revolution, but was then brought back into political favour in 1973 by Chou Enlai, becoming both Vice Premier and Chief of Staff of the PLA in 1975. Media attacks by the Gang of Four in the same year saw him removed yet again from office.

With the death of his political mentor, Zhou Enlai, in 1976, his political future became inextricably involved with the growing momentum for more balanced and stable forms of leadership within the CCP. This was confirmed in 1976 by Hua Guofeng's call for his rehabilitation and the formal revision of the fifth five-year plan which was then in turn to be locked into the earlier call to adopt the Four Modernizations. In 1977, Deng Xiaoping was formally restored to his previous posts in government at the 11th CCP Conference. His return to office allowed him to lead the processes of selection and election of party officials who had opposed the excesses of the Cultural Revolution. In December of the following year, the future of reform in China was set on the track it has since followed with a stress on the strategic objectives listed in Figure 1.1.

From an ideological perspective these proposals were reinforced at the Citizens' Congress (CCPCC) during the now famous Third Plenum. The Cultural Revolution was formally designated a natural disaster, with Mao's decisions categorized as a left mistake. More importantly the further statement that he had been correct for 70 per cent of his time in office was clearly intended to demythologize his status, which had reached semi-divine proportions in some segments of, especially, rural society. The most important aspect of the strategy was the call for the abandonment of the mass movement approach to economic development, which had finally emerged as a much needed stable counterweight to the period of confusion that followed after Mao's death.

- Expansion of rural incomes and production incentives.
- Encouragement of experiments in formulating the enterprise autonomy.
- Reduction of the total reliance on central planning.
- Establishment of forms of direct foreign investment in China.

Figure 1.1   Strategic Objectives Emerging from the Four Modernizations

Adapted from: *Focus on Asia Studies* Vol. VI, No. 1 (New York: Columbia University 1984).

In 1979, Deng set forth the four cardinal principles (Figure 1.2) which were to guide the processes of political reform. It is noticeable that their formulation gave stress to the view that reform was not a structural break with the past, but rather a natural change of direction which sustained at its centre a stress on ideological continuity. In other words the liberalization process was to stop short of any form of change that would alter the hegemonic role of the CCP as the primary agent of change.

Underlying these slogans was the resultant decision that the chosen instrument to initiate and develop the reform process was going to be the CCP itself. As we will see in later discussion this has remained a consistent principle over time, despite the continuing presence of factions of both conservative and moderate ideological persuasions

The final confirmation of Deng's status as the acknowledged leader of the new reform process came in 1980, when he became an appointed member of an operational triad which included the Secretary-General of the CCP, Hu-Yao Bang, and the Premier Zhao Ziyang. Deng himself retained his Vice-Premiership as well as his membership of the Politburo. His key position however was his post as PLA Chief of Staff. Unlike his successors in the third and fourth generation Deng did not during his lifetime, become either President or Premier of the PRC, though lack of such status did nothing to diminish his real authority.

In the administrative and managerial sense of the term, what was created by 1980 was a balance of power that had not been possible during the 1960s under the leadership of Mao Zedong. From the perspective of the pragmatic reform camp that was now assembled under Deng Xiaoping, a relatively strong degree of stability could be assured simply because the ruling triad had clearly constituted a degree of common purpose within what was really a PLA–CCP and bureaucratic coalition.

- Keep to the Socialist Road.
- Uphold the Dictatorship of the Proletariat.
- Uphold the Leadership of the Communist Party.
- Uphold Marxism–Leninism and Mao Zedong's Thought.

Figure 1.2   Four Cardinal Principles that Shaped the Political Reform Process

Adapted from: Deng Xiaoping (1985), *Building Socialism with Chinese Characteristics.*

The Instigation and Growing Momentum of the Reform Process

Beginning in the symbolic year of 1978, China's leadership asserted that they would abandon traditional ideological approaches to reform in favour of a search for truth from facts. What was heralded by this decision was the arrival of pragmatic solutions for definable problems as a real working strategy. This approach is reflected in Deng's much quoted comment that the colour of the cat did not matter as long as the mice got caught. What he meant to signal was the fact that in the future the superiority of practicality and efficiency over ideological purity was to be the primary driver of planning and strategy.

Despite the magnitude of the changes which were put in train by Deng, it is worth remembering at this point, that there remained at the core of the new pragmatism, a strong commitment to the continuity of the dominant role of the CPC as the governing force in the new politics. There follows a number of examples of policies that emerged as a direct consequence of Deng's leadership.

The Implementation of Major Reforms post-1979

The year 1979 was to see the National People's Congress (NPC) confirm the approval of strategies that would promote both foreign direct investment (FDI) and international trade. During the same year the Peoples Congress of Guangdong province, which contains the highly strategic Pearl River Delta (PRD) approved the designation of Shenzhen, Zhuhai, Macau and Shantou as initial special enterprise zones. (SEZs).

This process was to be extended in the coastal provinces over the next few years with some 14 coastal cities able to tap into the resultant inflow of FDI. In the 1980s the concept of household responsibilities was to be introduced, with the resultant removal of communes and work brigades. By 1984 government was addressing the very difficult question of how to change the formal and operational status of state-run enterprises (SREs). These had emerged under Mao as operational entities in which actual ownership was perceived to be ideologically vested in the masses, while the state provided the requisite management services.

Reform planning was to later include a provision that would allow under-performing SREs to file for bankruptcy, but this was not formally introduced until 1994, due to possible social unrest as unemployment inevitably rose. Success was achieved in another important direction by the fact that the introduction of a fiscal contract system in 1980 had become generally accepted in various formats by most of the former SRE sector.

Establishing the Modern Enterprise System

The 1990s was to mark an important ideological victory for deregulation as the basis of the ongoing reform strategy. At the core was the acceptance of the concept of a socialist market economy. This was to see a consequential range of reforms that virtually re-shaped business practice along market-based lines. After some major changes in banking practice, by 1994, the policy of grasping the large and releasing the small signalled the determination of government to introduce two important structural changes.

The first step introduced in 1995 called for 1,000 businesses which were already classified as successful large enterprises to be reduced through merger, acquisition and amalgamation, to 300 world class businesses, with an elite few of this final number able to compete successfully in global markets. In addition small SREs were to be either privatized, or see their businesses contracted out. Where neither option was viable, enforced bankruptcy was to become the ultimate tool of market clearance.

By 1998, at the 9th NPC, the success obtained by the pragmatic reformists reached a new pinnacle. The Congress approved an amendment to Article 6 of the PRC Constitution. As a direct consequence the traditional convention of ownership vested in the people was to be superseded by the concept of state ownership as the main form of control over the means of production. Through due process, SREs were to be re-designated as state-owned enterprises (SOEs). This was done on the grounds that individual, private and other forms of non-public ownership, according to Jaggi, *et al.* (1996), are important components of a socialist economy since they can effectively act as a supplementary force complementing the system of socialist public ownership.

This was a monumental change, since it endorsed and made possible both FDI in Chinese business and the further location in China of foreign firms wishing to maximize the wide range of market benefits that would (and have) ensued from such a move. A further and important endorsement of this course of action was revealed in 2001, when after 15 years of waiting, China was provisionally admitted to the World Trade Organization.

The period until his death in 1997, was to see Deng maintain his role as the dominant visionary of the CCP, despite the fact that did no occupy the conventional top offices of state. From a gradualist perspective, he had defined a continuing and progressive role for the CCP, while at the same time he had also shaped the future agendas of the next generations of leadership.

The Notable Absence of Fundamental Political Reform Strategies

The considerable changes wrought by economic reform in what is now termed the period of second generation leadership, were not emulated in parallel developments of any serious commitments to innovative and structural political change. This, despite the fact that Deng had very critically warned of the dangers of bureaucracy and the over-concentration of its power, together with a tendency to cling to outmoded organizational practices, as deleterious for the further developments of the reform programme. At the same time, one has to remember that Deng's reformism vision did not include a Russian style of approach in which the concept of *glasnost* had a primary role. Through his time in power, his basic concern was always the need to guarantee the continuity of the role of the CCP as the key agent and engine of structural change.

Unfortunately, discussions aimed at the development of a new reformist strategy, that would include over time possible democratic components launched in 1987 at the 13th Party Congress, were to be derailed by the Tiananmen Square protests of 1989. The focus by students and workers on corruption and the knock-on effects of economic deregulation as a cause of rising unemployment was perceived as a direct threat to the CCP's continuing position as a reformist party, and the PLA came down with extreme force in order to establish control over the demonstrators.

At the same time it is important to note that while the Tiananmen Square tragedy did considerably reduce the momentum of reform, it did not bring to a final halt subsequent and innovative attempts to change the constitutional and operational roles of the CCP in the interests of greater administrative and economic efficiencies. In that sense continuity was assured beyond the second generation of reform, which came to an end with Deng himself.

Leadership in the Third Generation and the Three Represents: 1997–2003

With the death of Deng Xiaoping the key leadership posts of the CCP, passed to Jiang Zhemin and Zhu Rongji, who were representative of the third generation of political leadership. As engineering graduates of two of China's most prestigious universities, Tsinghua (Beijing) and Shanghai Jiao Tong, their appointments marked a substantive change in the professional component of political leadership in China. The new appointees heralded a degree of technocratic shift in management since many of their colleagues in government had also had tertiary training as engineers in the Soviet Union as well as in China.

The new leadership emerged from the Shanghai party base, known colloquially to this day as the Shanghai gang, where they had held office in turn as Mayor and Party Chief. It is a matter of no small importance that when in office as President and Premier respectively, they did not enjoy very cordial relationships at the personal level. On the other hand, their time in mutual office between 1998 and 2003, saw a period of major economic growth, with Zhu Rongji as the primary agent. In turn Jiang Zemin, whose somewhat flamboyant personality and multilingual skills were not popular with some of his Politburo colleagues, did much to advance China's diplomatic relationships overseas especially with the United States and Russia.

From an ideological perspective Jiang's concept of the Three Represents was to become official dogma at the 16th Congress of the CCP in 2002. It called for the party to become a focus for China's advanced social productive forces and its emergent culture as well as the locus of membership for the vast majority of the country's citizens. It seems that what Jiang had in mind was an image of the CCP as a truly national ruling party, rather than as the traditional vanguard of the revolution. The implicit presumption that open membership signalled access for the growing number of capitalist roaders that were emerging with the acceleration of economic growth also meant that critics of these changes saw the model proposed by the Three Represents as little more than the legitimization of capitalism which was represented in the practical sense by a rapidly burgeoning business class.

The further and more contentious argument has also been advanced that what Jiang really had in mind was a more democratic form of government, rather than a strictly Communist system. It appears however that the significant ideological shift proposed by the Three Represents did not gain much traction since it did not make large-scale and material progress either within the CCP or the larger populace, despite the fact that it was officially endorsed as a successor and extension ideology of Dengist thought. With the retirement of Zhu Rongji in 2003 to be followed by Jiang Zhemin in 2004, the stage was set for the emergence of the fourth generation of leadership and with it the introduction of a socio-economic ideology with what is effectively the current brand image of the CCP.

The Contemporary World of the Fourth Generation: 2002–12

The 16th Congress of the CCP which convened in November 2002 met under some degree of political uncertainty. Many China watchers believed that the event was expected to test the ability of the party to successfully manage the transfer of power to the new fourth generation incumbents. The reason for this assumption was the anticipation of a possible attempt by Jiang Zhemin to attempt to extend his term in office. In fact, the internal party struggle to avoid this possibility went on from 2003 to 2005. By that time, Hu Jintao and Wen Jiabao who had taken office in late 2003 were in firm control. The result of this development was a tactical shift in the focus and direction away from economic growth and toward social harmony.

The Introduction of the Concept of Scientific Development

The prevailing view of the current administration that stresses the central need to seek a harmonious society was endorsed as official policy at the 17th CPC Congress in October 2007. Hu Jintao as President called for the development of democracy, the rule of law as well as a better relationship between the people and government. The shift in emphasis is in a very large sense a recognition of some acute problems. These range from the lack of individual rights, widespread official corruption, a widening gap between the wealthy and the poor, the chronic underdevelopment of rural as opposed to urban areas, serious unemployment amongst the very large number of unskilled workers and the need to overcome repetitive industrial disasters, notably in the mining industry, as well as severe and growing environmental pollution.

The new leadership came to power, with a strong awareness of the dangers of political unrest caused by a growing dissatisfaction within the large element of the national population that has yet to obtain any real benefit from 30 years of reform. The party response can be found in Premier Wen Jiabao's public pledge in 2005 to spend significant state funds on policies relating to the re-employment of public service workers and others affected by the cracking of the iron rice bowl. In addition he promised the introduction of the abolition of farmer taxes, as well as educational subsidies for poor rural children.

Specific reference was also made to the large number of rural migrant workers, who are constantly moving between their home villages and the major industrial centres of China. As unskilled workers they form the lowest component of China's low cost labour market. They are also found in significant numbers in forms of unskilled employment, which are no longer sought after by those urban Chinese who are enjoying upward labour mobility in terms of their employment choices. Their vulnerability in the workplace is reflected in the power of the small employer to dismiss virtually at will. The effects of this are also revealed by the fact that they are owed a backlog of unpaid wages, believed to be as high as $12 billion and growing.

It now appears that the application of policies under the social harmony strategy has had somewhat diverse results. Regional governments as well as factions in the Politburo Standing Committee (PSC), continue to stress the primacy of economic growth over the need to attend in policy terms to the undoubtedly high social costs that flow from the apparent uneven national distribution of the material benefits of reform to date. Meanwhile, as later discussion will reveal the structural shift in the nature of employment following the reforms of the former state-run enterprises, has left a very significant number of former Danwei workers without employment, assessed by some estimates to be as high as 40 million.

The Evolution of Generational Leadership – Some Important Implications

It is noticeable that the procedures for political succession to the supreme posts in the CCP leadership have evolved quite significantly since 1997. It can now be said that in historical terms Deng Xiaoping was, in a very real sense, the last strong man to take power as an individual leader. This is reflected in external analysis of the 17th Party Congress, which despite its range of often contradictory evaluations of policy outcomes revealed the growth of a strong consensus on the need for collective leadership.

There is growing assumption that the formal composition of the CCP's Politburo and especially its key Standing Committee has a crucial role in the determination of the political trajectory that the country will take at any given time. As a consequence any changes in the personnel of that body attracts considerable media attention, particularly since committee agendas now place a growing emphasis on collective leadership. As a sign of the current times Hu Jintao in his role as General Secretary of the Politburo called for a new emphasis to be placed on the improvement of collective leadership with division of responsibilities amongst individuals. This in his view would assist in the prevention of arbitrary decision making by an individual or a minority of factions within the CCP.

It seems that a new succession model has now emerged with the process that will seek and lead to the endorsement for the fifth generation appointments at the 18th Party Congress in 2012, led by dual candidates for President and Premier, rather than a single person endorsed as a designated heir apparent. The implications of this important procedural change will be discussed in somewhat more speculative detail in the final chapter. In summation and before we move on to consider the administrative changes that have occurred as a function of market deregulation and reform, it is worth comment that the processes of governance in China are not reflective of a traditional neo-Marxist and static authoritarianism, but rather of change and evolution within the prime mover of structural reform, the CCP itself.

The Parallel Evolution of Central Administrative Reform in the PRC

After the formal ratification of his executive power at the end of the 1970s, Deng Xiaoping began the necessary procedures to instigate administrative reform in China. He was motivated by the important realization as observed by Ngok and Zhu (2007) that any attempt to modernize the national economy would need to replace the inefficient, overlapping, duplication and often wasteful functions of both party and state agencies. This led to two rounds of major administrative reforms in the period 1982–87, these were followed by further changes in the periods 1988–92 and 1993–97 and then from 1998 to 2002.

The target of consistent and continuing attempts at administrative modernization was to be the State Council of the PRC. This super-agency is both the highest executive organ of state power and, in addition, the highest administrative agency in China. It is charged with responsibilities relating to the application of official policies as defined under the principles laid down by the PRC government as well as the formal implementation of laws and regulations approved by the NPC. The full extent of the State Council's brief is extremely wide, since its concerns include: internal politics, diplomatic matters, national defence, finance, economic issues as well as cultural and educational activities.

While the process of administrative reform has followed an evolutionary path in parallel with the political reforms introduced by the four generations, the key years when formal promulgation of proposed changes occurred have been 1982,

1988, 1993 and 1998. Throughout these reform cycles, the primary activities carried out related to downsizing, streamlining and functional reorganization as well as labour market reforms intended to reduce levels of dysfunction due to the continuing existence of labour market regulations that allowed for the permanent employment of cadres. These structural changes are described in order and more detail in Figure 1.3.

1982 Reforms

- The number of institutions in the State Council were reduced from 100 to 61.
- State Council staff reductions were made, from 50,000 to 30,000.
- Age limits were imposed on the duration of appointments in the civil service.
- The process of the professionalization of public service employment appointments was formally introduced.

1988 Reforms

- Separation of the CCP's organizational apparatus from that of government was approved.
- Ministries of Personnel and Supervision were set up to develop managerial reforms and standards of performance and professional behaviour.

1993 Reforms

- Reductions were made in the number of departments specializing in economic management.
- Corporatization was introduced with the China Aeronautics and Space Corporation replacing the Ministry of Aeronautics and Astronautics.
- The reformed system of work in the civil service as a professional career was introduced.
- The 1998 reforms were to see the number of civil servants cut by half.

1998 Reforms

- Fifteen industrial ministries were abolished and replaced with four ministries charged with macro-sectoral management.
- The State Planning Commission had its role restricted to long-term developmental planning plus the macro-management of regulations.
- The role of government in the delivery of social security and social services was enhanced.

Figure 1.3   Measures Introduced in the Administrative Reforms of 1982–98

Adapted from: Ngok and Zhu (2007), *International Review of Administrative Sciences.*

The actual speed of administrative reform continued to be beset by factional uncertainties throughout the entire period. The 1988 series for example became subject to strong resistance from the bureaucracy and from CCP cadres and with the chaos that followed the 4 June incident in 1989, progress toward implementation was effectively halted for over two years.

In response to the loss of reform momentum following the events of 1989, Deng's Southern Inspection Tour of 1992 and his many addresses delivered on route finally brought to an end what had become a period of political stagnation and loss of economic momentum. The period that followed down to the present was a time of concentration on the processes and means whereby the economic consequences of change could be deepened and expanded (Figure 1.4).

It is interesting to compare the structure and performance of the Chinese economy near the end of the first decade of the twenty-first century, and the economic conditions that prevailed after the end of the Cultural Revolution. After the sometimes controversial progress of reform during four generations of political leadership, it appears that the ensuing leaderships have attempted to meet three major objectives.

Beginning with the changes sought by Deng Xiaoping, the direction taken involved a search for immediate solutions to overcome the problems created by financial weakness, bureaucratic inefficiencies, and a dominant reliance on Marxist–Leninist principles in economic management, which saw economic reform only in ideological terms.

This led on into the 1980s with the concentration of attention on the effective redesign of institutions in the interest of increasing efficiencies. As these bedded in and China's identity as a major new economic player began to fully emerge in the 1990s, there also developed a subsequent need to define more clearly the active roles of governmental agencies. The outcome especially with the growth of FDI led to a significant process of socio-political emancipation for China's

---

The 2003 Reforms

- A Structural Shift in Government's Role from Micro-management to Macro-regulation.
- The Strengthening of State Asset Management Systems.
- Improvements with regard to the Macro-economic Control Regime.
- The Reinforcement of the Market Regulatory System
- The Unification of the Domestic and International Trade Regimes.
- Enforcement of Food Safety/Production Safety Regimes
- The Creation of Specialized Commissions and Administrations

---

Figure 1.4   The Reform Programme Continues into the New Millenium

Adapted from: Yang, D.L. (2004), *Remaking the Chinese Leviathan.*

emergent, growing and now very successful capitalist class. Finally, and with the advent of China's entry into the WTO in 2001, there emerged the further need to adapt government's role to accommodate the fact that China is now identified as an emergent and big player in the increasingly expanding world of international business.

Throughout this entire period as has already been noted in previous discussions, the acknowledged role of the CCP as the leading force in the achievement of the socialist market economy has remained unchallenged to date. China remains by definition an authoritarian state in which the CCP and the Chinese government have dual roles involving leadership on the one hand and the efficient execution of policies of state on the other. How far China can sustain this approach in the future remains essentially outside the current terms of this discussion at this time, but further commentary will address some of these issues in later chapters.

It would appear that the logic of market development may inevitably in the future call for an agenda to be developed that will lead to significant political and constitutional changes beyond the terms of reference that currently apply to the reform process. Whether it does so would seem to depend upon the ultimate definitions of managerial roles and scope that future leaders might apply to the ongoing search for socialism with Chinese characteristics.

The focus and direction of discussion thus far in this chapter, has attempted to establish the political and economic context within which civil aviation in China is formally embedded. The balance of discussion of will now attempt to identify and outline the legal, administrative and operational context within which the General Administration of Civil Aviation of China (CAAC) is currently required to operate.

What follows prior to more detailed discussion of various topics in later chapters is a chronological commentary which divides the structural reform of the CAAC into two distinct historical periods. The first involved a search for more operational efficiencies as offered by what was generally perceived to be a move toward a corporate model. The second after some manifest failures to actually change the industry, may be described as a process of consequential rationalization, which is still going on at the current time. We can now begin discussion below with some comments on the primary functions of the CAAC.

The Authority and Responsibilities of the CAAC until 2008

In 2008 the State Council of the PRC announced its decision to advance major structural changes in the state services which would take the form of some five super-ministries. This currently affects the administration of the civil aviation industry since the CAAC is now located within the new Ministry of Transportation. The following and initial discussion will cover the evolution of the CAAC down to the present time, from a macro-institutional perspective

The modern CAAC is the primary aviation authority of China responsible for national civil aviation affairs. A ministry level organization directly under the State Council of the PRC, its powers to act is defined by China's Civil Aviation Law of 1995. Under this statute, the agency is authorized to enforce the regulation of the civil aviation activities of the whole country and in accordance with laws and State Council decisions, to issue regulations and decisions concerning those civil aviation activities within its jurisdiction.

Apart from a very broad spectrum of regulatory duties the CAAC is also responsible for any international agreements negotiated between China and countries wishing to develop bi-lateral agreements for airline market access. Located under CAAC control are seven regional administrations whose responsibilities include the administration of civil aviation affairs (see Figure 1.5). Within the State Council institutional classification they are recognized as department-level organizations. The distinction is very important since to a large extent it separates the regulatory functions of the CAAC, from the managerial activities of its departmental units.

In addition and within the system of regional administrations there are to be found some 26 Safety Supervision Offices (SSMOs), whose task it is, is to represent their regions in matters relating to safety supervision and market regulations. These duties relate directly to the airlines and airports which are actively operational within each regional location. In turn, current rules permit a degree of managerial autonomy over unit activities as prescribed by the changing role of the CAAC itself.

The First Phase of the Reconstruction of Civil Aviation

Historically the CAAC was formed in 1949 after the CCP came to power, with responsibility for managing all non-military aviation activities. After a long period in control the PLA Air Force (PLAAF) was required in 1980 by Deng Xiaoping to abandon its command style management system as a first step toward the

---

- CAAC Northern Regional Administration.
- CAAC Northeast Regional Administration.
- CAAC Eastern Regional Administration.
- CAAC Central-South Regional Administration.
- CAAC Southwest Regional Administration.
- CAAC Northwest Regional Administration.
- Urumqi Regional Administration.

Figure 1.5   Regional Administrations of the CAAC

Adapted from: CAAC.org.cn.

development of a corporatized form of operational management for airlines. We can describe this as the opening stage of the modern reform process. Needless to say despite good intentions the new strategy did not proceed and evolve without difficulty.

From a political perspective the PLAAF, was not anxious to abandon the operational status quo. Through the period of Mao's ascendancy, the CAAC had carried out three primary functions: the control of the national airlines, the management of commercial air traffic and the administration of airports. All of these functions were directly linked to the PLAAF's military role. In fact throughout its history the bureaucracy in charge of the CAAC has, according to one analyst (Chung, 2003), tended to be operationally subservient to the military, even when an operational activity technically required a dual military–civilian unit as controlling agent.

The reformist agenda also aimed at the development of a corporate culture to replace the long period of monopoly management, which had proceeded with little or no concern for profit or operational efficiency. The concept of specialized airline corporations was introduced with the requirement that the new generation of airlines should be financially responsible for profits or losses. In addition CAAC was to be allowed to retain 90 per cent of any above-plan profits and attendant foreign exchange earnings. After the initial meetings in 1980, it took four years, according to Chung (2003), before the decision was taken to establish commercial airlines.

Finally, after a further three years, 1987 saw the launch of the first of six core regional carriers. It appears that the choice of locations for this first generation of airlines had little to do with the conventions of market research. In fact the development was really reflective of CAAC's degree of absence from the mainstream of reformist change. The cities chosen demonstrated that civil aviation in China still adhered to the post-civil war division of the country into greater administrative regions, which was first introduced by Mao Zedong. This first round of corporatization proved largely unsuccessful. Despite the game plan, the airlines remained subject to budgetary support from government and consistently failed to meet the official requirement that they actively manage their own finances.

The overall confusion was compounded by the fact that central government actively tried to encourage the provincial and municipal authorities to establish their own airlines through the grant of an empowerment to do so. This led effectively to the kind of duplicate construction programmes that had been prevalent during the Maoist era. The initial cost requirement for entry was only RMB5 million and, as a direct consequence, by 1995, more that 40 airlines were operational, some with fleets of less than five planes and many of which were past their use-by date. Even worse, some nine aircraft crashed in the 18 months between July 1992 and December 1993, due to such seriously negligent factors as the inadequacy of safety regulations and a serious shortage of professionally qualified and experienced commercial pilots.

The overall effects of this expansion were not felt across the total population of China. By 1999 only 135 cities actually had an airline service. There was also evidence of extensive over-capacity since the three leading players – Air China, China Eastern and China Southern – carried 56 per cent of all paying passengers in 1997, which meant that the core carriers were controlling 79 per cent of the overall domestic services. Further problems emerged from the beginning of discount wars between the airlines which saw tickets sometimes sold at 50 per cent of the official listed price. Corruption also actively emerged as travel agents' fees, which were officially set at 3 per cent, ballooned in some cases to between 11 per cent and 20 per cent at the time of purchase.

In turn, smaller airlines which attempted to launch short distance routes, found themselves in direct and failing competition on travel costs with the emergent and fast growing rail and road systems. When Shenzhen and Shantou in the Pearl River Delta opened their super-highways it is estimated that air passenger movements between the cities was reduced by 90 per cent. At the same time the cost of a flight between Shenzhen and Wuhan was priced at RMB780 while a new railway service between the same cities charged RMB250 for travelling the same distance by rail.

These resultant problems were compounded by the fact that the CAAC during this period of reform remained literally frozen in the role of a corporate monopolist. As a direct consequence of these major failures a more rational approach to the problems began to develop with the introduction of a dual strategy that included de-concentration and de-centralization as the motivating force. What was being sought through this initiative was a critical mass scenario, where market competition would emerge and with it increased efficiency.

The Second Phase of the Reconstruction of Civil Aviation

The government began a second round of restructuring in 1999, with limited results. This led in 2002 to a major disclosure by CAAC, that the ten carriers controlled by the agency would be voluntarily re-organized and merged into no less than three major conglomerates – Air China Group, China Eastern Group and China Southern Group – each of which in turn would become the main holding corporations for the airlines in question. This reform gave the new giants control over 80 per cent of China's aviation market, with a total value of US$18 billion. In addition, three major service companies were to be formed: China Civil Aviation Information Group (CCAIG), China Aviation Fuel Group (CAFG) and China Aviation Equipment and Export Group (CAEEG).

With the completion of the necessary change processes, CAAC was required to permit operational autonomy for the three airline groups to allow them to become viable, efficient and increasingly competitive. In turn, as a ministerial agency, CAAC would retain a purely regulative role, thus removing itself from the daily operational and overall managerial duties it had been required to perform until the new reforms were instigated.

The End of Monopoly

The year 2005 marked the end of an era for the Chinese airlines. In February CAAC announced that the government was going to permit private capital as well as foreign investment to enter the airline sector as much needed equity investment. The underlying purpose as officially stated by the Ministry of Commerce (2004) was to allow market forces to determine the allocation of airlines' resources in the future. A further strategic intention was to make air travel more available to the citizens of the PRC. An additional and underlying motive for this very significant shift in policy after some 50 years of state control was to attempt to offset the competitive effects of market entry by foreign carriers as required by the terms of admission requirements for China's membership of the WTO. Yet another aspect of China's response to increasing internationalization was signalled in 2006, with the public disclosure that it had completed a very large number of bilateral agreements for reciprocal air space usage and related route access with foreign countries.

With the beginning of the 11th five-year plan in 2006, the PRC was further publicly advised by the CAAC that the agency planned to remove its formal control over the operation of domestic air routes by 2010. The need to change was defined by the ministry as a response to the fact that the formal liberalization of air transport is a global trend, which China as a major new player fully intends to pursue.

When the 2010 reform is finally in place and operative, domestic carriers would no longer be required to go through the conventional forms of application for flying rights on specific routes. Instead, they would simply need to advise CAAC that they intended to offer what would be in effect a new service. The official purpose of the reform is to allow small private airlines together with joint venture carriers to compete with the big three, who currently enjoy very favourable oligopolistic conditions, on profit-making trunk routes.

It remains to comment at this point that, from a Western perspective, Chinese aviation reform often tends to send very mixed messages, notably to the airlines. An excellent example of the frequent gaps that can occur between government intention and managerial execution occurred early in 2005 when the government mandated a freeze on new aircraft orders. The decision was really intended to reduce the multiplication of new airline launches which were essentially a market response to rising passenger demand.

The CAAC faced serious problems because the relative speed of service expansion raised serious questions with regard to the availability of current airports in sufficient numbers to handle the rising passenger demand. The led to an assumption by CAAC that a moratorium on new fleet acquisitions would offset a rising tendency for bottlenecks to occur on some of the busiest routes. In the event by the end of 2005 the existing Chinese carriers had broken their own record for new orders with some 590 requests for fleet additions placed mainly with Boeing for its 737 range and with Airbus for the A320.

It is also important to place on record, that the undoubtedly explosive growth of demand for airlines' services has not been accompanied over time by a relative growth in profit margins. China Southern for example made a net loss of RMB964 million in June 2005, followed by a profit in the third quarter of RMB852 million. This trend emerged in parallel with the losses incurred by China Eastern. What is remarkable however is the fact that during this period, record higher fuel prices, greater competition and significant costs arising from small carrier amalgamations within the three main airlines were also being reported.

The government also made decisions that ran directly counter to conventional international market wisdom and practice. It actively sought to protect the principal state-owned carriers, suggests Wang (2008), through currency de-pegging, restrictions on the formation of new LCCs and a willingness to absorb fuel price hikes through airline subsidies. It was the investor who had the last word, however, with major airline share prices falling from between 20 per cent to 50 per cent during the February 2005/06 year on year time period. Despite these setbacks and the fact that aviation services face growing market competition from an increasingly sophisticated railway system as well as a massive road building programme that continues to make super-highway access a norm for major inter-city transport, the CAAC to date has been determined to deepen the market reform process for the balance of the current national plan and beyond.

It has been the primary purpose of this chapter to present a descriptive view of the major political, economic and administrative policies that have shaped the PRC since the advent of the revolution of 1949. An important reason for doing so has been to further demonstrate, albeit in a limited and selective manner, the various, complex and often unstable dynamics that have accompanied China's attempts at political, social, cultural and economic reform through its long and often troubled history. The fact that serious tensions and pressures are still present today is clearly evident despite the sometimes Herculean efforts of four generations of political leadership.

It follows that if we are to fully understand the various factors that continue to shape China's civil aviation policies over the last 30 years, we must also be aware of the manifest uncertainties identified by Nolan (2003) and Garnaut and Song (2005) that accompany the need to balance the forces making for structural change and modernization with those that seek to sustain political stability through control from the centre. As noted earlier this will remain a constant and repetitive theme throughout the balance of the following chapters.

Having described the larger geo-political framework of reform and development that has profoundly influenced the civil aviation industry since 1949. It is now necessary to consider some further macro-economic, social and organizational aspects that have shaped the role of civil aviation as a field of policy much influenced by major changes taking place in the other substantive areas of national transportation policy. This will enable further consideration to be given to specific aspects of the aviation industry in its dual roles and wide range of functional activities.

Before doing so, it is important yet again to give further emphasis to the fact that within the ideological parameters of the CCP, the concept of continuity in China's search for consistency and balance in the political management of a highly complex and volatile country, stretches back far into the past as well as forward into the future. The experience of Edgar Snow a noted foreign observer and supporter of the revolution in 1949 is worth recalling at this point. On the opening page of his later study of the period published in 1956, he recalls seeing the opening of the door to an ancient bell tower in Beijing by a CPC Commissar seeking to plant the revolutionary red flag on its roof. On closer inspection, the belfry revealed a series of cupboards, with many and various banners, signs and flags that in sum illustrated how very often, over many centuries, the tower had had to welcome a revolutionary change involving many forms of government.

There is a very modern order of consistency to be found in this ideological view of the essential uniqueness of the Chinese revolution as a continuous political process. The sequential introduction of the Three Represents and the Concept of Scientific Development by the third and fourth generations of CCP leadership is now officially perceived to be formally linked directly back to Mao Zedong's thought. In fact the claim is frequently made that 1978 denoted a pragmatic change of direction, and not a direct break with the revolutionary past. This of course allows the CCP in turn to claim formal historical legitimacy as the constitutional leader of the People's Republic.

It is now time to make a fundamental change in the direction of discussion that will accommodate the fact that the current and future development of Chinese civil aviation lies in two distinct dimensions. We can identify the first dimension within the larger search by the PRC government for a modern, successful and multimodal transportation system. The second lies in the development of a modern civil aviation industry that has a multifunctional role as both a domestic and international player in the global world of aviation services. The next chapter will attempt to describe and analyse the first of these dimensions.

Chapter 2

China's Continuing Search for an Efficient Multi-modal Transport System

The main themes addressed in the opening chapter revealed that the political and economic reforms progressively developed by the Chinese government over the last 30 years have been driven by a constantly evolving need for political, economic and social changes of a structural order and a liberalizing magnitude. In the process the continuing search for effective strategies has involved some occasional shifts in both the ideological and political directions taken by the PRC. This has tended to be a developmental constant since the search for socialism with Chinese characteristics began under Deng Xiaoping, and it has been continued through what have been sometimes large, but often small incremental improvements over time. It has also been subject to some quite significant changes in policy direction that have been influenced by both specific group differences over strategy and objectives within the CCP, as well as the various technological and geopolitical realities that have faced three further generations of party leadership, since the death of Mao Zedong.

The need to develop the national transportation industry comprising road, rail, ports and waterways and aviation, as a multi-modal combination of sectors has been an important focus of state planning by the national government of the PRC literally since the inception of gradualism as a developmental methodology. The expansion of the market economy and the growth of industries have placed in turn, an increasing pressure on the transportation infrastructure as the demand for both domestic passenger and export cargo services has emerged in response to rising popular and economic expectations. Given the primary role of exports as probably the most significant factor driving GNP growth in China, during the current decade, the need to develop more client friendly and efficient forms of aviation services, especially in small load high value markets throughout the world is in the process of becoming a major imperative.

China has also seen the deregulation process lead to a substantial increase in private as well as public business and industrial activities. This in turn has impelled the various transport sectors to respond to the associated and expanding needs of businesses seeking logistical and supply chain services. As a result the government's medium- to long-term transportation strategy has placed strong emphasis on the development of a multi-modal arterial framework as proposed by Zhou and Szyliowicz (2004) and Nogalis (2004). This has required in turn and over time that a very significant priority be given to investment in road and rail services as Table 2.1 reveals.

Table 2.1   Fixed Asset Investment in China's Transportation Industry

Year	2000	2001	2002	2003	2004	2005	2006
Value ($ billion)	41.5	47.7	55.0	61.3	76.1	90.2	103.41
% total public investment	–	–	9.83%	8.75%	8.62%	7.27%	6.72%
Ports & Coastal	2.4%	3.2%	3.1%	4.9%	5.5%	8.0%	9.9%
Inland waterways	1.6%	1.3%	0.9%	1.1%	1.2%	1.6%	2.3%
Highway Construction	68.9%	69.1%	72.1%	74.8%	76.3%	76.0%	87.3%
Trunk highways	32.2%	29.7%	29.1%	27.4%	28.4%	35.8%	43.6%
Other road networks	27.6%	30.1%	32.0%	31.0%	27.2%	20.8%	21.2%
County/ Township Roads	9.1%	9.3%	11.1%	16.5%	20.2%	19.4%	22.4%
Railways	23.5%	23.2%	21.6%	16.7%	13.7%	10.7%	n/a
Domestic Loans	34.2%	38.4%	41.0%	41.3%	40.4%	45.1%	45.1%
Self-financing	49.8%	43.1%	37.0%	40.6%	44.0%	37.6%	39.6%

Adapted from: An Overview of China's Transport Sector – 2007. World Bank East Asia Sustainable Transport Enquiry (EASTE) Working Paper No. 15, Final Report, 19 December 2007, p. 1.

Conventional models of transportation systems range across five categories of activity: road, rail, maritime, air and pipelines. As Table 2.2 indicates the same model has been largely followed by the PRC. The Chinese experience, however, as the distribution of investment reveals, has tended to give key priority to the domestic road and rail systems which have grown their networks at a very high annual rate of expansion. With this important development in mind discussion in this chapter will focus first on rail and road development in China, before concentrating attention on the parallel and rapid emergence of civil aviation as both a key domestic form of transportation and later as a major player in the global industry.

A more detailed examination of the structural changes that the transportation industry has undergone since the commencement of the national reform strategy will comprise the first part of the chapter. It will comprise a short review of the overall pattern of expansion that has been experienced by all modes of transportation, since government began the developmental process in 1980.

The Overall Growth of Passenger Travel by Modal Sectors: 1980–2005

There has been a consistent growth in passenger use of the various sectoral transport systems over a significant period of time as Table 2.2 reveals. As the data shows, highways are the major focus of passenger travel, a development reinforced by the rapid expansion of automobile purchases, especially in the major cities. The numbers reveal a pattern of passenger movements, which appears to verify the view that increasing consumer use has matched the growth in available services.

The notable exception to the trend is found in the waterways mode, which has retained a busy cargo-based service, but reveals a quite distinct fall over time in passenger use. By contrast the ports and coastal services have enjoyed growth based on the expansion of the PRC's maritime sector, which now sees successful companies such as the China Overseas Shipping Corporation (COSCO) commencing the building of a new fleet of mega carriers. The purpose is clearly to maintain the modal role of shipping as the primary source for the inward flow of imports and the outward flow of exports on a very large scale, as measured by tonnages carried. The result is the creation of container ships with tonnages up to and even in excess of 280,000 dwt, able to carry up to 12,000 standard 40-foot containers

The growth and impact of China's continuing investment in its transportation system is reflected in the fact that only the waterways mode reveals a steady financial decline over the time period. By its nature the Chinese waterway system is a natural consequence, over many centuries, of the growth of communities linked by their physical proximity to the rivers and their tributaries. They continue to retain a viable role as cargo carriers however through their ability to supply linking services between the emerging industrial clusters within special enterprise zones and the large provincial cities, which are expanding throughout the major river deltas of the eastern and southern coasts.

The consistent if somewhat volatile growth trend for civil aviation is also very interesting given the fact that, as discussion in the opening chapter has indicated, the industry actually went through often uncertain periods of deregulation followed by a return to consolidation. These experiences will be discussed in more detail in a later chapter when the managerial role of the CAAC becomes the focus of examination.

Table 2.2   Growth and Distribution of Travel by Mode: 1980–2005

Sector/Totals/Millions	1980	1985	1990	1995	2000	2005
Railways	1,383	2,416	2,613	3,546	4,533	6,062
Highways	730	1,725	2,620	4,603	6,657	9,292
Waterways	129	179	165	172	101	68
Aviation	40	117	230	681	971	2,045

Adapted from: World Bank EASTE Working Paper No. 15, Final Report, p. 2.

Emergent Issues of Modal Management in a Liberalizing Economy

The relatively high speed and direction of domestic market growth in China gives rise to some further big questions relating to the managerial aspects of development. As economic growth continues the quality of administrative and managerial inputs take on an important new operational perspective. In most Western economies managerial success seems to be a function of the degree and extent to which autonomous strategic and managerial control will produce quality outputs while keeping pace with those major market changes that reinforce the need to advance the growth of effective decision-making techniques.

This issue has particular relevance, especially in the case of aviation, given China's quite recent emergence and now general recognition as a future global market leader. It also has important implications for foreign direct investment as well as emergent strategic alliances and joint ventures. A problem arises at this juncture, since China is yet to fully develop a consistent and universal set of concepts of managerial control, which permits some optimal degree of executive autonomy to emerge that is usually commensurate with higher degrees of operational efficiency.

In fact as later discussion will demonstrate, governmental control and ownership is still a powerful constant and operational presence in both state-owned and indigenous Chinese businesses and particularly in transportation on the state bodies such as railways. It must also be noted according to Wang and Li (2006) that the Chinese concept of what constitutes an administrative system has always had inherently political components, sometimes to be found in quite unofficial relationships such as *guanxi* that can exist between business managers and public officials.

In effect, this means that efforts to obtain some degree of systematic integration of managerial understanding between the various transportation modes can be often lost inside a wide range of ministries and agencies, each with some claim to ultimate managerial control over decision making. In China management of transportation as a business has been shared between no less than ten government departments, as Table 2.3 reveals.

The serious problems that emerge from such a diverse number of organizational responsibilities distributed between varying levels of authority have already been previously described by Wang and Li (2006). There is a current lack at the national level of a properly unified and coordinated transportation management system. This leads as a result to some confusion with regard to the popular identity of individual modes as well as a high degree of monopolistic controls over operations that then tend to impede market competition. In turn, investment funds are mainly supplied by central government, which reduces local agency ability to respond to specific public interest priorities.

Table 2.3   Distribution of Ministerial Responsibilities for Transportation

Ministries Responsible for Managing Transportation Modal Sectors	Designated Business Management Roles
State Development Commission	Business Coordination, Project Establishment, Pricing Discussions
Ministry of Railways	Railway Transportation
Ministry of Communications	Highway Transportation
Civil Aviation Administration of China	Air Transportation
SINOPEC and CPCC	Petroleum Pipeline Transportation
Ministry of Construction	Urban Transportation
Ministry of Public Security	Transportation Enforcement
Ministry of State Land and Resources	Land Examination and Approval
Bureau of Environmental Protection	Project Environment Examination and Approval
State Council	Overall Coordination of all sectors

Adapted from: Wang and Li, (2006), *World Transport Policy and Practice*, Special Issue on Transportation in China, 12(4), September, 29.

Further structural contradictions also exist between these different transportation modes and as a result any integration and coordination between them is weak. Their existence also gives increasing emphasis to the need for greater integration between the functions of government and the market mechanism that drives transportation. Finally the sheer complexity of what is obviously a highly diverse and complex managerial system makes it difficult for urgent matters such as current resource consumption and environmental pollution to be factored into any further developments that aim at a more efficient and multi-modal growth strategy.

The immediate themes of the discussion that follows, will examine in turn the current developmental status of the rail and road sectors in the PRC. The primary focus will then shift in the latter part of the chapter, to a brief and introductory consideration of the emergence of the aviation sector as a major and growing force in the international aviation industry as well as its increasingly important strategic roles in China, covering domestic services for both passengers and cargo.

The Railway Sector: The Persistent Demand for Continuous Growth

It is interesting to find that the origins of railway building in China actually date back to the end of the Qing dynasty. The first railway line to be built began life as the Woosung Road, which connected Woosung with Shanghai. It was constructed by the Hong Kong firm Jardine and Matheson, who unfortunately did not seek permission from the requisite public officials. Needless to say, after it came into service in 1876, it immediately incurred the wrath of the imperial bureaucracy. The result was formal condemnation of what was referred to as an iron monster, which led on to its purchase and demolition in October 1877. The event is indicative of the serious limitations imposed on industrial innovation by the Mandarinate until virtually the final decade of the nineteenth century.

The continuing history of the Chinese railways after 1895 is one of rapid development with serious initiatives based on Beijing as the hub of a potential national system. Efforts to build a viable system were very much subject to the geo-political problems China faced in the period immediately before as well as following the fall of the Qing dynasty in 1911. These involved the cessation of control over cities such as Shanghai which reinforced the growth of domination by the Western powers. China also faced recurring conflict with Japan, which was to extend in various forms until well into the twentieth century. It can therefore be said with some confidence that the Civil War which ended in 1949 probably marked the real beginning of a consistent and national railway development programme. This was in turn subject to the various industrial constraints and limitations faced by the PRC, as it sought to develop a viable and national economic system during the first generation period of Mao Zedong's leadership.

The major reforms that have consequently shaped the modern railway sector of China began after 1978 under serious pressure to develop both capacity and efficiency. At the end of 2006, the railway system as described by the China Agenda 21 studies, comprised a 77,000 km network of which, 63,400 km comprises the national system and 13,600 km a localized series of joint venture services. The system is further serviced as reported in a national review by KPMG (2008) by some 5,420 railway stations of which 23 per cent are using computer interlocking systems. It is also currently experiencing the steady introduction of computerized ticketing services at many of the main city locations.

The Current Response to Developmental Demands

In 2003 the Ministry of Railways (MOR) began a research programme to identify the investment needs for further expansion of the national railway system through to 2020. After due consideration the Mid and Long-Term Railway National Plan (MLRNP) was finally completed and tabled for review in 2004. The State Council then approved the plan which includes both the designated programme for development through to 2020, and strategic proposals for the further inclusion of an investment programme that would include both domestic firms and major international companies.

The discussion that follows, will attempt to highlight some of the major changes proposed to be in place by 2020. It will then look at the second and important question of the total cost of the exercise, bearing in mind that the PRC must be compliant with the requirements of WTO membership, that includes as a basic free trade principle, international access to Chinese businesses for trade and foreign investment.

At this point it is important to be aware of the fact that in the macro-context of planning for the further development of the national economy, the government has also called for the progressive economic development of the western provinces of China, to be given serious priority. While the manifest and serious effects of the Sichuan earthquakes must clearly be taken into planning consideration at this time, it may be said with some confidence that the overarching priorities for western development will remain under very serious consideration by the administration. In fact the Chinese Prime Minister on a three-day visit to the northwestern provinces of Shaanxi and Gansu as reported by Xinhuanet.com (2008) expressed the government's hope that reconstruction can be completed by 2010 and to the required technical standards, with future safety to be targeted as the main priority. The effects of this strategy in terms of the roles to be played by the aviation industry will be reviewed in more detail in the next chapter.

The Physical Dimensions of the MOR Expansion Programme

What has emerged with the MOR proposal is the biggest plan for a national railway system to emerge from any country since the nineteenth century. The plan calls for a total track length of 100,000 km, with two separate and high-speed passenger and freight routes located on the main north–south and east–west corridors. Some 50 per cent of the system is expected to be either double tracked or electrified and in some cases both modifications will be introduced. This plan, as already noted above, also calls for the progressive development of the total network in regions that are under-supplied with rail transport services. The western region's existing tracks will be expanded to 40,000 km by 2020. The total programme also calls for the development of a country-wide intermodal network of some 18 hub-sized container terminals supported by a further 36 smaller sites.

The Passenger Network Developments

This has been planned to comprise four vertical and four horizontal train corridors with maximum train speeds of between 200 and 300 kilometres per hour. In addition urban rail systems are seeking to comply with a growing demand for commuter services requiring increases in their regular schedules. An inter-city regional passenger network is also planned, which will cover all towns and cities within the physical ambit of the major conurbations comprising the key centres of the golden triangle (see Figure 2.1). It will also introduce new forms of high-speed technology, which will progressively shorten the journey times of passengers. The intention on completion of the project is to have an urban fast passenger network, with an operational length of some 12,000 km.

Nodal Conurbation	Primary Cities in Group
Bohai Sea Ring	Tianjin, Beijing, Qinhuangdao
Yangtze River Delta	Shanghai, Nanjing, Hangzhou, Ningbo
Pearl River Delta	Hong Kong, Guangzhou, Shenzhen

Figure 2.1   Inter-city Major Conurbation Services

Adapted from: World Bank EASTE Working Paper 15, p. 23.

Development will also include the comprehensive upgrading of the existing system, as well as the introduction of dedicated freight services, notably for key clients such as the coal industry, which will require such rail lines to service China's ten major coal fields. In addition further commitments call for the upgrading of some seven major inter-city corridors, some of which, for example, Shanghai–Yunnan, require a service that runs from the Yangtze Delta in the northeast to the China–Vietnam border in the southwest.

The Task of Funding the MLRNP

The current internal funding sources available to the MOR, includes the railway construction fund, which is generated by a surcharge on the railway freight tariff. To this there can be added national construction bonds raised for western development as well as funds raised by local and provincial governments and their subsidiary businesses. The ability to draw on national retirement funds is also officially available.

There have also been important contributions from both domestic banks and multilateral agencies such as the Asia Development Bank (ADB) and the World Bank. On the other hand the estimated financial requirement for the project through to 2020 is in the order of RMB2 trillion (US$250 billion). This raises the inevitable and further need to develop significant private sector investment from both domestic sources and when possible from international investors.

The primary plan also allows a degree of flexibility with regard to the various forms of investment which can range from railway construction bonds, long-term commercial bank loans, public offerings of common and preferred stock and specific joint ventures. It also interesting to observe that the right of majority control by foreign companies over freight ventures has been in place since 2004, with a further removal of total restrictions on foreign ownership of freight services taking place in 2006.

There is also evidence drawn for example from recent professional research that a number of urban rail projects have already benefited from foreign joint venture participation. It must be borne in mind at this point in the discussion that expenditure on railway development is more centrally coordinated than is the case for highways and roads programmes. This raises some important questions for investors given the increasingly positive climate for private participation. Perhaps the most serious question involves the degree and extent to which the managerial and executive functions of the MOR can be separated from its ministry functions as a controlling agency.

The massive scale of the overall project will clearly require a highly diversified strategy for external financing. It is suggested in turn, that the need for structural changes that will allow the MOR to develop its own investor-friendly environment is already well understood in the ministry. The key question still remains however, how far and to what extent will China's developing model of a socialist market system, permit the entry and growth of new market-driven joint ventures and other forms of competition? In conclusion and given the notable fact that the proposed plans for a set of five new 'super' ministries, which will be considered in more detail later in this study, currently does not cover the MOR, it will be interesting as a consequence to see how far the increasing calls for a higher degree of autonomous managerial and operational control over what is becoming the world's largest railway system will lead to the industry getting its own super ministry. This is a question apparently in the minds of the managers of the other transportation industries that have already experienced amalgamation

Highways and Roads: The Consequences of Active Decentralization

The dramatic growth of China's national system of roads and highways had its origins in the decision of the CCP to give road development a very high infrastructure priority. As a consequence the period 1990 to 2006 according to the ADB (2007), which also coincides with the 8th,,9th and 10th FYPs, saw the National Transportation Highways System (NTHS) developed to cover some 44,000 km of high grade toll-based expressways. During the current 11th FYP, which ends in 2010, a further extension is planned which will have 66,000 km in place by that date.

The current growth target includes the completion of 12 inter-provincial expressways, which will connect all of the various capitals as well as cities with populations over 500,000 inhabitants. While the NTHS provides the main focus linking major centres with Beijing, the regular network has also been steadily growing. The aggregate length of the national system by 1990 was just over 1.03 million km, by 2005 it had reached 1.93 million km, and the target set for 2010 is 2.3 million km. Unlike the railway system, China's record rate of growth has been based on a decentralized model of infrastructure delivery, which was instigated under the Highway Law of 1997. The principal structure of the system is two-tiered as illustrated in Figure 2.2.

First Tier: The Ministry of Communications (MOC)

- The principal role of the MOC is to give formal guidance and technical support in the translation of national policies, regulations, and design and construction standards to provincial governments

Second Tier: The Roles of Provincial Governments and Agencies

- Each provincial government has a duty under various legal requirements to carry out the construction and maintenance of roads and highways within its physical boundaries.
- They have additional responsibilities for the administration and management of road-related activities
- They do so through their Provincial Communications Departments (PCDs) who report in turn to the Provincial People's Committee, and who are authorized through their Transportation Administration Bureaus (TABs) to carry out regulative and administrative duties.
- The TABs regulate road administration and road safety requirements as specified by the Ministry of Communications (MOC).
- They are also responsible for the licensing of transport operators, trucks, buses, drivers and inter-city bus services. Their mandate does not cover city bus services which come under the regional agencies of the Ministry of Construction (MCon)
- It should be noted that there are equivalent bodies with PCD responsibilities in both the Municipalities and the Autonomous Regions.

Figure 2.2   Principal Agencies Directing Roads and Highway Development

Source: *Policy Reform in Road Transport*, Manila, ADB 2007.

The Administrative and Technical Classifications Applied to the National Road System

China's national road system is subject to two important methods of technical classification. The first involves classification of the various components of administrative responsibility. The second goes on to establish a rating for individual roads based on the quality of their design standards and pavement strength. The various definitions which constitute the overall system can be found in Table 2.4.

The number and variety of classifications listed in Table 2.4 are dependent in turn on their locational contexts. These range from urbanized multi-lane inter-city expressways, to tracks that are so remote and basic as to fail to meet any existing standards for road engineering, as witness the aggregate numbers listed in Table 2.5.

Table 2.4   Administrative Classifications of the Road Network

Class of Road	Aggregate Number in Class and Percentage km of Class Total
National	129,815 (7%)
Provincial	227,871 (12%)
County	479,372 (26%)
Township	945,180 (50%)
Access	88,424 (5%)

Note: Access roads are designed as forms of entry and egress to industrial and business locations and sites.

Adapted from: *Policy Reform in Road Transport*, Manila, ADB 2007.

Table 2.5   Technical Classifications of the Road Network

Technical Classification	Aggregate Number in Class and Percentage of Class Total
Expressway	34,288 (2%)
Class I	33,522 (2%)
Class II	231,715 (12%)
Class III	335,347 (18%)
Class IV	880,954 (47%)
Unclassified	354,835 (19%)

Adapted from: *Policy Reform in Road Transport*, Manila, ADB 2007.

The Various Sources of Development Funding

The process of decentralization has required that provincial governments also raise the required funding for roads within their territorial jurisdictions. In doing so their activities gain support from a variety of financial sources which include, local government funding, state bonds, a vehicle purchase tax set at 10 per cent of the market price of a given vehicle, domestic loans and access to foreign capital. At the present time, the requirement to meet the costs of development under the targets set for the current FYP, when the aggregate estimates for planned development are considered, has created a significant problem for some communities..

According to recent statistical evidence the estimate for the period 2006–10 are set at RMB1.830 billion ($221 billion) of which RMB846 billion is required for the expressway system. Available revenue taken from user taxes at RMB840 billion and highway tolls at RMB50 billion reveal a shortfall of RMB940 billion. An ideal plan to overcome this discrepancy would be to encourage private funding based on a sequence of build, own and transfer (BOT) contracts. Unfortunately, investors have proven to be unwilling in a thriving economy, to tie up capital for the significant period of time that a BOT project requires. This raises the question of sourcing further development from foreign investment as a possible solution to any capital investment shortfalls.

The Potential for Sourcing Road Network Growth from FDI

With its admission to membership of the WTO in December 2001, the PRC incurred a number of important obligations, such as the opening up of the domestic market to international competitors, as well as the subsequent accrual of FDI benefits. In effect this meant that China was required to allow market entry over time by firms and businesses from the WTO member states, in the underlying interests of the development of free trade.

In response to this obligation the MOC and the Ministry of Foreign Trade and Economic Cooperation (MOFTEC), promulgated and introduced Decree 9, which required foreign firms entering China to enter into joint business venture contracts with a Chinese partner. This required that such investors become the active managers of such joint ventures if they wanted to move into the road transport industry, a rule which also applied in varying formats to all other industries. Figure 2.3 sets out the terms of the decree covering the alternative opportunities open to overseas companies.

Further conditional requirements where the enterprise involved passengers included the need for the proposed enterprise to be engaged in business in the PRC for more that five years. The FDI share in turn was limited to 49 per cent, and more than 50 per cent of the registered capital was required to be devoted to infrastructural development. The equity limit was raised in December 2002 to 75 per cent, and later policy modifications allowed foreign firms to move their investment above that level, where the business was devoted to container and express shipping as well as car rental services. The extension was also made available to firms wishing to locate their business centre in the western provinces.

The fact that the decentralization of the road transport system allows a high degree of local control over operational management, gives rise to the potential for conflict between national and regional interests over time. The major problem lies with the main objectives of the regulations. They are in the wider sense intended to achieve an adequate standard of service provision, without creating excessive capacity and within acceptable safety standards. An important problem that can arise, given the dispersal of control, is often caused by the fact that directions from the state agencies to the local authorities do not always include advice with regard to precisely what those standards are. Confusion can also arise where cognizance

- Foreign firms wishing to take either an equity interest or create a joint venture with a Chinese firm.
- Foreign firms wishing to take either an equity interest or undertake a contractual joint venture with a specialist firm.
- Foreign firms wishing to launch its own 100 per cent equity firm, engaged in freight, cargo handling and storage, or other services relating to road transport including vehicle maintenance.

Figure 2.3   Prescribed Requirements for Joint Venture Market Entry and Project Development by Overseas Firms

Adapted from: MOFTEC requirements of Decree 9 (2001).

is not taken with regard to specific local conditions. Before turning attention to the primary role of civil aviation as the focus of discussion for the balance of this chapter, it remains to consider recent research which has raised some interesting new arguments for defining specific policy distinctions, that address the growing urban–rural divide in China.

In assessing the impact of government strategy for the national road network Fan and Chan-Kang (2005) found that low-quality and mainly rural roads have benefit-cost ratios for national GDP about four times greater than those for high quality roads. It applies in both the agricultural contribution to GDP and in the rural non-farm GDP. These findings have important implications for the basic question: Is the aim of the programme to create economic growth or reduce poverty? Given the fact that any further extension of the current policy would appear to be an economically sound decision, it also raises another question: If an extension occurs when will the marginal returns from such investments begin to decline?

It is important as we switch the focus of attention to the key issues facing civil aviation to identify the degree of priority that was attributed to the aviation industry by the 11th FYP in terms of the proposed key strategies. According to the various duties attributed to the transportation industries, the main tasks facing aviation call for the optimization of the operational layouts of civil airports and the enhancement of airline networks. We can now consider these somewhat generalized objectives in somewhat more detail.

The Reconstruction of Civil Aviation in China

We begin discussion with a more detailed review of the reconstruction of China's civil aviation industry by returning to issues and points that have already been raised in earlier discussion. In the pre-revolutionary period during the final years of the Republic of China, the airlines operating passenger services were three in number. Domestic interests were represented by the Civil Air Transport Company and there were two joint ventures actually operational. These were represented by Pan American and Lufthansa, both of which had the Republic of China as the other partner. The entire system had some 36 airports in total, most of which could not service large aircraft.

The modern era of civil aviation in China really began in 1949, when the new government created the Civil Aviation Administration of China (CAAC). The agency was initially established suggests Wei (2007) by the Political Bureau of the CCP Central Committee. Its status was further defined as a subordinate organ of the People's Military Commission on 2 November 1949. The new agency was to be responsible for the management of all non-military aviation activities and was destined to be principally managed by the PLAAF, which had overall responsibility for the control of the national airlines, air traffic regulation and airport management. All of these activities as identified by Chung (2003) were really subservient to the PLAAF's fundamental role of maintaining the air defence of the PRC.

The first two domestic air routes were formally launched in 1 August 1950 with services offered from Tianjin to Chongqing and Tianjin to Guangzhou. In turn the Sino–Soviet Civil Aviation CO (SKOGA) was founded on 1 July 1950 as a joint airline offering three international services to Chitta, Irkutsk and Alma-Ata, all located in the former Soviet Union. The venture lasted a bare five months and was abandoned when the Soviet partner returned its shares to the Chinese government on 1 January 1951.

Before 1978 air travel, as noted in earlier discussion, was a social rarity for the average person. In addition the required technologies for air traffic management were of a primitive order that required frequent grounding during bad weather. The ensuing 30 years were to see very slow growth and development as witnessed by the fact that by 1981 only 15 new and relatively small carriers had been added to the 12 that were operational in 1951.

In 1980, as we have already seen, Deng Xiaoping called for the abandonment of the command style management of civil aviation activities. The aim of the reformist agenda as we will see was to replace what had been a long period of monopoly management with a more liberalized administrative role set as a means to increase operational efficiencies. It must also be kept in mind that the commencement of the period of structural reform post 1978, the bureaucrats, who staffed the CAAC were largely ex-military officers and despite their responsibility for the management of a reformist civil aviation industry, they were to reveal little or no concern for matters such as profit, economic growth or organizational efficiency.

Reconstruction and Market Reform: 1980–2005

The government began the reform process with the introduction of the concept of specialized corporations. This involved the creation of a new generation of airlines, to be financially responsible for both their operational profits and losses. In addition the CAAC was to be allowed to retain 90 per cent of any above-plan profits and attendant foreign exchange earnings. The continuing demands for compliance with existing regulations imposed by the bureaucracy after reform was introduced were, in fact, to see the final decision to establish new commercial airlines actually delayed until 1984. The launch of the first six carriers was then further postponed until 1987.

It appears that these delays had little or nothing to do with conventional market or management research and planning. In reality they were more reflective of the fact that the CAAC was not really located within the mainstream of agencies carrying out the CCP total reformist programme. It is also important to observe, as already noted earlier, that the cities chosen to host the new airlines were selected, not for demographic reasons, but rather on the basis of the post-civil war division of the entire country by the CCP into a number of greater administrative regions.

Given the apparent and total absence of serious research on traffic movement or other potential planning variables, this first round attempt at industrial corporatization was to prove unsuccessful. As a consequence despite the game plan which called for internal fiscal management by the existing airlines, the newly launched carriers remained consistently dependent throughout their operational existence on constant budgetary support by the central government. Operational problems were further compounded by the attempt made by Beijing to empower provincial and municipal governments with the authority to establish their own airlines. The cost of market entry was only RMB5 million and by 1995, there were 40 such airlines flying, some with fleets of less than five aircraft.

As earlier discussion has already noted, and it is worth repeating at this juncture, between July 1992 and December 1993, some nine aircraft crashed, with the resultant investigations revealing causal factors such as inadequate safety systems and a serious shortage of experienced pilots. Further problems of corruption also emerged when the airlines began a series of discount wars, which saw tickets often being offered at 50 per cent below the listed price. Further opportunities for under the counter dealing also emerged with the standard travel agency fee of 3 per cent sometimes rising to between 11 per cent and 12 per cent over time.

Smaller airlines also began to see serious competition from the expanding railway and road systems, especially on shorter routes. When for example the cities of Shenzhen and Shantou opened their linking super-highway, passenger movements fell by 90 per cent. In turn, the cost of a flight between Shenzhen and Wuhan, listed at RMB780, faced direct competition from the railway express service which charged RMB250. Chinese railways also had the advantage that they both developed and still maintain the practice of scheduled services departing exactly on time on the main inter-city trains.

It also has to be remembered at this point, that the overall expansion of a commercial passenger system was not really being experienced across the total population. By 1999, only 135 cities across China possessed a daily commercial passenger service. There was also clear evidence of an emergent highly skewed pattern of service demand by specific carrier. This is reflected by the fact that as late as 1997, Air China, China Southern and China Eastern, were carrying 59 per cent of all the passengers who embarked in that year across the entire industry.

The Changing Responsibilities of the CAAC

The somewhat dysfunctional state of the civil aviation industry was to a large extent compounded by the fact that the CAAC remained stuck in the role of an administrative monopolist. It was officially defined as a ministry level organ, with responsibilities for national civil aviation affairs. Its authority to act as such is found in the Civil Aviation Law of the PRC. Under the statute, it is required to carry out both enforcement duties in accordance with both the law and State Council decisions. It is also authorized to issue regulations and decisions concerned civil aviation activities under its jurisdiction. The latter requirement covers, air safety administration, market regulation, macro-control of air traffic management and international collaboration with international aviation agencies

The Major Reforms of 2002

The process began with the disclosure by the CAAC that the ten carriers controlled by the agency would be voluntarily reorganized through mergers. The result saw the emergence of the 'three pillars' – Air China, China Southern and China Eastern. Under the broader specifications of their intended new role, they became major industrial conglomerates as well as holding corporations, with aggregate control over 80 per cent of China's aviation market. The new system required that the CAAC should permit a degree of operational autonomy for the new mega-carriers. In addition, as a ministerial agency, it would retain as designated, a purely regulative role, leaving managerial and operational matters to the new airlines.

The CAAC nomenclature was also destined to be changed to the General Administration of Civil Aviation in China (GACAC) though the term CAAC has remained in common usage. It was also announced that under the CAAC by decree No. 110, 2002, new provisions for foreign investment in civil aviation were to come into force on 1 August of that year. This decision was related to the need for capital to be used for the expansion and opening up of the system. In addition the scope of foreign direct investment included airports, airlines, general aviation enterprises and projects related to air transport. The expatriate investor was not permitted however to take up equity in ATM projects. Meanwhile, in other categories of aviation activity, investment conditions approximated those relating to foreign investment in road and rail transportation.

Further major reforms were introduced when, in April 2004, it was announced that airfares would no longer be formally set by the central authority. Instead they would be subject to a degree of market competition, according to benchmarks that would allow competitive discounting within a given price range. This was followed in 2005 by a CAAC advisory message to the industry that private and foreign investment in Chinese airlines would be permitted in future. In that same year Chengdu's United Eagle, Shanghai's Spring Airlines and Beijing's Okay Airlines, following the popular international trend, obtained official approval to offer low-cost services. Some very large questions remain with regard to the continuity and direction of market reform as Chinese airlines have become increasingly identified as major players in the international market in their own right. These in turn, have a further implication for China's domestic market, as the fastest growing aviation market in the world attracts attention from an increasing number of foreign carriers now seeking potential route entry into China. These matters will be taken up in turn as appropriate themes in later discussion.

The primary focus of this chapter has been centred on the overall development of transportation reform in China as a multimodal strategy, within which civil aviation is intended to play a number of important roles. It has also been intended to demonstrate some important similarities in the developmental experiences of each mode. Perhaps the most common problem shared by each transport sector has been the way in which the concentration upon liberalization and the freeing up of markets sometimes conflicts with the basic political intention, namely the development of socialism with Chinese characteristics. This opens up the core question that will be raised consistently and repeatedly in the following chapters as to how far government is willing to permit its civil aviation sector to go in terms of the degree of integration between the liberalization of market rules and the necessary corporate and managerial autonomy.

The balance of the following chapters will now attempt to analyse and evaluate in more depth, the current dynamics of China's civil aviation industry as the key sector under primary focus. In doing so managerial strategies and their effectiveness will be examined, within the various dimensions of macro- and micro-activity that constitute the processes that now drive the active and international modernization of civil aviation. Also the examination will be continued of the key perception of modal reform as the need to seek a balance between a stress on domestic and international commercial growth and that of aviation as a vital industry for national development.

Chapter 3
The Roles of Civil Aviation Industry in the Great Western Development Strategy

The direction of the discussion contained in the last chapter was intended to locate the active role of civil aviation in China within the larger context of multi-modal transportation services development. It was clear from the evidence available that the first priority by government to date, within the context of a growing focus on overall national needs, has been given to the development of a viable road and rail system. Another formative theme will now be addressed, within a further developmental context, that has been given a high degree of priority within the current administration of the PRC.

It involves the increasing engagement of the civil aviation industry in the decision taken by Beijing to advance economic development on a massive scale in those provinces that have yet to fully share in the economic and social rewards of market liberalization and reform. The decision to act, which was taken by President Jiang Zemin during his Presidency, has given both birth and impetus to what has become known in the Chinese bureaucracy as the Great Western Development Strategy (GWDS).

In order to fully understand the urgent strategic emphasis that is now being placed by the national government upon the development of the central and western provinces, as well as the more remote autonomous regions of China's north and northwest, it is first necessary to first review the sequence of events that underpinned the decision to bring the regions named into the mainstream of economic development. In January 2000, the government of China announced a major strategy for the economic development of the western provinces, as an important series of immediate tasks to be completed during the 10th FYP (2000–05). The proposal originated in 1999, through the offices of the then President of the PRC, Jiang Zemin, and was then passed through the necessary procedures for formal ratification. The prescribed reasons for government action were formally attributed to the chronic geographical imbalance in terms of the misdistribution of the material benefits of market liberalization that was evident in the history of China's economic reforms since 1978.

The heavy concentration of attention devoted to the economic modernization of key provinces in the southeast and coastal regions had virtually left the central and western provinces outside the national development equation. It had also left government, as reported by Gelb and Chen (2004), with the politically unpalatable fact that least a quarter to a third of China's population were awaiting some material benefits from the opening up and liberalization of the national economy.

The degree of urgency in dealing with these matters was heightened by the fact that a growing inequality was emerging over time, in terms of relative income levels, between the developing and underdeveloped provinces. This was further reflected in rising unemployment and a growing urban–rural migratory drift toward the southern and eastern provinces by unskilled workers. It must also be noted that urban labour markets were affected negatively, as we have already seen, by the decision to reform traditional employment practices, which had the effect of raising long-term urban unemployment by a substantial measure. It is clear that central government saw political dangers for further large-scale political unrest, in the cumulative effects of these very negative social as well as market conditions.

The effects of this decision taken in the mid-1990s led to the plan to lay off some 40 per cent of all workers employed in the state-run enterprises (SREs). The question of future employment for a significant proportion of the working population required in turn, that structural changes needed to be made within the larger market context of the reform process. As a consequence the opening discussion will first revisit some of the human resource issues as a background to a further consideration of the GWDS.

The Growing Inequality of Employment Opportunities in China

The reform process until the mid-1990s had done little to change the fact that during the period of the command economy China did not really have a conventional labour market. All workers, as indicated by Naughton (2007), were covered by public employment regulations that simply divided the work process into a dual system of urban and rural activities. Further evidence noted by Williams and Williams (2008) indicates that the original model of employment regulation set wage levels in a stepped series of categories with an operational division between cadres and factory workers. In the various work categories attributed to the cadres, there were 25 to 28 wage levels that could be attained thoughout a given career. By contrast the career-long reward system for factory workers was set at eight wage levels.

The placement of a given worker on the first step of the wage scale was subject to formal evidence of each individual's level of educational attainment and work experience. Under what became known as the Danwei system, workers were also given the right to full-time employment for life. No cognizance however was either given or taken with regard to questions of productivity measurement or the establishment of work performance standards. This failure later became a major reason for the passing of a series of employment laws and regulations, as well as a subsequent driver in the push toward a more efficient production system.

It was also a mandatory condition as set down in the original legislation, that state-run enterprises should be required to sustain the total cost of lifetime social services for their employees. The effect of a large fixed cost per worker existed under the guise of a social premium and was set at 41.5 per cent of the total salary in any grade. What was in effect an impost package then required that these employees be fully covered for retirement benefits, medical insurance, unemployment benefit and costs incurred through industrial injury. All of these conditions comprised the ingredients contained within the famous iron rice bowl.

State unemployment was still growing says a leading international expert on the reform of China's labour markets (Malcolm Warner, 1996, 2008) well into the 1990s and with it the attendant costs of lifetime unemployment benefits for those rendered redundant by the reform process. At the same time and beginning in the middle of the decade, the government decided to actively deregulate the private sector. This resulted according to Hassard, *et al.* (2006) in the privatization of many state-run organizations, and led to some 40 per cent (50 million employees) in the public sector workforce being declared redundant.

The Decline of Employment in Rural China

The distribution of the working population in China has tended to follow the various initiatives to promote economic development in urban locations. By contrast, while there is a significant proportion of both Han and ethnic minority citizens located in the central and western provinces they have tended, without up to this time any significant investment in industrial development, to be largely employed as itinerant workers in agriculture. In the period down to the late 1970s, two-thirds of rural employees, according to Hanxian (1985) were to be found in the countryside, where communes and work brigades that have now been replaced in many rural areas by semi-autonomous town and village enterprises (TVEs) worked the land as a part of the Danwei system.

After the failure of the Great Leap Forward, tight controls were placed on rural–urban mobility. It is also a somewhat ironic consequence of later reform changes that the vesting of leasehold rights in farmers and their families raised unit productivity, but at some considerable cost to the landless peasants, who were often replaced by various forms of mechanization, under the direction of the managers of the TVE system.

While the dissolution of the agricultural work brigade collectives has literally seen the creation of millions of household farm businesses, and the employment of more efficient systems of production, the rate of GDP growth per capita in the central and western provinces, is still only around some 60 per cent of the national average. It is also important to remember that the relative growth of unemployment in urban centres is matched in the rural countryside. Estimates of a rise of up to ten million displaced rural workers in the period 2001 to 2010 may in fact be conservative.

Awareness in Beijing of the political dangers of a continued economic and social imbalance of this kind, leading to the development according to Loveridge and Mok (1979) and Wilkinson (1981) of a dual and fragmented labour market has tended to grow with the parallel rise of a significant and highly successful urban middle class. It was these growing pressures on government's perceptions of political stability, as an earlier comment has indicated, that gave administrative birth to the Great Western Development Strategy (GWDS). In fact as further discussion below will indicate, the geographical span of the GWDS actually covered not only the western areas, but also those central provinces such as Sichuan, which have figured so tragically in the recent natural disasters.

It is also important to be aware, that the movement into the west has important geopolitical implications. China of necessity must protect the political integrity of its national boundaries, which are coterminous with a number of states and regions, where a significant degree of political instability is the current norm. In addition many local populations in the border provinces comprise a high proportion of non-Han minorities; races, with religious, cultural as well as political expectations that do not fit the general model as prescribed by Beijing.

The analysis and discussion that now follows will first consider the details of the developmental strategies that have continued to evolve through what is now the 11th FYP (2005–10). In doing so it will attempt to present a perspective on various roles and tasks that have been allocated to civil aviation, as the policy-makers struggle with the age-old tasks of creating an efficient transportation system, in one of the most geographically difficult and complex sub-regions in the world.

Aviation's Modal Role in the Great Western Development Strategy

The relative social and economic state of the central and western provinces at the commencement of the GWDS programme is reflected in three statistics. The regions in sum according to Nizhe (2000), accounted at the turn of the current century, for 57 per cent of China's land mass, 23 per cent of its population and 14 per cent of its GDP. If the autonomous regions like Inner Mongolia are added, the figures rise to 71.4 per cent (6.85 million km^2) of landmass, 23 per cent of population and 17.5 per cent of the national GDP.

While planners of the reforms called for a degree of urgency in implementation, the plan itself is part of much more medium to long-term expectations, which will require several generations of effort. In fact the decision to develop the region fits into the larger assumption commonly held in Beijing, that it will be 2050 before China is a really fully modernized economy as befitting its assumed role as a major international state. With this in mind the initial developmental period of the GWDS, has called for activities that would begin the process of modernization, through rural development, the urbanization of key cities, the enhancement of natural resources and the attraction of investment from both national and international sources (see Figure 3.1).

All of these activities were intended to be buttressed in turn by a steady influx of skills, investment and strong government support. By 2006, some US$125 billion had been spent on more than 70 infrastructure projects that the various designated

- Infrastructure Construction including Transportation.
- Ecological Environment Protection.
- Industrial Restructuring and Prioritization.
- Development of Science, Technology Education and Social Causes.
- Investment Development.

Figure 3.1   The Five Initial Contexts of Western Reform (FYP 2000–05)

Adapted from: The State Council Office of Western Development, Beijing 31 October 2000.

agencies have under development. In addition some 226,000 km of highways and over 4,000 km of railways had been completed. Further developments were also identified as being in the planning state for aviation and considerably more land-based developments.

In September 2006, the National Committee of the Chinese People's Political Consultative Conference (CPPCC) held a delegates conference in Beijing. As a consequence the opportunity was taken by the National Development and Reform Commission (NDRC) to announce that for the balance of the 11th FYP attention would be focused on no less than eight key tasks aimed at achieving new progress in key areas. The announcement also signalled a new strategic context. While the initial plan to develop western China had stressed some economic and social objectives, the first priority was now to be focussed, as identified by Linbeck (2006), on the facilitation of the construction of the new socialist countryside (see Figure 3.2).

It is noticeable that the second phase of the development of the GWDS calls for transportation development to have a high priority. As a consequence while road and rail development have in the central and western provinces followed sequentially, the evolutionary progress of expansion to be found in other regions has tended to be seriously neglected. Civil aviation has attempted to develop both a primary role as a major supplier of the means for quicker population movement and been committed to the supply of a variety of logistics and supply chain services by air and in support of a wide range of industrial infrastructural projects.

The industry has also been engaged in a broad spectrum of activities to be found in the key areas of airport development, expanded airline services, and the location of outsourced activities relating to aircraft manufacturing, as well as other industrial developments. In addition the city of Chengdu in Sichuan Province, which is already a major strategic airport hub in central China, will now continue to be developed as a key national and international centre of aerospace research. It has also been revealed that further primacy has been accorded the development of airports as a strategic imperative, for the obvious reason that the ability to service the movements of passengers and goods by air requires an effective airport network. The balance of the chapter will examine some of the organizational and operational consequences of this requirement.

- The socialist countryside was to be advanced through agricultural development and a rise in rural living standards.
- New projects in transportation and civil aviation were proposed together with the expansion of telecommunications.
- The pillar industries in the provinces were to be further developed.
- The development of key sectors was to be accelerated, especially in the areas of cross-regional zones such as the Chengdu–Chongqing axis in Sichuan.
- Ecological and environmental protection was to be given priority.
- The need to raise the general standards of efficiency in the public sector was duly recognized.
- The further need to meet serious shortfalls in remote service locations, by offering a range of incentives and allowances including training.
- To establish and improve the long-term mechanisms of state support, regional coordination, enterprise development, resource development, management, foreign economic exchange and cooperation and government services.

Figure 3.2   The Eight Tasks for the Future of Western China Development

Adapted from: Li Shen, The Eight Key Tasks for Future Western China Development, Chinagate.co.cn.

Western China's Airport Development in the 11th FYP (2005–10)

The game plan for civil aviation development in China's western provinces call for the development of 37 additional airports during the current FYP. Of these, six will be relocated and 31 either rebuilt or extended. The intention is to respond to the growing demand for airline services. As a further result, airport construction in some outlying areas now tends to rank ahead of rail expansion as the key policy initiative. According to official sources the developmental budget (US$6.5 billion) is larger than that allocated for further construction projects to be located in the eastern provinces.

By 2007 the GWDS region had some 54 civil-use airports identified by the *People's Daily*, which amounts to 38 per cent of the national total. Further developments include a second airport for Tibet which already operates domestic services to all major cities, from a plus 4,000 metres altitude site in Lhasa. Now work is reported to be in progress on a new airport in the even higher Ali region of Tibet, which will no doubt rank in the *Guinness Book of Records* as the highest airport in the world and which will serve an area not accessible to land transport, because of adverse weather conditions for up to five months of the year. In turn Inner Mongolia is scheduled to have some 20 airports in civil use by 2010, located at sites ranging from the eastern pasture land to the western wilderness. It is now time to take note of the fact that the GWDS also embraces the central provinces, especially Sichuan which brings two important cities into the developmental equation, as what might be termed the key bridgeheads of the programme.

Chongqing and Chengdu as a Developmental Epicentre

The cities of Chongqing and Chengdu are located at a key central point in the central province of Sichuan. Their dual roles as gateway cities to the west are based on a very high level of interactive urban dynamics which are materially assisted by strong arterial linkages. With the advent of the GWDS they have now taken on primary roles at the strategic operational centres of the programme. Chongqing for example has seen its population grow substantially both as a major industrial city and as a target location for itinerant workers seeking release from constant unemployment in the more remote regions and provinces.

In turn, Chengdu has become a major location for modern industry including new aerospace ventures as well as acting in tandem with Chongqing as a linked and dynamic location for further economic development. Both play an important role as potential international as well as domestic locations for the civil aviation industry, especially in the airport sector.

Key Changes in the Management of Airports

The management of airports has also been progressively transferred over time from Beijing to provincial governments. In 2004, for example, CAAC handed over control of four civil airports – located at Lanzhou, Dunhuang, Jiayughuan and Qingyang – to the provincial government of the Gansu Province. In order to stimulate passenger demand in the small-scale operational centres that are to be found in the western and some central provinces, some of which currently report a 90 per cent plus operational loss rate, the CAAC has also implemented a period of fixed-term operational subsidies.

Case Examples of Key Airports now Serving the GWDS Region

The focus of discussion will now turn to a set of operational examples, involving a sample of four key airport sites. It is important to be aware that each site has a very strategic role within its individual location. The areas of choice will cover the two major cities in central China, which have already been commented on and two other cities, one in the southwest and one in the northwest.

Case One: Chengdu International Airport

Chengdu is an important city in the province of Sichuan which shares, as we have already noted, a major development role with what has become the municipality of Chongqing. Both have experienced migratory movements of population from the west, and are also growing centres of industrial development, based on both public and private investment. Chengdu's role in the aviation industry dates back to both the second Sino–Japanese war and World War II, which in the former case led to its designation as a military airport in 1938.

The international airport is managed by the provincial government and is accessible by an expressway, which will be eventually linked with the metro subway system currently under construction to service the population movement needs of the growing city. It will transfer passengers from the terminal to downtown Chengdu, a distance of some 16 kilometres. This type of development fits very comfortably into the larger context of national urban transportation planning, since light rail services of this type have already either come into operation, or are currently in the planning stage at locations which contain other major aviation hubs.

In 2007, the airport was rated sixth busiest for air cargo in China. It also acts as an important hub for both Air China and Sichuan Airlines. Client carriers using services on site include the two other majors, China Southern and China Eastern. Seven other domestic carriers are also active, including both provincial and private airlines. Destinations served from Chengdu cover all of the major cities of China as well as the GWDS urban centres. Foreign carriers with scheduled slots now include KLM–Air France, Thai International, Asiana, Orient–Thailand and Silk Air. Both the Dragonair and the Silk Air's schedules are also rated as international flights.

Case Two: Chongqing International Airport

Chongqing has a growing population of 30 million plus and shares with Shanghai the official classification as a municipality rather than as a metropolitan city. It also shares with its sister city, Chengdu, a role as a military airport during wartime. The first phase of airline operations, which are now under public management, began in 1990, and the second began in 2004. Two terminals currently service domestic and mainly international flights, with operational capacities for seven and one million passengers respectively. A third terminal is in the planning stage, with a second and third runway to commence construction during 2008.

It is clear, as with the example of Chengdu, that the airport is increasingly a major entrepot for the important industries that are now growing within the locality. The airport acts as a hub for Air China as well as Chongqing Airlines, Sichuan Airlines and services will extend to Shenzhen Airlines when it opens a new hub on the site. Both China Southern and China Eastern service the region and there are numerous other carriers also listed as clients.

Air China, as in the case of Chengdu, services Japanese, Korean and Thai destinations from the airport. At the time of writing Asiana was the only foreign carrier using the airport services, since Philippines Airlines withdrew from its scheduled flights to and from Manila. Meanwhile Dragonair, Hong Kong Express and Shanghai Airlines are also rated as international flights. In 2007 the airport handled some 10,355,730 passengers and was ranked the tenth busiest airport, nationwide.

Case Three: Kunming International Airport

Kunming is the capital of Yunnan province and an important strategic location in the southwest of China. There is a shared border with northern Vietnam, and the western Mekong region which is itself undergoing important infrastructural development. The airport dates back to the early days of flight, since it was founded in the 1900s, by the local warlord General Tang Jiyao. During World War II it became a major base for the famous Flying Tiger squadron under its legendary commanding officer, Clair Chenault, who was later promoted to the rank of General.

Kunming has developed a growing importance as an industrial centre and also as a tourist venue. It has a very significant minority population and enjoys a great deal of popularity with domestic as well as foreign visitors. The current site is under considerable pressure from the growth of the metropolitan area of the city, which is increasingly encroaching on the amounts of land available for its further development. In the light of these limitations, airport management and the local authority have a new site planned; which they hope will be in operation within the next five years.

Passenger traffic through Kunming in 2007 reached a new high of 15,725,791 which helped the airport to gain the ranking of the eighth busiest in China. It also shares a common pattern of domestic services with China's central cities. The list of user clients includes several private carriers, for example, Deer Air Spring Airlines and Okay Airways. International clients include Korean Air, Malaysian Airlines System, Lao Airlines, Thai International and Vietnam Airlines as well as Silk Air and Best Air out of Bangladesh. This concentration is a further indicator of the strategic value of Kunming's location in relation to the countries of Southeast Asia.

Case Four: Urumqi International Airport

Urumqi is by far the most remote airport location in China. It is the capital of the XinjJiang Uygur Autonomous Region in China's northwest and shares a border to the west with a number of the former central Asian member states of the Soviet Union. Meanwhile to the east lies Outer Mongolia with the result that XinjJiang province is really an enormous land based peninsula. The airport was opened to foreign traffic in 1973, when it became an emergency landing site for airlines en route to Europe and west Asia.

The site now has a recently opened runway which can take aircraft types up to the Boeing 747-400. The airport is also under public management with the CAAC as the controlling agency. International operations began in 2005, with Korean Air offering a seasonal service to and from Seoul. A PIA service from Islamabad started at the same time but was suspended in April 2000. Urumqi is used by China Southern as a major domestic hub, while China Eastern services the western airports. Air China in turn runs services to Beijing and Chengdu. The balance of scheduled flights is offered by a combination of provincial and private airlines.

Inevitably, the overwhelming number of international carriers flying into Urumqi carries a strong regional identification. They include Ariana Afghan, Azerbaijan, Dalavia, Tajik Air and Uzbekistan Airways.

***

The case examples that have just been described are based on the findings of Bounova *et al.* (2006) and are useful in the sense that they reflect the official emphasis being given to the strong growth of airports as the first step in the building of a viable civil aviation presence within the larger framework of the GWDS. It is interesting to note that while the three major national carriers are found in each location, the presence of significant provincial players like the former Hainan and Xiamen Airlines as well as the emergent private carriers, signals the beginning of growing market competition between state-owned and private players in the western and central provinces.

The Emerging Importance of Cargo Services in the Great Western Development Strategy

In line with the basic assumption that the role that civil aviation is expected to play in central and western China is embedded in the overall economic and social development of the region, it is important to remember that while airports as reviewed by Yang and Gakenheimer (2007) are becoming increasingly multifunctional on the landside, they still have a primary obligation to service carriers in the twin dimensions of passenger and cargo movement. The balance of discussion will examine the latter question of cargo services, bearing in mind the fact that the development of high technology industries in the GWDS region also predicates the need for rapid and customer-driven supply chain systems.

The ability to service market needs more and more quickly is a fundamental driver of supply-chain management research. At the current time the logistics and supply chain industry in China is confronted with some urgent developmental problems, since current domestic services tend to be predominantly urban centred, short-haul and road-based. It is also important to add at this point the fact that many of the emergent high technology industries in China, as is common internationally, are often producers of small loads with significantly high value. It is perhaps an awareness of these market changes that is driving the major aircraft manufacturers to add a freighter classification to the design of many new models of varying sizes and types.

With these factors in mind its is also worth putting on record at this point in the discussion that recent research has indicated that the amount of air cargo requiring passage is expected to grow at the rate of 11.2 per cent per annum to 27 million tonnes by 2020, of which 15 million tonnes are expected to be carried by Chinese dedicated aviation cargo services.

The Expectations of Rising Demand for Air Cargo Traffic

The CAAC strategic development plan for the period to 2020, which will coincide with the 12th and 13th FYPs, assumes that there will be a two-tiered infrastructure system servicing air cargo in place by that date. This assumption as discussed by Jiang, *et al.* (2002) suggests that the rate of airport throughput will call for three dedicated international hubs: Beijing – Capital; Shanghai – Pudong; and Guangzhou – Beiyun. A series of second-tier hubs would then be located at key geographical points throughout China, namely Shenyang, Wuhan, Chengdu, Kunming, X'ian and Urumqi. By implication these in turn would eventually be serviced over time by flights from outlying locations which might constitute in turn, a third level of operations. This possibility is of course very dependent on the rate and growth of industrialization in the more remote regions, which would require in turn access to regional points of entry into a fully functional domestic system. In regards to the required developmental traction needed, it is clear that the planners are anticipating further growth in the GWDS provinces and expect that in the future the autonomous regions will also expand at the forecast rate. Table 3.1 gives some indication as to the distribution of the growth patterns.

In the immediate term, it would appear that the total contribution of the GWDS region would reach 6.793 million tonnes over the period until 2020. On the other hand the possibility arises that the projected growth of movements in locations such as Kunming might be unduly optimistic, since the airport is serving a local market that as its maturity increases might slow down over time.

It now remains to examine the official media report that China has a national plan for the development of an aviation cargo sector with the year 2020 again as the target date for full-scale operation. The completed plan calls for the building of 97 new airports as well as the consolidation of smaller sites and the upgrading

Table 3.1   Projections of Cargo Throughputs by Central and Western Airports 2002–2020 Unit: 000 tonnes

City-Airport	2002	2005	2010	2020 Plus Cumulative Total
Shenyang	57	75	118	295/545
X'ian	65	84	130	305/584
Chengdu	162	219	362	985/1,725
Kunming	122	195	424	2,001/2,742
Wuhan	52	58	70	102/282
Urumqi	43	53	75	150/321
Chongqing	71	91	135	297/594

Adapted from: Hong, *et al.* (2002), Table 3, p. 9.

of certain key locations. The proposed budget involves a massive investment of some $64 billion.

The proposal which has emerged from the new super Ministry of Transport which was formed on 24 March 2008 and which includes the CAAC, now redesignated as the Bureau of Aviation, makes further calls for the administrative reformation of airports in China into clusters according to their various functions. These are classified as international, domestic and feeder locations. A further and planned intention is to reach a state of balance with targets involving better coordination and greater efficiency through the required introduction of hub and spoke operations.

Of the 97 new airports, more than 50 per cent are scheduled to be built in the southwest and the northwest. The basic and reported intention is to speed up the further development of domestic services. In addition Kunming has been identified as a gateway airport for trade promotion linking China to Southeast and South Asia. Support for the airport to play this role effectively, will also be forthcoming from the Chengdu and Chongqing hubs. Urumqi which is also tasked with the same role for trade between China and Central Asia, will also gain support from the X'ian and Lhasa hubs which are to be cast in the same type of supporting role.

The proposed developments for civil aviation in the western provinces also reveal a broadening in the various roles and functions needed to support and sustain viable aviation services, both domestically and internationally. A notable working case example involves a major aviation engineering services joint venture to be located in Chengdu on the site of the Shuangliu International Airport. In addition a second case study will examine the joint venture involving the leading international airport company Fraport AG and X'ian Airport which has been described by various news media as a further indicator of strong responses to the market entry opportunities now being signalled in western China.

Both of these ventures are specifically aimed at the future as well as the current potential for the expansion and development of new market opportunities. They also seem to indicate a preventive trend to move outside the more conventional locations that have traditionally attracted new investment opportunities. How far this reflects a search for lower cost advantages, especially in the matter of labour costs, remains a matter of some conjecture at the current time The projects are now described in some detail below.

Current Case Studies on the Development of Support Services for the GWDS

First Case Study: The Taikoo-Sichuan Aircraft Engineering Services Company Ltd

The growing need for a full range of aviation service industries to support the expansion of passenger and cargo operations into the central and western provinces is reflected in the establishment of a new company which will be located at Chengdu Shuangliu International Airport. The project is a joint venture and comprises the partners set out below. It is also on record as constituting the first Sino–foreign joint venture on the mainland to specialize in Airbus aircraft maintenance.

First Partner: Hong Kong Aircraft Engineering Company Ltd (HAECO)   HAECO the project leader is recognized internationally as a major player amongst aeronautical engineering companies. Its primary role at its Hong Kong base covers the total range of maintenance, repair and overhaul (MRO) functions and in addition it is active in aircraft modification. In sum HAECO offers a comprehensive package to clients covering transit, technical services and full hanger support at HKIA. The firm is listed on the Hong Kong Stock Exchange. It also holds a 40 per cent equity share in the new venture.

Second Partner: Taikoo (Xiamen) Aircraft Engineering Company (TAECO)   The company is a subsidiary of HAECO, and provides heavy maintenance services on both the Airbus A320 and Boeing 737 aircraft types. Its functions also cover passenger-to-freight conversions for client airlines as well as line maintenance for a number of mainland airports. The firm's equity share in the new venture is 9 per cent.

Third Partner: Sichuan Airlines Group   The group is a large-scale state-owned enterprise and the largest of the civil aviation groups in western China. It also has the Sichuan Airlines Company as a subsidiary and holds a 20 per cent stake in United Eagle Airlines and a further 33 per cent in Northwest Airlines. The Group is the largest shareholder in the project with 42 per cent of the equity.

Fourth Partner: Sichuan Haite High-Tech Co. Ltd   The firm was founded as a large-scale privately owned business in 1992. It was charged with a range of maintenance tasks relating to the servicing of modern airborne technologies. Its activities range from the maintenance of airborne equipment, aircraft power systems as well as the development of technological products and information software. The company is able to transfer its developmental activities directly to client airlines, through the marketing of equipment. It is also able to provide supply chain services for over 40 aircraft types as well as Boeing and Airbus. Its share holding is 9 per cent of the project total.

The Primary Role of Taikoo-Sichuan Co. Ltd

The purpose of the development is to bring on line an operational facility that will cover heavy aircraft maintenance, technical management, aircraft conversion, line maintenance, fleet technical management and inventory services management, as well as a range of other engineering requirements. The total investment will range between RMB1 billion and RMB1.2 billion and will be developed in a series of timed phases. The first phase will require two single-bay narrow-body hangers, at a cost of RMB150 million with the first one scheduled to come on line by June 2010. The location will be found at the north end of the main runway and will cover an approximate area of 450 hectares. When complete it will be able to accommodate four A340s and four A320s at the same time. This in turn will require the deployment of over 3,000 technical staff.

The CEO of HAECO in his address at the launch of the new company pointed out that the actual delivery of a comprehensive maintenance service was to be aimed at accommodating not only domestic airline clients flying Airbus services, but other potential airline users in India and Southeast Asia. In his turn the Chairman of the Sichuan Airlines Group suggested that the project had important local ramifications for the maximization of Sichuan's role as a major industrial province in western China. This assumption is based in turn on the further ability to leverage off the growing importance of Chengdu as an industrial location with a strong civil aviation base. He also noted that the development of the new company fitted within the national plan for the future of civil aviation in China.

Second Case Study: The X'ian Xianyang International Airport Company Ltd

A formal ceremony occurred in X'ian on the morning of 9 September 2008. Its purpose was to celebrate the launch of a new German–Chinese joint venture in which the foreign investor was one of the world's leading international airport companies, Fraport AG. The overseas partner will hold 24.5 per cent of the equity and is the first foreign airport operator to invest in a Chinese airport which is not currently listed on a stock exchange.

The CEO of Fraport gave considerable stress in his speech at the launch to the great importance Fraport attributed to its work in China. He further endorsed his comments by advising his audience that Fraport had several projects in the development stage in other parts of the country. From these comments there emerged the impression that two important considerations appear to have influenced the Fraport decision. The first involved the now popular view that China was potentially the world's largest market for aviation services.

From the CEO's remarks there emerged the further assumption that X'ian enjoyed a central geographic position which made it highly likely that as air traffic increased over time, it would grow into a potential hub, not only for the northwest, but also for international traffic. This latter assumption it became clear, was also based on the fact that X'ian has enormous tourist potential, both as a former imperial capital which is symbolically reflected in its famous inner city walls and as the home of the Terracotta Army, a UNESCO World Heritage site.

It is clear that Fraport drawing on its vast experience in international airport development sees great potential in the future tourism market, in conjunction with its local partners and the regional and local authorities. The firm is also anticipating that over time, there will be a significant growth in landside retail and real estate facilities at the airport which will produce a valuable and on-site rental market.

It now remains to record the fact that in conjunction with the launch of the new company, Fraport also advised the domestic Internet world of its presence with the launch of its new Chinese language web-site.

***

These case studies reflect the growing investment both in fiscal form and in terms of professional expertise that is taking place in the designated key cities of central and western China. It is also important to be aware of the fact that implicit within the plans of the two new companies described above is an essential balance between national civil aviation policies and the market expectations of these new players. From a corporate and strategic perspective this new order of joint ventures signals to the participating firms as well as many other aviation companies seeking new locations in central and western China that they will also need to become involved in a dual-market strategy.

In the first instance they will be required to fit within the prescribed parameters of the government's western policy. In the second they will clearly be involved on a corporate basis, with the development of both domestic and international routes. Such activity would be expected to permit direct access to and egress from the major international airports outside China which would then be linked with the key industrial cities that are currently under further planned development under the auspices of the GWDS up to 2025.

It is clear that civil aviation has played and continues to play a leading role in the expansion of the Chinese economy into the considerably underdeveloped central western and northern provinces. Meanwhile the growing financial crisis of 2008/09 has produced some manifest and serious uncertainties as to the future management and control of civil aviation in China, which is beginning to impose new problems with regard to the real time accuracy of exponential market growth projections. These matters will form a part of the various thematic issues that will figure initially in the next chapter. They will also be an important part of the review of major issues that will form a part of both later themes and programme evaluations.

Chapter 4
National Administrative Reform and its Consequences for Civil Aviation

There will now be a significant change made to the range of topics that have been covered thus far. This means the balance of themes and issues from now on will be more directly focused upon the various operational aspects of the civil aviation industry. At the same time discussion will take active cognizance of the developmental parameters that have been set by central government as the primary agency driving the search for what is really becoming a mixed market economy with a specific and Chinese socialistic character.

The CAAC has in more recent times become an active agent in the search for socialism with Chinese characteristics despite the fact that its organizational culture had developed within an environment in which the strategic role of aviation was historically shaped by a largely military agenda. This may be partially explained by the fact that its institutional status within the national bureaucracy has changed, bringing it closer to the centre of power within bodies such as the State Council. At the same time there can be no doubt that the period since the reforms of 2002, has seen an increasing awareness of civil aviation as an important component in a modern and growing economy.

As earlier chapters have noted there is a high degree of scholarly consensus that the pattern of events that has driven the emergence of the PRC in the twenty-first century as a major international player in civil aviation have their basic origins in the larger processes of gradualism in market reform. At the same time, the precise nature of the changes needed to produce a modern and efficient industry have been subject to an often considerable degree of conflict and misunderstanding, largely over the precise administrative and managerial direction that civil aviation should take in its active search for progressive efficiencies.

The assumption that China has larger geopolitical objectives and has also been seeking an ideological, political and economic direction that is commensurate with its emergent and important role as a major player in world politics comes back into focus at this juncture. It has been argued by many scholars that China has been engaged on this search since the nineteenth century and is currently busy in making up for time lost during that period when the hegemony of Western industrial power in Asia was moving toward its zenith. How far that argument holds true with regard to the potential supporting role that the aviation industry can play under such a mandate, remains an important issue for both the strategic policy makers and those charged with turning policy into various forms of operational reality.

With the civil aviation industry now in central focus, this chapter will first examine the influence of the larger macro-issues currently driving the totality of economic and social reform as background to the increasingly detailed specification by government of the developing role of air transport as an important economic and political agent. The context of discussion has been evolving to this point through earlier chapters which have given consideration to the major forces that have driven generational political reform since 1978. Previous discussions have also tried to locate civil aviation within the larger reformist perspectives of China's multimodal transportation strategies.

The current intention is to establish an initial context which will allow civil aviation and its various componential activities to then be examined more fully in later chapters, as part of their expanding role as agents of economic and social reform. This will involve, of necessity, a further examination of the way in which professional sector institutions like the CAAC have themselves become subject to the dominant requirements of the political reform process. The intention will then be to allow the balance of the following chapters to consider, sequentially, the effects of change on airlines, airports, air safety, as well as manufacturing and geopolitical alliances within the larger contexts of the global industry.

As a prelude to a more detailed discussion of specific aspects of industrial reform in civil aviation, it is important to be aware that market liberalization by industrial sectors as a process, has in turn been located within the political and ideological context of a much larger reformist initiative.

This can be best described, as earlier discussion in Chapter 1 has indicated, as a primary shift away from ownership by the people toward ownership by the state, motivated by the need to overcome the manifest failures of the economic policies of the period before 1978. The fact that these aims are still undergoing growth and development will be considered below as an attempt to widen both the context of reform and to elucidate the best means whereby the CAAC can ensure a more positive approach to the maintenance of successful forms of operational progression.

The Political and Ideological Constructs of State Ownership

The concept of state ownership which is still embedded in the manifest role of the CCP retains an important ideological status and has been present in the ideological consciousness of the Chinese people for 60 years, and will now be revisited in somewhat more detail below. It is worth recalling at this juncture as an example of what Beijing has described as a continuous commitment by the CCP to an ideologically seamless reform process dating from 1949, that what 1978 signalled was not a massive change in political intention but rather the exercise of a flexible choice with regard to political form and style. In other words the intention to reform begins in 1949 and has continued ever since.

From an historical perspective that with the advent of the CCP's accession to political power in 1949, the first step in reform taken by the new Chinese government was to see the formal emergence of Mao Zedong's concept of democratic centralism take on a human form. Its primary definition can be found in the Trade Union Law of 1950. The purpose of the law in Mao's own words was to progress the enfranchisement of the working classes of China, so that they can play their proper role in the construction of the new democratic state. The ultimate goal was to make workers the masters of the means of production, while setting them free from unemployment and capitalist exploitation.

During this period the economic infrastructure of a socialist economy was intended to be put in place. This development has already been the subject of comments in previous chapters and further discussion below is intended to flesh out the operational aspects of that system. At the core stood the state-run enterprise (SRE), which became as a direct consequence of governmental action, the central focus of urban life. The working population following the Danwei strategy, was divided, as we have already seen, into cadres and workers. Members were entitled in addition to wages, to a range of state benefits that included health insurance, housing, educational and hospital services and canteen and bathing facilities. Production was organized on a factory or plant basis, in the urban centres and around the large state farms in rural areas. This meant that the staff had their living quarters located in and around a given SRC. Employment in the Danwei as a consequence saw management also play the role of community leaders, since work and social life both tended to come together over time.

The operational basis of the Danwei rested on three key symbolic elements.

* Job tenure (the iron rice bowl);
* Egalitarian wages (big rice bowl);
* A comprehensive range of welfare packages.

Under the constitution of the PRC, Danwei members were entitled to various ongoing subsidies in both cash and goods, which tended to create a very high level of social dependency. This condition was compounded by the fact that low wages were common at plant level and any real degree of labour market mobility, based on the individual choice of a worker to seek employment elsewhere, was completely absent.

Exit opportunities and job transfers were either minimal or simply did not exist. As a consequence workers were physically restricted to the locality in which they were employed. In fact any involuntary departure from a given location by a worker could lead to serious problems, since eligibility for Danwei services was subject to formal registration as a worker in a specified plant or as a member of a given work team in a given rural location. This rule still applies where itinerant workers are concerned since movement to a given city can often mean loss of any benefits or services, in the absence of any formal documentation certifying an individual worker's locational rights to be in that urban vicinity.

Finally the absence of market competition between firms led to low productivity and a tendency to overstaff the required work teams, by the direction of multiple workers into prescribed duties that could be reduced in terms of operational efficiencies into the workload of a single employee.

There also developed a tradition of occupational inheritance known as *dingti* in which an employee reaching retirement age could then relinquish a given job in favour of a son or daughter. As already noted in Chapter 1, the decision to undertake market reform was strongly influenced by evidence that the organization of the production system of the PRC did not take into consideration important matters relating to economic efficiency and productivity. In fact economic reality presented a somewhat cosy situation, as one critic has described it, where the SREs ate from the big iron pot of the state and the members of the Danwei from the big iron pot of the state-run enterprise.

The Domestic Problems that Influenced the Reform of the Danwei

It has already been observed in an earlier chapter that rising unemployment as well as major organizational inefficiencies within the SREs tended to dominate as key issues during the last years of Mao Zedong's leadership. Scholars have suggested that its causes can be attributed to population growth, economic stagnation during and after the Cultural Revolution and a massive return population flow from the country of the young people sent there to learn from the peasants.

As a result it has been estimated that by 1979, approximately 5.4 per cent of the urban labour force was actually unemployed. It is also important to take note at this point of the opinion of a leading Western expert (Warner, 1996) that by the time the state-run enterprises (SREs) had formally become state-owned enterprises (SOEs) in 1993, the ratio of SREs that were technically bankrupt was 1 in 3. This problem was initially addressed by government through the passing of the Enterprise Bankruptcy Law, which allowed insolvent state enterprises to formally declare bankruptcy. At the same time, the magnitude of the human resource problems facing market reform is best illustrated by the fact that in 1980, the SRE system accounted for 80 per cent of all jobs to be found in the urban labour force.

In the period from 1985 until 1993, the central focus of reformist attention was taken up with two major strategic tasks. The first involved the need to both introduce and develop the structural and organizational changes that would create state-owned enterprises from the former core businesses of the Danwei. The second and seminal requirement was to effect a seismic shift in the organization of the national economy from a centralized command structure to a mixed market arrangement by which the goal of China's entry into the WTO would be finally attained.

In the event the processes of SRE deregulation as well as the downsizing of work units, were to extend virtually to the present time, as the government tried to retain welfare responsibilities through continuing state subsidies for the laid-off workers who were seeking re-employment. The situation was further complicated by the fact that in the period from 1986 to 1992, the total labour force actually increased by 17 per cent. This literally left 100 million people seeking some form of employment in urban centres.

The First Initiatives to Advance Organizational Reform

In 1988 government passed the Enterprise Law, which attempted to codify relevant policies, rules and regulations that would accommodate the fact that the PRC was facing a new and complex series of problems, relating to the growing momentum of market reform. It was the first attempt to respond to market realities since 1949. It also faced the planners with no less than four distinct types of business organization. These included a diminishing number of SOEs, foreign investment firms, private Chinese–foreign joint ventures and firms located in the burgeoning private sector.

By the turn of the twenty-first century the CCP was ready to move on regulations to formalize this operational status quo, encouraged by the conditional entry of China into the WTO in 2001 and subject to the government's ability to meet a set of confirmatory changes with regard to its market conduct and behaviour. The following year was to see the creation of the State-owned Assets Supervision and Administration Commission (SASAC). This body was charged with five major tasks aimed at both maximizing market liberalization and completing the final phase of SOE reform (see Figure 4.1).

By December 2006 the SASAC was in a position to specify those industrial sectors where the state economy should have either absolute control, a leading role or simply a strong influence. Non-performing SOEs were scheduled to have left the market by 2008, leaving some 80 to 100 still operative by the due date. It is anticipated that of these, between 30 and 50 should be major corporations that would be internationally competitive in world markets by 2010.

Quite clearly the latter policy is based on the government's perceived need for the PRC to plan for a significant group of very large indigenous firms to become strongly competitive in both domestic and international terms and with the further aim of maximizing both their status and market identities alongside their major foreign competitors. In a sense the consolidation of the three major state-owned airlines fits this developmental profile, and in doing so they set the civil aviation industry comfortably within the liberalization process

The focus of the discussion thus far has attempted to identify the larger contexts of political and market reform that has been evolving in China both before and after the accession to national leadership of the CPC by Deng Xiaoping in 1978. The intention has been to establish the important formative influences of the ongoing search for socialism with Chinese characteristics within which the reform strategies driving civil aviation have been embedded. The balance of the

---

- To permit domestic stock exchange activity involving both domestic and foreign capital investment.
- To encourage large SOEs to develop a merger-acquisition strategy with a view to becoming enterprise groups that are internationally competitive.
- To maximize the effective market clearing of uncompetitive SOEs by elimination through selection or competition.
- To create an effective group of SOEs, capable of integration into the global economy, through the location of overseas production as well as mergers and acquisitions. These to be further supported by consultancy services, legal protection and listings on international stock and asset markets.
- To develop a legal environment and property rights system, that will allow foreign enterprises to be active in mergers and acquisitions in the China market.

Figure 4.1   The SASAC's Role in Market Reform

Adapted from: *People's Daily* 20 November 2003.

chapter will now attempt to further establish the functional identities of the reform processes that have driven the growth of civil aviation in China and shaped its new role as an international player in the modern era. In doing so it will also set the scene for the detailed further examination of the various operational aspects of the industry in China, and the means and ways they have been shaped by economic and various geopolitical forces.

The Origins of China's Civil Aviation Industry

It is now time to return in somewhat more detail to the historical origins of civil aviation in China, which in its earliest period developed in parallel to some extent, with the evolution of airline services in the West. The first commercial flight is recorded as having taken place in 1920, but the major wars which began in 1927 impeded further any real and further progress. The Republican government began a tentative developmental policy in 1929 as identified by Jin *et al.* (2004) with the foundation of the Shanghai–Chengdu Aviation Administration. As a consequence three domestic airlines were operational by 1933. They were China Airlines (Sino–US). Eurasian Airlines (Sino–German) and Southwest Airlines, an all-Chinese venture. By 1936, the available network had expanded to cover cities across China, with the exception of the northwest. Further development came to a halt in 1937, with the war against Japan and what was in effect an enforced moratorium on civil aviation development. This continued beyond the defeat of Japan in 1945 and on until 1949, as a consequence of the Liberation War.

Civil Aviation in the Post-revolutionary Period: 1950–80

The end of the civil war in 1949 saw the aviation industry in a state of total disarray. The existing three airlines as identified by Le Thuong (1997) ceased operations and there was a wholesale departure of both expatriate and Chinese pilots and technical staff. Services were not reintroduced until 1950, when the Civil Aviation Bureau (CAB) began operations. The new administrative agency was nominally under the control of the Ministry of Communications, but in fact its real control rested with the military. This meant that until the age of reform dawned, the management of a somewhat embryonic airlines industry was really under the command of air force officers. This tradition as we have already seen was to be further sustained until sectoral reform began in earnest with the return to a consolidation strategy that produced the current major carrier group.

The year 1953 was to see the launch of the first FYP (1953–57). It was a period of national development in which the Soviet planning model was adopted based on mandatory production targets and rigid governmental controls. Great reliance was also placed on the fact that the Soviet Union was very active in the developmental process supporting the new communist state with substantial economic and technical assistance, including over time the supply of both military and commercial aircraft.

In 1954, the government merged the two existing airlines a Sino–Soviet joint venture and Chinese carrier into a new state-owned monopoly. In addition the CAB was transformed in the same year into the Civil Aviation Administration of China (CAAC). Given its existing managerial links the administrative style of the CAAC was to remain somewhat subservient to military considerations which have tended to be paramount until fairly recently. These developments according to Zhang (1997) reflected the CCP's existing perception of the role of civil aviation as an instrument of government policy.

That it was not successful is demonstrated by the fact that the period 1950 to 1980, saw domestic inter-city traffic volume stalled at 1 per cent. It must also be observed at this point that in any real sense commercial passenger services simply did not exist. As a consequence those travelling by air, tended to be either government officers or cadres working in the larger SREs, who were required to move about the PRC on official business.

From the perspective of the industry's administrative roles and activities, it is possible to draw a strong parallel between civil aviation and the other SREs in the period from 1953 to 1978. Every aspect of activity was regulated with rules relating to all the conventional aspects of operational performance. In addition the CAAC had a degree of final authority over route entry, flight frequency, ticket pricing and passenger eligibility to travel. As a direct result, the industry experienced some 14 years of persistent financial losses, despite the fact that government subsidies were available and actively sought after at all times during the same period. The period 1968–74 alone saw consecutive failure to balance costs and revenues and resulted in a total loss of RMB360 million.

The Expansion of the Reform Process to the Civil Aviation Industry

The reform process got underway at the start of the 1980s with the first new regulations that would give CAAC the primary responsibility for promoting civil aviation at the national level. In 1981, the central government introduced into the SREs the concept of self-responsibility for losses and extra profit retention. Instrumentally this put in place a RMB1/RMB9 division of revenue to be shared between the airlines and the CAAC. As a result the airlines got one RMB and the CAAC the nine-RMB balance on each transaction.

In addition at the second level of CAAC's administrative hierarchy, the six regional civil aviation bureaus located in Beijing, Shenyang, Shanghai, Guangzhou, Chengdu and Lanzhou (later relocated to X'ian) were given responsibilities for recording both their profit and losses. The regional agencies were also given more autonomy in decision making and the controlling authority over revenue was further extended to a third level of authority, the 23 provincial bureaus.

It should be noted here, that the expected outcomes were both limited and restricted to some extent by the fact, says Chung (2003), that the CAAC was a relatively weak bureaucracy, traditionally overshadowed, as we have already seen, by the military. The suggestion that the CAAC–PLAAF relationship be uncoupled, with the former to be placed under the exclusive control of the State Council, inevitably met spirited opposition from the air force. It required as noted earlier the personal intervention of Deng Xiaoping for the CAAC military style command system to be restructured in the reformers favour.

But in fact, after the changes were introduced only some aspects of airline management became subject to an exclusive form of civilian management. Control over route utilization remained largely within the domain of the PLAAF, while the active demilitarization of airports has also tended to remain formally categorized as needing to be subject to a medium- to long-term change process. During the period down to 1987, the CAAC remained as the operational agency for all scheduled flights as controller of airports and administrator of the national ATM service. As a consequence, this left the question of the retention of monopoly control by CAAC formally outside the general debate on market reform.

The Report on Civil Aviation Reform Measures and Implementation: 1987

It was the primary intention of this report, duly ratified by the State Council and as described in some detail by Zhang and Round (2008), to progress the active separation of the role of the CAAC as a governmental, administrative and regulatory agency from all activities involved in the day-to-day operations of airlines and airports. The policy initiatives included the following major changes.

The existing four levels of administration were replaced with a two-tiered system that linked the CAAC head office in Beijing with each of the regional aviation bureaux. Six independent airlines were to be founded linked to each of the regional bureaux. Ownership was to be retained by the state, but functional operations in turn, were to be totally under the active control of each airline's management. In addition the carriers were to be encouraged to consider the expansion of their own networks through the search for and the development of new routes. The range of administrative responsibilities being passed to the airlines are listed in Figure 4.2.

Between 1987 and 1991, the six trunk airlines that had been proposed in the reform strategy began operations. They comprised, with their hub locations: Air China (Beijing, July 1988), China Eastern (Shanghai, June 1988) China Northwest (X'ian, December 1989), China Northeast (Shenyang, June 1990) China Southwest (Chengdu, December 1987) and China Southern (Guangzhou, February 1991). All of the designated airlines were in the nominal ownership of the CAAC as a

---

- Researching and developing the guiding principles, policies and strategies for the development of civil aviation.
- Developing plans for the industry's long-term development.
- Formulating policies, rules and regulations for flight safety.
- Developing standards and administrative rules for operational certification in all professional sectors of the industry.
- Developing the operational functions relating to airworthiness, overall licensing activities and the rules that apply to each activity.
- Formulating ATM regulations and their operational application.
- Formulating standard rules and regulations for the construction of airports and their certification.
- Developing compliance requirements for both domestic and international air safety regulations as protection against unlawful acts such as terrorism.
- Developing rules and regulations for the operation of air transport and general aviation.
- Researching and developing pricing policies and economic regulations for the civil aviation industry and monitoring for approval various budgetary, purchasing and leasing strategies as well as salary specifications for all entities affiliated with the CAAC.
- Acting as leader for the various regional administrations, SARs and municipalities as well as those educational institutions providing guidance on training and education.
- Acting as the national representative in all matters relating to foreign countries, as well as agencies such as ICAO and IATA. Acting as agent for government in the development and signing of air service agreements with foreign countries.
- The designated role of the CAAC also covered duties relating to ideological and party activities as well as other matters assigned by the State Council.

Figure 4.2   The Extended Responsibilities of the CAAC

Adapted from: CAAC.gov.com.cn.

ministerial agency representing the central government. Their launches occurred and were paralleled by further expansion of new airlines which were also intended to operate at the regional level. These carriers were either founded by local governments or as joint ventures with the CAAC.

The regional and trunk carriers remained under close supervision by the CAAC with regard to service provisions, market entry, route entry, service frequency and ticket pricing. As a consequence any hope of serious market competition was dashed. Indeed until 1996, the only competitive elements in the market were based on the quality of cabin in flight services as well as a given airline's flight safety record. The consequences of these structural changes in terms of any increase in competitive efficiencies were thus to prove disappointing from the reformist point of view.

In the event China was to see during the late 1980s and into the 1990s, a period of significant market entry by newly launched airlines, which inevitably led to increasing market fragmentation until the government finally moved to really consolidate the market in 2002. A more detailed examination of these events will inform discussion on the domestic airline sector in the next chapter.

The Changing Role of the General Administration of Civil Aviation

In 2002 the State Council ratified an emergent aviation system reform programme. A major consequence was to see the CAAC, elevated to the status of a ministerial agency and administratively reorganized. The resultant two-tiered system was to contain seven regional civil aviation bureaux, all subject to semi-autonomous management. The provincial bureau locations were abandoned and in their place some 26 aviation safety offices were created. This meant that the role of CAAC and the regional offices were for the first time clearly defined. The primary focus was on safety management, aviation market management, ATM services management for commercial services and responsibility for all matters relating to administrative relationships with foreign carriers. In the future the agency was not to be permitted to interfere in the internal affairs of any individual civil aviation transport enterprise.

The restructuring of the airlines and the aviation services followed with the regrouping of the current carriers into what now constitute the three primary state entities: Air China, China Eastern and China Southern. In turn the management control of some 93 airports was transferred to their provincial governments with the exception of Beijing Capital and the Tibetan locations. It was also decided that with finance and operations now the responsibility of the provincial authorities, that private investment in airport development was to be actively encouraged. While the CAAC in public declared the completion of this reform in 2004, there has been no indication of the cessation of reformist activities. In fact early in 2006, under proposals for changes within the 11th FYP, the agency signalled its support for the widening and deepening of civil aviation reform, with a set of key guidelines.

The document *Guidelines on Deepening the Civil Aviation Reform*, issued by the CAAC, anticipated the removal of control over operational rights on all domestic routes. A registry-for-record system will be expected to be in operation for all airlines by 2010. Domestic carriers seeking new routes will then not be required to go through a formal approval procedure and will be only required to report the decision to fly on a particular route to the CAAC. The plan also contains a strategy to encourage Chinese airlines to engage in all forms of cooperation with foreign carriers, including membership of airline alliances.

This follows the 2004 decision by China and the US to remove code sharing restrictions over time, from their new bilateral agreement. As a further consequence of the push for cooperation with the international airline industry, China Southern joined Skyteam in 2007, while Air China and Shanghai Airlines in turn, joined the Star Alliance. Work is also in process to promote the membership of China Eastern into the oneworld alliance.

This is clearly a response to the government's own signal that it intends to widen and deepen the institutional reform process and will pay very specific attention to the key services sector. The National Development and Reform Commission (NDRC) recognizes the essential weakness of overall aviation services as a tertiary industry, which has negative effects on key development projects, employment opportunities and a growing state of international competitiveness. The purpose of deeper reforms call for the establishment of a civil aviation industry which will conform with the needs of economic and social development, have a rational structure, operate smoothly, develop scientifically and establish an open, unified, competitive and orderly civil air transport market.

The New Plan to Place the General Administration of Civil Aviation in the Super Ministry of Transportation

In 2007 it became apparent that the CAAC is now in the process of further transformation, when it was announced by the government that it intended to advance further down the consolidation track, through the development of five super ministries. The planned intention is to streamline government department functions by the large-scale amalgamation of some of the key ministries. The anticipated result will be bigger departments charged with the task of strengthening macro-economic regulation, national security of energy supply, the integration of information development and industrialization. A new Ministry of Transport was anticipated which will include road, water and civil aviation. From the civil aviation perspective, the intention was to bring the CAAC under the aegis of the new ministry, with the status of a State Civil Aviation Bureau. It also appears that railways will continue to operate separately, on the grounds that their development has special characteristics.

Returning momentarily to the discussion on the ideological principles that were adopted by each successive generation of party leadership, we find that the current leadership of the PRC are strongly motivated by the concept of Scientific Development. The goals being sought involve sustainable development, social welfare, increased stress on individualism and increased democracy. These elements are connected by the notion of the emergence of a harmonious society as the social expression of socialism with Chinese characteristics.

It is clear that the relative economic unevenness of the geographical distribution of the benefits of market reform, and the consequential effects this would continue to have on public order, was an important factor in the decision of the CPC to engage in yet another programme of major liberalization. The primary initiative which was reported officially at the 11th NPC has been inspired by problems of overlap between government departments as well as a serious dichotomy between power and responsibility. As a consequence a plethora of ministries, commissions and bureaux tend to reflect low levels of operational efficiency. Ongoing research by Liu Quong (2006) has produced an interesting example, with evidence, that any matters relating to the growth and consumption of cabbages may involve the administrative expertise and full consideration at some stage of no less than 14 government agencies!

According to the Director of the CAAC, Li Jiaxiang, it is anticipated that in future passenger access to new airports will be integrated into the urban transportation systems of the cities they are intended to serve. It has also been suggested that the new Civil Aviation Bureau, will retain a degree of autonomy within the larger ministry. The ongoing discussion in China with regard to further reform developments also anticipates that various aspects of the technical management of major operational functions as prescribed in the 2002 reform of the CAAC will remain within the new ministry.

More general administrative and human resource functions are however likely to be merged within the larger ministry. It is also anticipated that the ministry bureau relationship will ultimately replicate to some degree the United States aviation management system as reflected in the fact that there are, at the current time, a number of ongoing advisory roles being played in China by the Department of Transportation (DOT) and the Federal Aviation Authority (FAA), all under the terms of the existing China–USA bilateral agreement.

Discussion thus far has attempted to describe and analyse the macro-contexts of political, social and economic reform that have been active in China since 1949, but more specifically since 1978. It is now time to begin the more detailed examination of the various operational components that constitute China's civil aviation industry. Before doing so it will be useful to first summarize the themes covered in the first part of the study. The intention will be to establish a theoretical framework in which the more industry-specific themes that will inform later discussion can be set.

The Specific Role of Civil Aviation

By contrast with the first three chapters it has been the purpose of this chapter to separate the administrative evolution of civil aviation management from the larger structural shifts taking place across industry in general. We have already seen with regard to practical policy developments, that a strong stress has been given to transportation as a multi-modal system. Quite clearly civil aviation has a substantive role, as noted by the key importance of airports in the Great Western Development Strategy. It has also been demonstrated that when formally tested on a sectoral basis with regard to its receptivity to reform, aviation shares with the automobile industry an operational classification as a most progressive industry.

According to one leading analyst (Chung, 2003) the general reform process post-1978 has moved through two distinct phases. These in turn, tend to demonstrate significant alternative shifts in policy direction. In the first phase the process of freeing up market activity clearly drove government's strategy in its decisions relating to the massive changes that took place with the abandonment of the Danwei. In the second phase the strategy now appears to have turned 180 degrees with a shift toward consolidation reflected in fewer but much larger and consolidated corporate entities.

First Phase: The Response to Over-centralization

This is most clearly illustrated by the deregulation of the Danwei and the ongoing reforms of the SREs. A high degree of devolution was encouraged and with it the growth of individual firms. In the absence of clear directions with regard to open market practices, the reform process as pointed out by Liew (2005) ran into what economists following Liebenstein (1966) tend to call a variety of soft budget constraints. These were compounded in turn by the retention of key roles by the various bureaux involved in the industry.

Second Phase: The Return to Consolidation

The decision to return to what is in effect an attempt to recreate centralization through amalgamation and conglomeration, was clearly influenced by the difficulties CAAC encountered in trying to control the operational behaviours of the airlines. This need clearly became prevalent at the regional, sectoral and local levels of activity. In effect aviation has gone successively through processes of partial demilitarization, corporatization, de-concentration and reconsolidation as well as various attempts at competitive marketization.

The Dimensions of Reform as Contemporary Organizational Restructuring

It is now time to focus attention on the major themes relating to the effects of market reform on a number of specific sectors of the civil aviation industry. Primary attention will be paid to the growth and development of operational services in both the domestic and international dimensions of the industry. Due cognizance will also be taken of the fact that Chinese aviation now constitutes an industry with several major dimensions. These include rapidly growing domestic and international airline services, a growing international identity as a major customer for new aircraft, an emerging aerospace industry which is attempting to become increasingly integrated into the international aircraft manufacturing sector and a sought-after location for international carriers seeking new markets.

The various elements that constitute what has been popularly called the new 'super ministries' can be identified in the following pattern of amalgamations. The notion of fewer but larger institutions has clearly emerged as part of an attempt to remove the last remnants of the Danwei tradition and the over-specification of both institutional and human resource needs within the civil service.

It has also been driven by the constant need for central government to sustain and maintain control over social and economic problems generated by the fact that despite the relative success of industrialization and the undoubted fact that China's export sector has experienced significant growth, significant urban as well as rural unemployment exists and with it the potential for political and industrial unrest. This casts consolidation in yet another role as an agent of political control when it is needed.

The expected consolidation as seen in Figure 4.3 has been under discussion for some time and the new Ministry of Transport will take responsibility for 3.57 million kilometres of road, 148 airports and over 1,400 sea ports. It has attracted strong support from the national logistics and supply chain industry which is really crying out for greater integration as part of the solution to a growing demand for services. The absence of the railroads from the amalgamation process has led to some comment, which would indicate as noted earlier that it has been able to resist the reform process to date. On the other hand an important member of the expert team that drafted the new proposals (Wang, 2008), made a public statement in which he suggested that the railways lag considerably behind the other transport sectors in matters relating to administrative reforms. In the meantime its immediate organizational future remains independent from the new administrative integration of the other transportation modes.

In the case of the maritime sector, the head of COSCO, China's leading shipping line, expressed strong approval of the shift toward modal integration that was promised by the new reform, especially in relationship to the emerging possibilities that the current high-cost inefficiencies would be removed under more streamlined procedures. In turn and from a civil aviation perspective, it appears from a further statement by a Li Jiaxing, a former head of CAAC, that the agency saw considerable merit in the possibilities of modal integration, notably in a road and air format to be implemented through the possible integration of city transportation systems that will allow for direct linkages into each of the airport sites.

National Energy Bureau (under NDRC)

- National Development's Research Commission Energy Bureau.
- Nuclear Power Management Function.
- National Energy Leading Group Office.

Ministry of Industry and Information

- Ministry of Information Industry.
- State Council Information Office.
- State Commission of Science, Technology, Industry and National Defence (COSTIND).
- NDRC's Industry Administration and Project Approval Functions.
- State Tobacco Monopoly Bureau.
- Ministry of Environmental Protection.
- State Environmental Protection Administration.

Ministry of Transport

- Ministry of Communications.
- Civil Aviation Authority of China (CAAC) now State Civil Aviation Bureau.
- Ministry of Construction Transport Management Functions.
- State Postal Bureau.

Ministry of Housing and Urban-Rural Construction

- Ministry of Construction.
- Ministry of Health.
- Ministry of Human Resources and Social Security.
- Ministry of Labour and Social Security.
- Ministry of Personnel Administration of Foreign Expert Affairs.

Figure 4.3   The Organizational Outcomes of the Super Ministry Amalgamations

Adapted from: China Economic Review, com.cn. August 2008.

The precise nature, role, responsibilities and degree of administrative autonomy to be enjoyed by the new Bureau of Civil Aviation remains an open question at the current time given the fact that the post-launch period of the new agencies has been one of an intensive review of current practice. This has created for the relevant agencies the need to identify and evaluate literally hundreds of regulations and rules as a prelude to the further development of new, streamlined and integrated procedures.

It appears to be generally understood that this process will clearly have to precede any further and positive forward momentum to that time when the Chinese government will be able to give a date to the formal unveiling of a fully reformed super ministerial system. The processes of thematic identification and discussion will now progress into the more detailed investigation of the various sectoral activities that constitute China's civil aviation industry. As a consequence, the emphasis in later chapters will cover the various and specific aspects of the civil aviation industry which will each be addressed from a specific operational perspective.

Chapter 5

The Reform and Modernization of the Domestic Airline Market

The application of the market reform process to China's airline industry as it has been carried out through the CAAC can best be described as a process fraught with trial and error. This is perhaps the best descriptive term for what has clearly been an often confusing and problematic period in China's aviation history. The process of evolutionary reform in civil aviation administration was addressed in the latter part of the previous chapter, with a review of the changing administrative processes that shape the operational and structural role of the CAAC.

In this chapter we will begin the process of study and analysis that will then continue throughout the balance of the following chapters. The sequential focus will be on the examination of the various and specific aspects of the industry through a continuing examination of the evolving reform process as it was and continues to be applied. This will extend the review perspective initially and specifically to China's domestic airline system, and then due consideration will also be given to the international and often geopolitical arenas in which China's civil aviation increasingly finds itself.

The Application of Market Reform Processes to the Domestic Airline System: 1987–2008

Commencing in 1987 China's civil aviation industry was to see a period of tension and conflict between CAAC as the managing agency and the emergent and burgeoning airlines. It appears to have surfaced as a consequence of two linked problems. The first involved a manifest failure by CAAC to find a consistent balance between the market change process and some efficient set of economic outcomes. At the core of this problem could be found the soft budget constraints that were imposed largely by a centralized tradition of management, and in turn staffed by people whose quasi-military background meant that they lacked any real or normative experience of competitive market conditions.

This problem was further compounded as later discussion will reveal by the inability of the managing agency to either obtain or enforce operational compliance from the various airlines. It is apparent as events were to demonstrate that their initial response was to compete against each other, not on conventional grounds which usually involves competition over fare prices coupled with the ability to match demand with regular and convenient route schedules, but rather, in the absence of any real experience of competitive market conditions, on the relative number and quality of their in-flight services.

It is an historical fact, worthy of further examination below, that the period of often controversial responses to reform initiatives in China particularly after 1997, were actively mirrored some 21 years previously in the much larger world of the American airline industry. In 1978, the United States Congress passed the Airline Deregulation Act, a legal event that was to structurally reform the largest civil aviation market in the world. In doing so it also set in motion what became a virtual international agenda for the expansion of what became described internationally as new market freedoms.

In the history of the United States airline industry, the institutional role of the original managing agency, the US Civil Aeronautics Board (CAB) from the late 1930s until 1978 was to exercise what can best be described as absolute control over the airline industry. Under the aegis of a highly politicized system of leadership which became subject to manipulation by government the CAB had controlled United States air space with a management system that bears significant comparisons with the Chinese experience until 1978.

The CAB literally designated the number of airlines permitted to operate in any given region of national air space. In addition it had control over both the rules of admission and the selection of applicant airlines seeking market entry. It also set the levels of ticket pricing and granted route allocations to the various carriers. In the latter process, the common practice was to balance the losses made by a given airline on mandatory but thin, money-losing routes (dogs), with the compensatory grant of thick, heavily patronized routes (plums). In sum the airline industry was insulated from conventional competitive conditions, since entry to the market by new carriers was very carefully controlled. As a response to inevitable market losses, airlines would simply offset high operational costs with unilateral increases in ticket prices, a practice often formerly ratified by the CAB.

With the passing of the 1978 Act, the CAB was dissolved and its administrative functions were passed collectively to the US Department of Transport (DOT) and the Federal Aviation Authority (FAA). The US industry thus faced for the first time in the history of commercial aviation, an open market situation in which competitive market pricing was to be the norm and market entry was to become legally open to new airlines.

The 1978 legislation was to set off what became a global trend. Given the fact that the United States was the largest and busiest of the world's airline markets, many Western countries followed suit with the adoption of various market deregulation. Inter-airline competition became the performance norm for an increasing number of players, especially in America. This was further compounded according to Chandra (2000) by the expansion of routes beyond national boundaries, especially by the larger carriers. The macro-effects especially with the later emergence of what has been described as the low-cost carrier (LCC) revolution, was to see the large-scale and increasing popularization of consumer use of airline transportation, an effect duly experienced by the Chinese domestic market in recent times.

The Theoretical Assumptions Underlying US Market Reform

It is a matter of emerging interest amongst scholars researching economic reform in China that, when the civil aviation industry becomes the main focus, there are major and important comparisons to be drawn with the United States. The successful progression of a market reform strategy into law in the US was in fact managed by a leading academic economist, Professor Alfred Kahn. It was he, according to a somewhat apocryphal story, who once described a modern airliner as a marginal cost with wings.

The aviation reformers were working at a time when significant academic research by economists was being focussed on the question of effective strategies that would avoid the need for anti-trust legislation to overcome the tendency toward market monopoly, or in civil aviation's case, oligopolies driven by a few controlling players. One important contribution to this debate took the conceptual form of what became known as contestable price theory. This model was found to be particularly applicable for testing purposes, with the emergence in the United States market of low-cost carriers led by the iconic Southwest Airlines.

Adapted for the civil aviation industry, contestable price theory proposes a market in which there is one major airline (a monopolist) which may be formally required to accept a marginal price ceiling for all routes. In addition there are no barriers or sunk costs involved with regard to entry or exit by new competitors. This allows for the important presumption that a new carrier could enter or leave without incurring cost liabilities through either course of action. In other words they would be able to continue business within the industry after leaving, though not directly in the LCC sector. It was further assumed that the active presence of new entrants would act as a deterrent for a monopoly airline seeking a return to competitive advantage, through the predative act of reducing its price to a point below that set by the new entrant. The dynamics of the model are covered in a stepped sequence which is described in Figure 5.1.

In the American case the model did not really work empirically, if only because there are very few markets which are really free of sunk costs and entry and exit barriers. There is no doubt that the market did expand very considerably and in the process brought air travel into popular use. But it must also be observed that many of the larger legacy carriers simply grew in size through mergers, takeovers and amalgamations, while the less successful members of what had been a comfortable oligopoly, notably Braniff, Pan Am, Eastern and TWA together with a number of new entrants like People's Express simply left the market, as competition increased. They did so through a variety of procedures including those listed in Figure 5.1 as well as through the inevitable fall into bankruptcy in some cases.

Those legacy carriers that remained active in market competition were later to be faced with the significant growth of the LCCs sector on an international scale. As a consequence their competitive reactions over time included fare discounting. The contestable price theory model did enjoy considerable attention, initially from economists especially when it was applied to the LCC market. In practical

- If we assume that the monopoly airline raises its ticket prices above the conventional marginal price for a given route, then the carrier will earn conventional monopoly (abnormal) profits.
- At this point new low cost entrants (LCCs) will be attracted into the market expecting to obtain a profit, from offering seats at a price below that set by the monopolist airline. (Note that both entry and exit are assumed to be costless.)
- As a response strategy the monopoly carrier might reduce the ticket price to a figure below the original marginal cost, as well as below that offered by the new competitor.
- The new LCC which is operating on a break-even cost strategy is unable to match the incumbent's new price, by reducing its original price. Since exit is costless the LCC now leaves the market.

Figure 5.1   A Five-stage Model of Contestable Pricing as a Market Entry Strategy

Adapted from: Baumol, et al., (1987).

terms however the LCCs in turn did have to accommodate real barriers to market entry often associated with control over terminal slot leases, the specific aircraft availability for leasing and the use of predatory pricing by those large incumbent carriers, who tended to also obtain significant non-competitive advantage from their domination of the available slots at various key hubs.

The American examples do have a degree of relevance in the discussion here, since some of the activities described were partially replicated albeit, one suspects, without deliberate intention as reform strategies within China's domestic airline market when it got under way. For example in the matter of slot control in the United States and Britain this tended to be in the hands of the dominant carrier or carriers at the given key airports, notably United at Chicago, American at Dallas Fort Worth and British Airways at Heathrow. In the Chinese case it stemmed in large part from government control over traffic in designated key airports such as Beijing Capital, Shanghai Pudong and Guangzhou Baiyun International. It was also influenced in turn, by the fact that the key hubs originally tended to be dominated by the large state-owned carriers both in scope and scale of services.

The Emergence of Domestic Services by Chinese Airlines

From 1997 onward, the Chinese airline industry was to face increasing challenges from foreign carriers wishing to enter the domestic market, as the range and scope of market entry for foreign direct investment (FDI) began to expand across industries. This was to a large extent a consequence of the fact that the world was experiencing a massive expansion of both domestic and international air travel. It seems that China was not to be exempt from this trend, as the rate of market growth during the current decade has graphically indicated. Faced by an emergent Chinese middle class, especially those engaged in corporate and professional business on both a regional and national scale, the airlines have also had to contend with increased consumer awareness which has been related to a growing demand for better services as well as competitive prices.

From an airline perspective, the domestic carriers also had to face the fact that as administrative prohibitions were relaxed, it was no longer possible to guarantee profits when necessity required it through the acceptance of a government subsidy. As a consequence, this made fluctuations in the level of revenues a further and growing problem. It must be kept in mind that government policies on the domestic airline industry were often inconsistent, both in form and intent, and as a consequence they simply added to rather than reduced the complexities that created the various controversies that were described earlier.

Challenges to the Role of CAAC as the Regulator of Domestic Air Fares

The year 1992 was to see the opening phase of what became a period of price relaxation. This was because during that year the State Council ruled that airfares would be allowed to vary within a range of 10 per cent of the formal set price. The practical effects of this change ran counter to expectations. This was because the airlines simply adopted the same price, according to Li (2001), through what was really a cartel arrangement and then instigated a unanimous price change under the CAAC's supervision.

July 1997 also saw the elimination of price discrimination against foreign passengers, when all expatriate business people and visitors who purchased their tickets in China, did so by paying a common market price. Later that year, in parallel with the international trend, CAAC introduced the concept of a single class of traveller with a ticket price that allowed for the practice of discounting. The general idea was to attract more passengers by following international conventions with regard to price discrimination in the matter of seat prices for given flights and on specific routes.

While the move signalled the beginning of price deregulation, it also set off a series of price wars between the airlines. There was also a serious predatory effect experienced six years later which was caused by the market activities of some of the airlines. They began to set prices below the marginal break-even point where the costs of a given flight are at least equal to the revenues obtained as fares. The consequence in 2003 was a massive aggregate revenue loss within the airline sector in the order of RMB3.5 billion.

In May 1998 CAAC issued a decision that was designed to enforce its authority as controlling agency and, at the same time, bring some degree of order to the market. The intention was to control the various forms of discounting that were by then common practice amongst the carriers by a prohibition on any airline offering tickets priced at more than 20 per cent below the conventional set fare.

Unfortunately the new rules did not carry any form of penalty to be imposed for default, and the price wars simply continued as before.

As a response to what was a direct challenge to the agency's authority, in February 1999, the CAAC introduced, says Huang (2000), a new strategy which effectively called for all airlines to stop discounting on fares. The penalty for non-compliance was to be a cancellation of the offending carrier's right to fly the route on which the offence occurred. Several violations took place notably involving Hainan Airlines, which then had the penalty imposed. Unfortunately offences over time became so prevalent the CAAC simply found it increasingly difficult to enforce the rules in a really stringent manner.

The Introduction of Revenue Pooling as a Final Attempt to Control Market Behaviour

The introduction of revenue pooling has been described by Zhang and Round (2008) as the CAAC's last-ditch attempt to restrict the airlines' freedom in practice to ignore the conventional rules of fare setting. The requirements of the new regulations targeted a selected number of high density routes and called for revenues earned by the individual carriers to be placed in a common pool, after which they would be subject to reallocation on the basis of the measured sales revenues of each carrier. The process was to be compulsory and any failure by the carriers to join the scheme made them liable for a penalty, which could lead to the cancellation of the rights of access to the route or routes to which the pooling requirements were applied. In practice, as will be shortly revealed, the scheme was to prove to be inherently counter-productive in terms of the need for effective market competition between the airlines. The operational aspects of the new regulations as they were introduced are described in Figure 5.2.

This policy was seriously flawed in the sense that while it reduced the decline in revenue caused by discounting below marginal cost, it also gave carriers no real incentive to compete for passengers. Consumer reaction was also extremely critical and attention was drawn to the fact that what was essentially a price-fixing strategy, simply did not work. In fact, as noted by Huang (2000), the allegation was publicly criticized on the grounds that CAAC's price-fixing strategy was illegal under the 1997 Price Law (c.14.1), which prohibited price collusion. After its implementation, however, the requirements of the new clause was simply ignored and revenue pooling went on to be introduced as an active policy.

The policy was also viewed with disfavour by those airlines that found themselves with a degree of comparative advantage in the market under normative conditions. Their strategic goal was greater freedom, rather than active compliance with restrictions which required them to sacrifice their own interests for the benefit of the weaker carriers. It also tended to impose limitations on carriers such as Hainan Airlines who serviced a regional tourism industry and which was beginning to move into an opening period of strong growth.

- Revenue aggregation was required by all airlines servicing 108 selected and high density routes.
- The 108 routes equalled 11 per cent of the national total and 50.5 per cent of all passengers carried.
- Sales revenue equalled the total of all passengers carried multiplied by 80 per cent of the normal fare.
- Reallocation was to be delivered by the designated CAAC Settlement Centre.
- The system favoured carriers with larger fleet types and more seats, since their reallocations were larger, even if seats were unsold.

Figure 5.2   CAAC's Revenue Pooling and Re-allocation Process

Adapted from: Zhang and Round (2008).

The CAAC also faced a much larger political dilemma at the turn of the millennium. China was entering into the last phase of preparation for formal admission into the World Trade Organization which required, as we have already seen, demonstrable compliance over time with international free trade market standards set by that agency. An attempt was made to retain control over-discounting when the pooling arrangement was reintroduced in 2001, but it was to remain active only on paper. A year later the CAAC signalled what amounted to the formal abandonment of revenue pooling.

The Scheme for Domestic Airfare Reform: 2004

Despite these repeated failures the CAAC still retained its role as a price regulator. With this fact actively in mind, the 2004 scheme was intended to do two things, first to set benchmarks for pricing while at the same time introducing a consistent pricing mechanism. The benchmark price in the domestic market was set at RMB0.75 per kilometre on the basis of what were deemed to be average carrier cost, market demand and an average of available consumer resources. It allowed the airlines themselves to set their own prices. They could set their price levels in a range of up to 25 per cent above the price ceiling, and 45 per cent below the price floor.

In practice these requirements tended to be ignored even before the regulations came into force with 70 per cent discounts offered on many routes. It is also interesting to observe that while confusion continued over the fact that what had actually taken place was a *de facto* deregulation, there was no serious attempt ever made during this period by the CAAC to actually codify the regulations and operational rules that were needed, if the airlines were to take advantage of the proposed increases in market flexibility.

The Deregulation of the Route Entry and Exit Process

Under the 1996 regulations on domestic routes and flights, airlines were required to make application in order to effect entry to and exit from given routes as well as for any intention to increase the number of flights that would service a given route. There is some official evidence supplied by the then Deputy Director of the agency that from 2000 the CAAC, as the designated authority, actually began a process of gradually reducing this formal and administrative stress on the need for permission to make changes to entry and exit criteria.

Approval procedures were simplified and applications were in reality very rarely rejected. From 2004, airlines with proven efficiencies in the key areas of better safety records, reputations for punctuality and in-flight service quality, were given priority in the opening of new routes and the expansion of flight frequencies. While the 1996 regulations had permitted the CAAC to require that an airline continue serving a thin route, in practice, they were quite often permitted not to do so, where losses on that service threatened a carrier's operational viability.

The expansion of operational freedoms continued to develop with the regulations on domestic routes that were promulgated in 2006. Excluding those routes with high traffic volumes as well as those linking with busy airports, carriers were now permitted to activate both entry and exit decisions without seeking prior agency approval. Instead they were simply required to register their decisions for the record with their regional civil aviation bureau. This also meant that airlines could enter most domestic markets without being required to go through the traditional reviews with the CAAC.

At the same time it should also be noted that the routes into and out of the eight busiest airports in the domestic system – Beijing, Shanghai's Pudong/Hongqiao, Shenzhen, Guangzhou, Chengdu, Kunming and Dalian – still remain formally under CAAC control. The reason for this type of constraint can be found in the fact that the airports concerned have a strategic geopolitical significance in terms of military control of air space. In addition it must be noted that the top 15 busiest domestic routes remain to this day under relatively strict forms of exit–entry control.

The Effects of FDI on the Development of Market Privatization in Civil Aviation

The possibilities for further economic growth stemming from the privatization of the civil aviation industry did not appear on China's reform agenda until the mid-1990s. In fact it was in 1994 that the CAAC, in tandem with the Ministry of Foreign Trade and Economic Cooperation, produced a policy statement relating to foreign investment. The terms of reference initially limited foreign capital to the purchase of a specific level of equity in the existing carriers as well as component investment in the construction of airports. Private investors were also allowed to establish general aviation enterprises classified as non-passenger and cargo business ventures.

The ability to invest in an indigenous carrier also carried restrictions which tend to parallel those applied by the US Department of Transport and Federal Aviation Authority (DOT–FAA), to foreign investment in American airlines. The investor would be limited to 35 per cent of the registered capital, with a limit on voting rights as company directors to 25 per cent. The cap on FDI in airports was later to be set at 49 per cent, under regulations promulgated by the CAAC and duly noted in its Annual Report for 2005–06. An important step forward in terms of the evolution of managerial roles and functions was also taken on 28 September 2005 with the formal launch of the China Air Transport Association (CATA). The organization was effectively the first non-governmental body to become active in the civil aviation industry, and its mandate included the coordination of developmental activities as well as the further advancement of industrial interests at governmental level through lobbying.

Despite these liberalizing trends and the advent of the CATA, a degree of caution still remained in official circles with regard to what was generally referred to as the policy of opening up. According to Le Thuong (1997) an acquisition of 25 per cent of the shares in Hainan Airlines was made by a US investment fund but the CAAC, at that time, was at pains to deny that this was to be treated as an indication that it was opening up private ownership rights in the airlines.

The agency's conservatism with regard to market privatization also became evident in the test case involving the possible stock exchange launch of shares in China Eastern. After a long, intensive and often acrimonious discussion involving the restructuring process undertaken by the CAAC and other government agencies in 1997, China Eastern Co. Ltd was finally launched on the stock exchanges of Shanghai, Hong Kong and New York.

The effects of this landmark decision were to signal what was to become an ongoing process of both privatization and diversification. Many of the overall effects of these changes will be examined in later chapters which will be dealing with other major institutional themes. From an airline perspective, as a capital-intensive industry, their managements now found in stock market launches a much more cost-effective way of raising capital. This was particularly true in the key matter of investment in new aircraft, an essential requirement but one previously limited by the higher cost of interest on bank loans.

Today foreign investment is actively encouraged in all domestic airlines, notably with the raising of the FDI maximum from 35 per cent to 49 per cent, although with the limit of 25 per cent of share ownership still applying to individual investors. There has also been an important development with domestic investors now seeking market entry through the active purchase of shares. In a real attempt to halt the development of monopolies in the emergent market sectors of the civil aviation industry, indigenous investors were also encouraged to purchase equity in airlines. Further protection was also introduced in regard to possible market entry by airport companies and the aviation oil/fuel supply firms, who were already operating as virtual monopolies. In effect the CAAC imposed restrictions on any attempts such parties might make to gain equity interests in the domestic carrier sector.

The Decision to Return to Airline Consolidation

The first Chinese airline merger in modern times took place in 1994, when the relatively small Fujian Airlines was taken over by Xiamen Airlines. With the Asian monetary crisis of 1997, many smaller airlines found themselves facing major crises and the possibility of imminent collapse. As a direct consequence there followed a number of further mergers, with notable primary acquisitions undertaken by two of the three leading trunk carriers, as well as by a private airline, as listed in Table 5.1.

The National Consolidation of the Domestic Airline System

The full return to consolidation was instigated in October 2002, when an agreement was signed that resulted in the emergence in the market of three major carrier groups and left a small group of independent airlines still operational. The integration of carriers also saw the key groups obtain significant and new control over regional and provincial locations.

Figure 5.3 has a geographical significance in the sense that it demonstrates the ways in which the three major groups now have a series of operational bases quite outside their traditional locations in the primary cities. It should be noted that a number of these sites, including Chengdu, have also become strategic locations for airlines like Air China wishing to launch new international services.

The distribution of domestic capacity shares between the main carriers and the secondary group is very interesting. By July 2007 China Southern was clearly the national leader with a 30 per cent share. China Eastern followed with 19 per cent and Air China was third with 16 per cent. Hainan Airlines which has begun international services leads the cluster that is found in the second group with 8 per cent, while Xiamen, which is incidentally, 60 per cent owned by China Southern,

Table 5.1   Examples of Mergers between Major and Regional Carriers

Major Carrier Mergers	Regional and Local Carriers Merged
China Eastern (trunk)	CGAC, Great Wall, Wuhan
China Southern (trunk)	Guizhou, Zhongyuan.
Hainan Airlines (private)	Chang'an, China Xinhua, Shanxi

Adapted from: Zhang and Round (2008).

follows with 7 per cent and Shenzhen closely follows with 5 per cent. Shanghai, Sichuan and Shandong are then found to be on 4 per cent, with some 4 per cent of the market taken up by other private carriers

The formal processes of consolidation drew to a close during 2004 and the CAAC began somewhat cautiously to issue new licences to operators. It was done so at a time when the major carriers themselves were struggling to convert strong demand into profitability. The industry faced higher fuel prices, increasing

---

Air China Group (CNAC Holding Company)

- Air China (Beijing)
- China Southwest (Chengdu)
- CNAC (Hong Kong)

China Southern Group (China Southern Holding Company)

- China Southern (Guangzhou)
- China Northern (Shenyang)
- China Xinjiang (Urumqi)

China Eastern Group (China Eastern Holding Company)

- China Eastern (Shanghai)
- China Yunnan (Kunming)
- China Northwest (X'ian)

Hainan Airlines (HNA Holding Company)

- Hainan Airlines
- Chang'an Airlines
- Xinhua Airlines
- Shanxi Airlines

Independent Airlines

- Shanghai Airlines
- Xiamen Airlines
- Sichuan Airlines
- Shenzhen Airlines
- Shandong Airlines

Figure 5.3   New Airline Group Concentrations and their Locations

Adapted from: Zhang and Round (2008).

debt levels, rising operational costs and increased staffing costs as the result of amalgamations. China Eastern is on record as the hardest hit of the major airlines, whose future has remained consistently uncertain ever since.

Its problems led into the recent extended, but finally aborted, attempt to obtain an infusion of capital and restructuring expertise by the sale of equity to Tamasek Holdings on behalf of Singapore International Airlines. In parallel with these developments the domestic airline market saw the expansion of the new entrants' intent on creating a private airline market. Their various experiences are described below.

The Emergence of the Private Airline Sector

While the emergent private carriers, in sum, have taken up some 4 per cent of the very large domestic market, no single airline has been able to take up a commanding position over its rivals to date. As an operational example, Spring Airlines, a high profile entrant, holds just over 0.5 per cent of the very competitive Shanghai market. It serves the metropolitan centres on a weekly basis, which is the common test for market growth in the private sector. The overall leader, Lucky Air, in turn, has been able to retain between 0.7 per cent and 0.8 per cent of market share. The key players are noted in Table 5.2.

It must be immediately borne in mind, that small operational size, and formal exclusion from the key volume markets, a current limitation which may be removed in 2010, has tended to shape the leisure and special market aspects of the growth of some private airlines. Fleet size leading to the inability to offer daily frequencies is also a factor that imposes a serious limitation on market growth. Its is also important to be aware that in terms of ownership, CAPA (2007) has made an important distinction between airlines launched on the basis of private equity and those sponsored and financed by government.

The developments described in Table 5.2 have been replicated to some extent by the launch of airlines in the second category of operational players whose financial support, has come from either government grants or from investments by state-controlled companies. All of these airlines are in the very early stages of their development, for example West Air and Chongqing Airlines were both launched in June and July 2007 (see Table 5.3).

It has also been reported by CAPA (2007) that at least 12 further airlines are in the project planning phase of their development, with three being actively prepared by their founders to enter into the cargo services market. Their emergence currently seems to indicate a search for niche markets, rather than the replication of new and successful market entries. While LCCs are clearly a source of interest for entrepreneurs, the realities after launch can dampen corporate enthusiasm. In the case of Okay Airlines, a return to a more conventional business model was reported by its President to have been influenced by operational cost levels which reached 80 per cent.

Table 5.2   Operational Profiles of China's Privately-owned Airlines

Airline	Business Focus	Owners	Current Fleet	Fleet Plans	Bases	Network	Classes
Shenzhen Airlines	Passenger Cargo International	80% private 20% Air China	43 737 series 19 A319 7 A320	70 in 3 years 100 in six years	Shenzhen Nanning Wuxi Guangzhou Zhengzhou	60 cities in China	Business and Economy
Spring Airlines	LCC	Spring Travel Agencies	8 A320	30 by 2010	Shanghai Sanya	24 cities in China	Single
Juneyao Airlines	Business travel Premier market	Juneyao Aviation Investment Group	2 A320 2 A319	6 by 2008 40 by 2010	Shanghai 2	21 cities	Business and Economy
East Star Air	Peak Business off peak Tourism	East Star Group	3 A319/20	Leasing incremental 7 A320 20 by 2010 10 leased	Wuhan	16 cities services to Hong Kong and Macau	First class Economy
Okay Airlines	Cargo plus passengers MRO and Logistics	Juneyao Group	3 737F 3 B737 2 Y-8	7 B737F 7 B737	Tianjin Int. Hanhzhou Xiaoshan	15 cities in China	Economy
China Express Airlines	Hongshan Industrial High Hero International Tampines International	Hongshan Industrial High Hero International	3 CRJ 200ER	30 aircraft and 6 bases in six years	Guiyang Chongqing	22 cities in China	Economy
United Eagle Airlines	Changed from tourist to business travel	80% 3 private investors 20% Sichuan Airlines	3 A319 1 A320	Not applicable	Sichuan Shuangliu Int. Airport	15 cities in China	First class Economy

Source: CAPA (2007) pp. 9–15.

The degree and extent to which central government will permit a really competitive market to develop still remains a somewhat ambiguous issue. The CAAC has signalled that full de-regulation will be introduced in 2010. Unfortunately, the key indicators for 2008 are not positive. Apart from the need to absorb the consequences of higher oil costs, there have been worrying signs of weakening discretionary consumption in the domestic market, even before the current global financial crisis. In turn the effects of the major earthquake in

Table 5.3   Market Entry by Government-supported Airlines

Airline	Business Focus	Owners	Current Fleet	Bases	Networks
Lucky Airlines	Tourism plus capital city services	Hainan Airlines	5 B737 plus one extra	Dali	16 cities in China
Grand China Express	Regional operations city services	Hainan Airlines	29 Dornier 328 Jet	Tiajin X'ian in planning stage	54 cities in China
West Air Airlines	LCC tourism model	–	–	–	–
Chongqing Airlines	Western market development Intending major city operations	China Southern Chongqing Development and Investment	3 A320	Chongqing	City pair with Shanghai

Source CAPA (2007) pp. 16–19.

Sichuan are estimated to have caused at least RMB1 billion in airline losses. The hardest hit appears to have been Air China, with Chengdu its third hub physically located in the epicentre of the disaster.

The Negative Pressures of Exponential Market Growth

In 2007 domestic passenger growth in China grew by 16.7 per cent in the first two quarters of the fiscal year. The result was a revenue return to the airlines in the order of US$11.46 billion. Despite the positive nature of the rate of growth, the CAAC found itself faced by a shortage of technicians and other aviation professionals, coupled to the existing limitations on capacity at various domestic airports. As a consequence it announced that from 15 August to 27 October some 336 domestic flights to and from Beijing Capital International Airport (BCIA) would be discontinued. The operational effect would reduce peak hour flights from 60-plus to 58. The CAAC went on to advise carriers that in the period November 2007–March 2008, peak hour flights would be reduced to 55 an hour, leaving approximately one minute between flights. Warning of the intention to reduce services had commenced in June 2007, with the cancellation of 120 flights and two services from Beijing Capital. The major burden of the cancellations inevitably fell upon the three leading carriers, Air China, China Eastern and China Southern.

Two reasons were identified as the causal factors that prompted the decision to cancel. The first related to concerns with regard to the possibility of delays at Beijing Capital in August of 2008, when the anticipatory traffic pressures exerted by the Olympic Games were taken into consideration. The second related to the significant fact that some 18 key airports, including Beijing, Shanghai Hongqiao, Shenzhen and Chengdu, were reporting that they were currently operating at maximum capacity.

The CAAC also formally announced on 15 August 2007 that it would not entertain any more applications for the registration of new airlines until 2010. This actually dovetails into the earlier decision to prescribe a moratorium on the purchase of new aircraft since airline fleet growth is assumed to be contributing to the increasing strains being carried by the main airports in the system. The vexed question of runway capacity also looms very large as a continuing problem impeding further growth, simply because there is no hub airport anywhere in China at the current time that has more than three runways.

It is also worthy of record that the further development of new airports in the west of China, which was discussed in an earlier chapter, has a direct influence on the growth of domestic services, since the number of scheduled routes will need to be increased in order to meet passenger and cargo demands in the more remote provinces. The new ban does, at the same time, have considerable loopholes, since cargo night flights and more remote weekly services are left out of consideration. The possibility has also been canvassed that the current ban will allow breathing space for increased market capitalization as well as an expansion of operational and technical upgrading.

Underpinning these significant difficulties there may be found some even more serious and emerging problems. If national transport is perceived essentially as a major set of public service systems it is possible to identify two acute social contradictions inevitably at play in the context of this discussion. They are to be found first in the conflict that is inherent in the pressures of economic growth, the imbalance in the distribution of economic and social benefits, and problems created by resource and environmental restraints. In turn the growing demands from citizens across society for an increasing range of public services is bedevilled by what has been called by Fulin (2008) the forces of under-supply as well as problems regarding the displacement of the provision of services. It would appear that the frequent and often contradictory attempts to date by government to resolve these problems through administrative fiats may require a more modern approach and a much clearer understanding of the forces shaping market change.

Discussion thus far has concentrated upon the evolution of reform in terms of its impact upon the domestic sector of airline services. It is now time to examine the questions raised by the application of market reform on Chinese airlines who are actively seeking market growth within the larger context of global market competition. As the evidence will show, this has seen the former role of Air China as the major international carrier, come under challenge from both the other two large state airlines as well as the growing regional carriers. The next chapter will examine a number of issues, including the strategic location of a new Chinese presence in the major airline alliances that now bring new forms of collaboration to the expanding world of ultra-long haul passenger transport.

Chapter 6

The Entry by Chinese Airlines into the International Passenger Market

The serious attempts by the CAAC to bring about airline reform and consolidation have seen Air China, China Southern and China Eastern emerge as the leading-edge carriers, now intent on taking China's civil aviation industry forward into a growing international market. They have been followed over time by a number of smaller carriers that have also been seeking opportunities to open up international routes. Reciprocal arrangements for entry have in turn led to a significant number of foreign carriers entering the Chinese market, usually under the terms and conditions of bilateral agreements (ASAs). This significant and parallel trend continues to develop to this day, subject however in the latter part of 2008, to increasingly uncertain changes in market conditions that will be the subject of later discussion.

This strategy which is aimed initially at moving the big three national carriers into the competitive international airline markets has also seen two of them successfully apply for admission into formal membership of the leading international alliances, Star and SkyTeam, while the third is in the process of negotiating a place in the third largest namely, oneworld. In doing so they have opened up a whole range of potential opportunities and benefits, which may be developed further as the international alliance system continues to grow.

The overall result of these various activities now places China within the operational environment of the primary market forces that are actively driving the expansion of an industry that, to date, has been playing an increasingly important role in the growth of international business and world trade. It has also had an interesting effect on the career expectations of some Chinese airline pilots as they become aware of the fact that their professional skills are in short supply on a virtually global basis. This has led to reports that a number of aircrew members are seeking to buy themselves out of their existing and career-long contracts at a substantial personal cost. Figures of up to RMB5 million have been quoted in the domestic trade press.

The primary focus of this chapter will be to examine what is becoming a very important issue in Chinese civil aviation – international route development, which is clearly intended to complement the growth of domestic airline services that was duly noted in the last chapter. The idea of having a viable international service driven by Chinese carriers also fits within the larger economic strategies that are intended to place those firms which are now the leading SOEs as active players in the international business sector.

At this point it must be borne in mind that China has a very high dependency on its international exports to such leading markets as Japan and the United States as one of the major components that sets the growth rate of its GDP. With these economic parameters in mind, it is now time to examine the various issues and concerns that face the Chinese carriers as they have sought to expand route development beyond the domestic parameters of the national market.

It is important to first record the fact that to date the presence of Chinese airlines, both major and regional, as potential competitors on important international routes has not brought the expected levels of revenue and yield that the decision to develop long and ultra-long-haul traffic is commonly assumed to provide. Further discussion will also seek to take account of the issues and complexities that are to be found in the highly competitive and increasingly technological world of the modern international passenger airline, especially with the increasing growth of airline alliances as a collective counter to contemporary market uncertainties.

The CAAC Policy on Structure Reform and Opening to the Outside World

Following the directions for aviation set by the 11th five-year plan for China, which called for an expansion of international services by the various Chinese carriers, the government found that by the end of 2006, it had amassed a total of 106 bilateral air service agreements with other countries. In addition new agreements had been signed which brought both Hong Kong and Macau SARs actively into the South China network. Further expansion occurred with the opening of a new Air China service between Chengdu and Amsterdam, during which event, the first and symbolic route between central China and Europe was established. The same year also saw a direct service introduced between China and Brazil.

At the leading edge of what became a rapidly growing activity were to be found the three major carriers, Air China, China Southern and China Eastern. Their progressive role and the growth of their international routes send a clear signal, suggests Doganis (2006), that the major carriers are now busily moving beyond the purely commercial advantages that accrue from agreements that emphasize the operational aspects of alliance membership. As a prelude to a more detailed examination of the role of Chinese carriers in the international market, some consideration will first be given to the nature of aviation alliances and the important distinctions that separate them in terms of both their size and their intended structure.

A Brief Historical Overview of Modern Airline Alliances

There has been a tendency over a number of years for airline alliances to be established across a wide and often complex variety of formats. The primary driver has often been the specific needs of the parties establishing the agreement.

Doganis (2006) reports that the process gained very serious momentum from the mid-1990s, driven by a series of international crises. They first emerged in late 1997, with the financial storm which struck the 'tiger' economies of Southeast Asia. The year 1998 then saw an economic slowdown in Europe which signalled the beginning of a general economic downturn. For the airline industry, the following year was to see a rapidly growing rise in fuel prices. The unstable cycle was then capped by the tragic events of 11 September 2001 which tended to deepen an already emerging crisis for American airlines.

According to a leading organizational theorist (Porter, 1990), industrial firms use alliances as transitional devices when they are confronted with adverse market conditions, such as escalating market competition or important structural changes. In doing so they are often being influenced by their management's fear that they are unable to cope with growing problems. This assumption as a total explanation for the motivation that drives the development of alliances, as Rigas Doganis points out, is really difficult to fit into the context of the airline industry, which has both complex and special characteristics and its own operational norms.

While the experience of smaller carriers may well reflect the uncertainties described by Porter, as international route networks grow in size and complexity, various synergies and market opportunities suggest new possibilities for the increasing formulation of very large and integrated mega-carriers as currently seen in the attempt to create even closer ties outside the existing and conventional alliance arrangements. A most recent if negative example of this trend is to be found in the abandonment at the last minute of what would have amounted to a special kind of merger deal between British Airways and Qantas. The immediate question that arises at this point is would the Chinese carriers in some presumptive future be allowed to consider such possibilities?

With the relative decline of the state-owned airline as the primary international service carrier there has also been outside the United States, at least until recently, a shift toward mergers as the classic strategy aimed at maximizing specific market share. This view tends to be supported by the history of contemporary innovative international airline agreements, indicated by the notable cases of KLM–Air France and Delta and Northwest in the United States. The merger model used effectively created a holding company as the organizational core, while the partners retain and maintain their comparative market advantages and identities as individual airlines.

A Brief Résumé of the Growth of the Regulative Process in International Air Travel

International airline agreements had their genesis in 1919, when delegates from some 26 countries formulated the Convention Relating to the Regulation of Air Navigation (see Vasigh, *et al.*, 2008). What became the Paris Convention introduced the basic principle of national sovereignty over the airspace contained within the geographical boundaries of a given country. Neither Russia nor the United States were signatories, but the US was present in 1928 at the Havana Convention, which set both the technical parameters of rights of passage, as well as the right of the specific state to set the routes for travel within its sovereign airspace.

The 1920s was a busy period for the ratification of the basic rules of international air travel. In 1929, the Warsaw Convention set the terms under which the operational process of international air transportation was to be defined. The terms included a definition of any liability incurred by the airline due to accidents in flight, and in doing so introduced the principle of contributory negligence. At the same time a given airline could claim immunity from liability for death or injury where it could prove that the causal incident was due to some kind of natural causes under the principles of *force majeure*. This procedure has been replaced under the Montreal Convention of 1999 by the rule that an airline has unlimited liability.

A landmark in the development of international regulations for the aviation industry emerged in 1944 when the Chicago Convention was both convened and hosted by President Roosevelt. His intention was to expedite the post-war developments of an agreement that would permit an internationally recognized freedom for open skies traffic. In the event he was not to be supported by the majority of the 54 countries that attended the Convention.

Under Article 6 permission to fly through the airspace of a given country became dependent upon a bilateral agreement signed between the airline's country of origin and the country whose airspace the airline was proposing to enter. The terms of the Chicago Convention superseded all previous agreements and remain the basis for all international aviation law. In addition the airlines chosen to deliver the service, tended to be duly designated state-owned or national carriers. This traditional arrangement became, in the view of many critics, a major restriction on airlines seeking greater freedom for market entry.

The Emergence of International Airline Alliances

The opening phase of alliance formation began in 1986, when Air Florida and British Island Airline (BIA) as identified in Oum, *et* al. (2000) signed a code share agreement which introduced the practice of the placement of passengers booked on one airline onto the scheduled flight of another carrier. In this symbolic example, Air Florida transferred passengers onto another aircraft scheduled to fly the BIA London to Amsterdam route. What began as a simple sharing agreement has grown to be a common practice, as the review of the flight information screens at any international airport will reveal.

Today the process of code sharing has evolved to the point where a given flight is often identified as having multiple carrier names and numbers, and passengers are welcomed aboard according to which airline number is on their ticket. The range of routes covered by such agreements has also expanded to include joint ventures and revenue sharing. Meanwhile the general practice of proration in revenue sharing has also increased the range and flexibility of code share options, especially within the leading-edge alliances. In turn the dynamic evolution of the major alliances has increased the formalization of agreements and expanded the range of activities and services that now form a part of collective membership.

What has become the global alliance system is currently dominated by three major players, Star, SkyTeam and oneworld. Their collective memberships combine a very significant number of the world's leading airlines, and the magnitude of their members operations are reflected in Table 6.1.

The three global alliances account for almost 80 per cent of the total world airline capacity (average seats per kilometre (ASK)), 78 per cent of the world's aviation revenue (revenue passenger kilometre (RPK)) and 73 per cent of all passengers carried. It is worthy of note at this point that the benefits to be obtained from admission clearly underpinned the decision by the Chinese government to allow their carriers to apply for membership. The rationale is further advanced by the following points that are taken from Air China's formal application to join. The CAAC formally recognized the following industrial realities.

- With economic expansion and open skies, the competition in the airline industry will become more and more severe.
- No one airline can create a global network by itself, although Emirates appears to be prepared to give it a good try.
- In order to survive and develop, airlines have to cooperate with other partners in various forms including when required, multilateral alliance cooperation.

Table 6.1   Major Global Alliance Membership in 2008

Alliance	Membership Numbers	Countries Served	Destinations Served and Departures (000)	Aggregate Fleets Numbers
oneworld	10 plus 20 affiliates	134	664, 8,951	2,228
SkyTeam	11 plus 3 associates	169	905, 16,786	2,496
Star	21 plus 3 regional members	162	975, 18,100	3,359

Adapted from: Airlines Issues and Trends: Airline Alliances, 4 September 2008, Tourism International.com.

Alliance Benefits, Advantages and Competition-based Problems

The ranges of benefits that accrue from membership include the ability to offer the member airlines an expanded network in which their market growth plans can be optimized. It also allows its members to offer services to locations which are not formally covered within their current route schedule. This allows for economies of scope and scale. To these advantages may be added cost reduction in terms of maintenance and other factors often obtained through bulk purchasing and resource sharing.

On the other hand a key requirement that members of a given alliance have an information system that is seamless and easy to use is addressed in quite different ways. The most notable example of the strategy is of course Star, which is the leading alliance and recognized by analysts as the group that has reached the most advanced level of membership integration. Further types of information creation and exchange are being developed, as a part of the process of increased consolidation. The assumption that this strategy signals that Star has a global game plan for organizational growth, is supported by a recent statement in *Air Transport World* (12 December 2008), that the potential development of this alliance from some 24 to over 50 member airlines is now considered to be a serious commercial objective. By contrast, while SkyTeam has not elected to follow suit, oneworld has developed and introduced an e-ticketing system that now operates across all its member airlines.

There are of course significant costs involved in the setting up of a permanent administrative structure to service alliance members. Again the Star group comes to the fore, with a full-time staff of approximately 70. While the largest of the global alliances obviously needs an administrative team, it is also an indicator of the strategic approach being taken by the Star group toward a master brand image. This is also reflected in the practice that each member should have one aircraft in operation which carries the logo and livery of the alliance, with the home brand usually on the nose. By contrast oneworld has a much smaller management team whose main function is to administer its e-ticket system throughout the membership group. In turn SkyTeam has yet to move in the same direction and is currently reliant on discussions between members in order to reinforce their alliance commitment.

It appears that an important problem can arise where member airlines who are strong market competitors for the dominance of some key routes enter into an alliance and are expected to comply with what has been described as a single contract as the condition for membership access. While the basic intention is to endorse collaboration and increasing degrees of economic integration, the reality may often be diminished by continuing competition between member airlines and with it a reduction of services where the route is being shared.

This has been particularly the case in the conflict between Delta and Continental, where the routes in question were thick competitive earners for the individual carriers before they joined the alliance. By contrast such conflicts may be balanced, in turn, by the fact that smaller airlines seeking to expand their international markets will see the material benefits from membership entry as a form of market protection, while they proceed to build their own collaborative networks.

We can estimate the percentage distribution of airlines that have entered each of the three global alliances by region as Table 6.2 reveals. We can also see by comparison the relative strengths as growth leaders by region of Star and SkyTeam in North America and the South Pacific. By further contrast it seems that oneworld's strongest growth has been experienced in the rapidly growing market of the Asia–Pacific region.

The membership distribution across all three leading alliances marks a clear distinction between those regions where national air transport systems can be described as both mature and still growing and those that are currently expanding their markets at a significant rate. It is also safe to assert that, as Table 6.3 reveals, by contrast, in the Latin America and the Africa and Middle Eastern areas some of the leading-edge carriers are still evaluating their basic choices in the matter of alliance membership versus any advantages that might arise from staying as an independent.

Table 6.2   Percentage Market Share of the Key Alliances by Region

Alliance	Europe	North America	Asia–Pacific	Latin America	Africa/ Middle East
Star	21	24	29	Nil	12
SkyTeam	22	30	11	15	2
oneworld	15	16	22	15	2

Adapted from: 'Alliances Overview' (September 2008) 24(9), *Airline Business*, pp. 36–7.

Table 6.3   Percentage Distribution of Alliance and Non-Alliance Airlines

Region	Aggregate Percentage Global Alliance members	Aggregate Percentage of Non-aligned Airlines	Plus/Minus Aligned/Non-aligned
Europe	58	42	−16
North America	70	30	−40
Asia–Pacific	62	38	−24
Latin America	30	70	+40
Africa/Middle East	16	84	+68

Adapted from: 'Alliance Overview' (September 2008) 24(9), *Airline Business*, p. 37.

A marked feature of the growth of global alliances, as earlier discussion has shown, has been an increase in the rate of interaction, notably in code sharing within the alliance groupings. This finds many carriers are now operating parallel relationships within alliances, a practice that will be described later after due consideration is given to the fairly recent decision to become alliance members made by Air China and China Southern. The events that followed the applications are considered in some detail below.

The Emergence of China's Major Carriers as Alliance Members

China Southern became the first Chinese carrier to be accepted into an alliance, with its admission to SkyTeam on 15 November 2007. It is clear from the various group perspectives that the possibility of access to China's massive domestic market by their members has also been an important factor underlying the invitation to the Chinese airlines to join. Following this initial entry, Air China and Shanghai Airlines have both become members of the Star Alliance. In addition Hainan Airlines – now China's fourth largest and private airline and operating under a new name, Grand China Airlines (GCA) – has also signalled a developing interest in oneworld membership.

The current situation leaves China Eastern yet to finally commit to oneworld, although the carrier does have links with several key players in the alliance, notably Cathay Pacific, Qantas, American and JAL, and has indicated an interest in joining the group. It has also been involved in protracted and difficult negotiations over an initial offer by SIA, to take an equity interests in the company. This initiative was abandoned by the parties at the last minute after the CEA shareholders turned down the SIA equity offer. This decision will be discussed in more detail later in the chapter.

Given the continuing role of the state in the ownership if not the management of both these leading airlines, it is unlikely that tensions between Air China and Shanghai Airlines will emerge over time. On the other hand they are faced with the competitive need to be very up to date in such key areas as the quality of in-flight services. The pressure is very acute given the increasing emphasis by the major Western carriers on all aspects of customer satisfaction as an important marketing strategy.

It is now time to begin a closer examination of those Chinese airlines that are building international services, both as members of the global alliance system and in a private capacity. Given the sheer scale of the Chinese market and the wide range of political, social and economic factors that have and will continue to shape the role of civil aviation in that country, the focus will be on the three major carriers and a selection of the regional airlines that have expanded their service offerings into the international market.

Air China, the International Market Leader

In the historical sense of the term, Air China has always had a primary role in international travel. This dates back to its origins as the international arm of the original CAAC. Today it remains the national flag carrier in the literal sense as the only airline permitted to use the national emblem on all of its aircraft. Its parent firm is the China National Aviation Holding Company (NAHC) in which the government is the major shareholder. The operational programme of Air China cover a range of activities as listed in Figure 6.1.

These activities include commercial ground services on offer to airlines flying into the key airports where Air China is located. In addition its subsidiary Air China Cargo operates a flight logistics service firm, while Air China Business Jet is also contributing to China's small but growing presence in executive aviation. Air China's core hub is Beijing Capital International, and it also operates from Chengdu's Shuangliu International as well as Pudong International in Shanghai. In addition it is servicing a range of cities with international capabilities such as Hangzhou, Xiaoshan, Chongqing Jiangbei, Tianjin Binhai and Hohhot Baita.

The Air China passenger fleet comprises some 155 Boeing aircraft ranging from the B737-300 series through the B767-300ER to the B777-200. The airline is also on record as having placed orders for some 45 B737-800s, 15 777-200ERs and a further 15 of the new 787-900 series. In turn it has some 68 Airbus aircraft currently operational, with types ranging from the A319-100 to the A340-300. Orders have also been placed for a further 20 A321-200s and an additional 21 A330-200s.

It is clear that Air China is seeking to anticipate a medium to long-term potential increase in demand, both domestically and internationally. As an example of its intentions, it has already nominated a further 12 destinations in Europe and North America it wishes to service in 2009, in addition to the current number of 185 destinations it has within its schedule. The overall average age of the current fleet is 7.8 years, which reflects its relative modernity. Given the pattern of formal orders for new aircraft, it would appear that Air China's plan for its future fleet specifications will also cover an important requirement, that of aircraft replacement.

- *Airline Operations*: The active provision of air passenger and cargo services
- *Engineering Operations:* Internal and commercial delivery of MRO services
- *Terminal Services:* A range of ground services covering all required activities
- *Support Services:* Supplementary services such as in-flight catering.

Figure 6.1   Air China's Divisional Operations by Function

Adapted from: www.airchina.com.cn.

Planning may also be strongly influenced by such factors as fuel costs and price hedging and the need for operational economies, together with the need for technologies that offset the potential environmental requirements of the future. As a final comment, according to comparative data, Air China is the fourth largest airline in Asia, the fifth largest in the world in terms of its domestic cargo traffic and seventeenth largest globally in the category of fleet size.

China Southern: From Domestic Dominance to International Competition

Measured by sheer size China Southern is the country's largest airline with a primary focus since it commenced operations in 1989 on domestic passenger, cargo and mail services. The Guangzhou-based carrier operates a fleet of 300 aircraft through China Southern Air Holding Company, which has just over the required level of government shares (50.3 per cent) in its portfolio. The balance is held by non-Chinese investors (H type = 26.84 per cent) and private Chinese investors (A type = 22.86 per cent). In comparative terms China Southern was rated the seventh largest passenger carrier in the world in 2007, the same year it joined the SkyTeam alliance, and is now seen to be the current operator of the largest fleet in Asia.

In 1996, the carrier entered the international passenger market when it began to service long-haul intercontinental routes commencing with flight that linked in sequence Guangzhou, Beijing and then Amsterdam. This was followed in 1997 by what remains its longest flight, non-stop from Guangzhou to Los Angeles. The opening up of the new service coincided with two other events. The launch of a public stock offering on the New York Stock Exchange which netted over $700 million and the first non-stop B777-200 flight to cross the Pacific. The initial emphasis on international route development also saw the primary growth of new destinations within the East and Southeast Asian region. In 2000 the programme was expanded to take in Sydney and Melbourne. Further service locations since have included Dubai, Lagos and Teheran.

What has been described by the Chairman of the China Southern Board, Liu Shaoyang, as a major shift in its operational priorities occurred in 2007. Government approval was granted to allow the carrier to develop its international networks and this led to ten new routes being opened into Europe and North America. The carrier also plans to develop further routes with services from Beijing to New York, London and Detroit and probably from Guangzhou to Vancouver, Paris, Riga and Moscow in the period from 2009 to 2012. In addition management recently announced that the further fleet requirements of this ultra-long-haul schedule will be met through the use of the five Airbus A380s and ten Boeing B787s that China Southern has currently on order.

Supporting the expansion of its international network, the airline has a growing pattern of code share arrangements with Delta, KLM, Japan and ANA. In the case of ANA, arrangements allows for domestic code sharing within both host countries. There is also the further possibility that ongoing negotiations with Air France with regard to a cargo joint venture, may lead to the introduction of a foreign strategic investor. While the airline is not currently prepared to name a possible partner, market analysts are picking the growing relationship with Air France as a potential signal.

China Eastern: The Constant Search for Market Stability

The airline (CEA) was first launched in 1988 and entered into an expansionary phase from 1987 until 2003. It began the process with a takeover of China General Aviation and during that year became the first Chinese airline to offer shares on the international stock market. The foundation of China Cargo Airlines in collaboration with COSCO was commenced in 1998. There then followed the further absorption of Great Wall Air in 2001 and the merger of Yunnan Airlines and China Northwest in 2003. It now also operates two further subsidiary carriers, China Jiangsu and China Eastern Wuhan.

The carrier's primary owner is the Chinese government with 64 per cent of the equity. Some 32.19 per cent of shares are held in the public H category and 6.7 per cent is held in the public A category. In keeping with the other two major carriers it also operates in a range of airside and landside services to airlines flying into its two Shanghai hubs, Hongqiao International and Pudong International. The CEA fleet is similar in its distribution between various aircraft types to what is virtually the norm amongst the big three carriers. Its 213 aircraft are to be found in both the Airbus and Boeing series with the main long-haul international routes covered by the Airbus 330-200-300 and Airbus 340-300-600 aircraft.

CEA has developed a strong international identity on routes in Asia, Europe and North America. In addition during 2007 it began its first African service to Johannesburg as well as a Shanghai–Brisbane service to Australia. While there are no problems with consistent rising demand until recently in China, China Eastern continues to face an expanding series of difficulties over time which is the product of serious managerial shortcomings. It is true that profitless growth has been the common experience of many international airlines, but in the Chinese case the situation is exacerbated according to a lead article in *The Economist* (2006) by such factors as high debt related to fleet expansion, and the inability of China's state carriers to seriously practice yield management. The existence of a domestic state-owned monopoly as the primary aviation fuel supplier, also translates into a 40 per cent average cost against a comparable 24 per cent for all foreign carriers.

In the case of CEA, the situation has been further complicated by what has been noted above as the now completed saga of its attempt to create an equity link with Singapore International (SIA). On 2 September 2007, it was announced that a deal had been struck with SIA and its parent company, the Singapore investment arm Tamasek Holdings. The terms called for the transfer of 24 per cent of CEA shares with 15.7 per cent equity going to the airline and the balance of 8.3 per cent to Tamasek. The quoted price was Sg$1.4 billion and from the buyer's strategic perspective the purchase would allow entry into the Shanghai market, which would in turn help offset the relative maturity of the Singapore market. From CEA's point of view, apart for a welcome injection of much needed capital, SIA would also have assisted in the positive growth of the airline through training programmes and other forms of development.

In the event CEA's shareholders turned the proposal down in favour of an alternative link with Air China. This involved an offer in January 2008 from Air China's parent CNACG, to buy 30 per cent of CEA's equity at the rate of $5 per share. The proposal in turn has failed to come to a satisfactory conclusion, and rumours abound that Air China has since been having merger talks with Shanghai Airlines, which both parties have continued to deny until fairly recently. It is also clear that CEA hopes that there will be future possibilities for further discussion with SIA.

In the meantime, it would appear that discussions on the now potential CEA–Shanghai Airlines merger are under way. Somewhat ironically given the current economic crisis that is now affecting China, despite the sheer size of its current trade and monetary surplus, it appears that the PRC government has suggested that a range of mergers might serve to consolidate the airline industry at a time of rapidly falling demand. In the meantime the existing alliance members are engaged in serious commitments with the alliance membership as noted in Table 6.4.

The Second Wave of Smaller International Carriers

The internationalization of civil aviation in China has also seen the growth of a range of smaller carriers managed by regional and major city administrations. These decisions to enter the market are also reflective of a range of activities, which have emanated from the national government's landmark decision to transfer operational management and administration to regional and local government. The following descriptive comments offer examples of this quite important and localized market system, which constitutes a secondary group of airlines servicing international routes.

Grand China Air

Now the fourth largest airline in China, GCA started life as Hainan Airlines and became China's first joint stock carrier in 1993. Its parent company the HNA Group is very well known since the famous billionaire financier George Soros is part owner. The carrier was formed under a new parent company Grand China Airlines Holding (GCAH) which merged Hainan, Shanxi, Chang'an and Xinhua. This gives the new airline a fleet of 120 with some 166 new aircraft on order.

Current plans call for a Beijing–Seattle service which will be GCA's first external route to North America. The airline also plans to introduce some eight Boeing 787-8s into its expanding North American service. It remains to note that under its old HNA Group name, GCA is the first Chinese airline to have achieved the quality rating of ISO 9000.

Table 6.4   The Distribution of Code Sharing Arrangements by the Big Three

Air China Star code shares	Air China non-Star code shares	Shanghai Airlines Star code shares	Shanghai Airlines non-Star code shares	China Southern SkyTeam code shares	China Southern non-SkyTeam code shares
Air New Zealand	Alitalia	Air New Zealand	Korean Air	Air France	Asiana
ANA C	Finnair	Asiana		Continental	Dragonair
Asiana	Korean Air	Lufthansa C		Delta	Garuda
Austrian	Kuwait Airways	Scandinavian		KLM	Japan Airlines
Lufthansa C	Qantas	United		Korean Air	Malaysia C
Scandinavian	Qatar				PIA
THY Turkish	Virgin Atlantic				Vietnam Airlines
United	Dragonair				
US Air C	Cathay Pacific				

*Note*s:

- The data is sourced from some 500 alliances involving 150 mainline passenger carriers. The sources are restricted to full members of the three major global carriers, and non-aligned airlines listed in the top 100 ranking of carriers.
- The letter **C** denotes the existence of a comprehensive code sharing agreement in which ten or more routes form the substance of the agreement. All the other arrangements involve code shares involving less than ten routes.

Adapted from: 'Airline Alliance Survey', *Airline Business op. cit*, pp. 47–52.

Shanghai Airlines

The airline was established by the Shanghai municipal government in 1985 as the first independently-operated local airline in China. In September 1997 government approval to fly international routes was obtained by the carrier. Shanghai Airlines maintains a fleet of 53 aircraft and is a member of the Star Alliance. The strategic plan is to have 100 aircraft flying by 2010.

Following a not uncommon pattern of development, Shanghai Airlines has developed a range of international services based on the fact that it is strategically located at the epicentre of the growing Chinese economy. It has also built up a strong set of code-sharing relations as well as valuable reciprocity arrangements with major international carriers. Current plans include applications for route entry to Seattle and Los Angeles as well as Vienna, Hamburg and Zurich. These are on hold however as the uncertainties confronting the international airline market are being strongly felt in China.

Xiamen Airlines

Xiamen Airlines has a special uniqueness in the sense that it is the first carrier in the PRC to be managed as a private business. It was founded in 1984, and equity rights are shared by China Southern with 60 per cent and the Xiamen Construction and Development Group with the balance of 40 per cent. Its fleet comprises some 45 Boeing aircraft in the 737-300-800 series with a further number of 737-800s on order. The balance of the fleet comprises eight Boeing 757-200s.

In addition the airline has ordered six new indigenous aircraft from the proposed ACAC ARJ21 regional jet series. Following what has been something of a Chinese tradition since 1978, Xiamen also serves a number of international destinations in East and Southeast Asia namely: Seoul, Osaka, Hong Kong, Macau, Singapore, Kuala Lumpur, Penang and Bangkok.

A Primary Problem with the China's Civil Aviation Infrastructure

The fact that airline services have tended to grow in response to an exponential rise in demand down to 2007 has drawn international attention to the growth potential of the Chinese domestic passenger market. This raises a serious question with regard to the need to create a clearer picture of the various groups of passengers that utilize passenger transport by air, from tourists, through groups such as itinerant workers, to the emergent and growing middle class who travel on business as regular airline clients.

There are also clear difficulties being currently experienced with regard to the rate of growth of airport development. As noted in Chapter 3, civil aviation along with other transport modes shares a developmental role in the government's western strategy. It has been suggested by some experts that the current rate of expansion is somewhat out of kilter. The difficulty arises from the fact that there is a chronic imbalance between the number of services scheduled for major trunk routes and those allocated to cover major regional routes.

The problem is further complicated by the timetables for localized services, some of which may only run on a weekly basis. These difficulties are further exacerbated by the fact that China's aviation system has yet to develop a systematic and national hub and spoke system to replace the current large-scale reliance on city-pair services. Finally, route allocation in turn is strongly influenced, as earlier comments have indicated, by the fact that some key areas of Chinese airspace still have military controls in place as a part of the government's prescribed plans for national security.

Further problems emerge from the fact that the current system tends to raise user costs to significant levels, in addition important business class travellers seeking fast inter-city services on a regular basis are possibly being lost in favour of other transport modes. The need to respond to this kind of issue may well await the terms of reference that will in future set the parameters of national civil aviation security somewhat more clearly than they are at the present time.

The development of international passenger air services both into and out of China has a developing overlap with the transit of cargo. This is because international wide-bodied jets are designed with cargo space which allows a spot market arrangement to be developed where an actual number of pre-flight users seeking rapid transportation for valuable goods permits. At the same time specialist logistics services do exist for both heavy lift freight, and for express deliveries which are now setting up their own terminals at the major airports. The importance of these trends has a serious multi-modal potential, given the fact that the development of a viable supply-chain system is still restricted in many locations to point to point road services only. A further and more detailed discussion of some these issues will be undertaken in the next chapter.

As a prelude to future discussion it is important to take note of the fact that China's airline industry now shares with the rest of the Asia Pacific region a developing downturn in demand for services which is clearly a direct consequence of the current global financial crisis. The effects of this extremely worrying global trend and its expected duration are extremely difficult to predict. The extent and range of the effects of this economic calamity is perhaps best symbolized by the fact that the US car industry represented by the CEOs of core companies General Motors, Ford and Chrysler, appeared recently in Washington to request monetary assistance to cover their large-scale debt imbalance from the federal government. They have since become virtually dependent on what is in reality a policy of state subsidization, under terms laid down by government and not the financial market. With these matters in mind it is now time to begin the examination of China's equally important as well as growing presence in the international air cargo market.

Chapter 7
The Growing Strategic Importance of Air Cargo Services

There is a general consensus amongst analysts engaged in the study of international business and world trade, that the carriage of cargo and freight by air enjoys some degree of comparative economic advantage over alternative modes of transportation. In fact it has been demonstrated in various studies and recently by Senguttavan (2006) that cargo airlines are closely associated with a positive growth rate for a country's trade and GDP returns over time. With the growth of cross-border production systems driven by a growing number of multinational enterprises, the traditional advantages of physical location in close proximity to both internal and external markets have been consistently losing their value as the only strategic option for businesses. Today it is quite common to find firms which schedule and plan product design and testing in say the corporate HQ, or through a specialist subsidiary, followed by component production in one overseas location, partial assembly in other overseas locations, final assembly in a chosen centre and sales of the final products in a fourth target market.

It is important to bear in mind that while air cargo accounts for 40 per cent of world trade by market value, when compared with the tonnage carried by the surface transport modes, the actual physical proportion is 1 per cent of the global total. It is at this point that the special nature of cargo carriage by air is revealed, since its activities are to be found in the servicing of firms offering a wide range of time-sensitive high value products, which can be divided into two major categories (see Bliss and Haddock, 2008). The first involves products that are subject to obsolescence, due to the effects of rapid rates of technological change during the shelf life, for example, of a computer, music player or cell phone. The second are subject to high inventory carrying costs and are to be found in a list ranging from medical devices, aircraft jet engines and critical manufacturing components for low-volume high market revenue products.

Air cargo services operate under a dual definition covering first, express freight in the form of high priority packages, which are carried from the point of immediate sale or procurement to the door of the customer's final location. In turn heavy cargo and larger volumes of product come under the aegis of direct air carriers and freight forwarders. Consequential revenue shares are divided in proportion on average with, for example, 31 per cent going to the express carriers, 48 per cent to the direct air carriers and 21 per cent to the freight forwarders in 2005. It should also be noted here that the freight forwarders handled some 80 per cent of all intercontinental freight measured by tonnage in the same year. The general trend is moving the industry toward an increasing dependence on dedicated freight carriage over combination flights where the main component is belly cargo.

The Air Cargo Market in its Operational Context

The air cargo sector has a set of specific and unique roles and functions within the larger context of air transport. The transportation of cargo by air has already been defined as a high value market, in terms of its weight and value per kilo carried. Defined by type, such cargoes range from expedited small package movements with door-to-door services offered by such household names as Fedex, DHL, TNT and UPS, each servicing an often highly time-sensitive client list. In addition many of the world's leading airlines are now introducing their own dedicated and specialized cargo fleets into the market.

It is now possible to define the various options for freight carriage as characterized by three specific operational groups, namely: emergency traffic, routine perishable traffic and routine surface divertible traffic, which can be switched between cargo modes. This indicates that the air cargo sector has a very wide distribution of market clients each with different price sensitivities and each requiring efficient service suppliers to help them to fully customize their operational strategies.

There has also been a general broadening in operational practice by logistics and supply-chain firms, many of which are now able to operate virtual port locations for the transfer and redistribution of cargo, often at some strategically placed airports. They are not totally dependent, for example, on the more traditional single modes of geographical access at a single entrepot. In fact they may utilize an integrated range of specific modes.

This chapter will continue with an overview of the various strategic aspects of the modern air cargo industry as well as the logistical infrastructure that underpins its undoubted advantages in terms of customer services set within a dedicated timeframe. It will then attempt to locate, analyse and discuss the stage of development that has been reached to date by China's air cargo sector.

The Comparative Advantages of Modern Air Cargo Services

From a cargo aviation perspective, research led by Kasarda and Green (2004) has indicated that in the period 1980–2000, the relative growth rates of GDP, trade and air cargo, in sequence, and over the 20-year period were 72 per cent, 132 per cent and 302 per cent. When the time period is extended to 30 years, from 1970 to 2000, the relative rates of growth are found to be 154 per cent, 355 per cent and 1,395 per cent. These results reveal that in the first period trade grew faster than GDP by 60 per cent, while air cargo grew by 230 per cent; whereas the growth of air cargo when compared with that of trade rose by 170 per cent. This long-term trend is reflected in the fact that when the time period is extended by a further ten years, the growth of trade over GDP increased by 201 per cent, while that of cargo over trade growth reached a massive 1,040 per cent.

It is also important to recall at this point, that the more recent growth of the air cargo industry, both as a passenger carrier-based spot market and as a specialist carrier service has been embedded to a large extent in the relatively high value sectors of various product markets. This is the level of operations where scheduled time of delivery to the customer, is based on wide-ranging international sourcing, matched with Just-In-Time (JIT) production systems that speed up production while reducing the costs of component storage.

Given the further fact that intermediate products and components are often now sourced in developing countries, the relatively higher cost of air transportation, when compared with road, rail and maritime services, can also be actively reduced through competitive mitigation. More importantly such costs lose their relative significance when compared with the market advantages of shorter delivery times for new products, and a resultant higher rate of consumer satisfaction.

The Air Cargo Strategic Value Chain

The point at which a specified cargo item is loaded into the belly of either a scheduled passenger flight, or a designated freighter hold, is the penultimate step in an increasingly complex set of network relationships that includes, apart from the carriers, transfer of the final goods to the customer, supported by a wide range of specialist activities such as the various operational contributions of brokers, handlers, road carriers, integrators, airports freight forwarders, suppliers and manufacturers and logistics service providers.

This complex pattern of activities in held together in turn, by information technology systems that allow for real-time decision making. The final point in the network is reached when the item is safely delivered into the hands of the customer. It is important to be aware at this juncture that the service is increasingly, and literally, from the producer through the shipper to the client on a door-to-door basis. We are of course describing the leading-edge systems that are to be found in the growing metropolitan areas of the world's leading market economies. From an air cargo perspective they constitute a key nodal airport as a hub, surrounded both in space and distance by a range of international companies seeking to be a part of an optimal distribution network.

Two examples from different sides of the world come immediately to mind.. Federal Express has developed Clark Air Force Base at Subic Bay in the Philippines into an important cargo service centre. It comprises a secondary airport in a free enterprise zone which has attracted some 200 international customers to the consistent use of its facilities. A further working example may be found in Amsterdam, where Schipol International has something of the order of 500 international firms utilizing its services in order to maximize added value for customers who are located in their European networks.

Current Trends and Prospects for International Air Cargo

Despite the fact that aircraft manufacturers Airbus and Boeing predict a rough growth rate for global freight traffic to increase by a further 6 per cent up to 2025, the industry is currently experiencing difficult times. Inevitably high fuel costs come to the fore as one important cause of this problem. It has also been suggested that the Asian market and India in particular now faces serious problems with overcapacity, resulting from very rapid growth in new market entrants. Despite a worsening international economy there can be no doubt that, in the long run, air cargo will continue to expand as the best choice for the transit of time-sensitive and specialist products. In passing, to this may be added some further developmental possibilities that may emerge in a future mixture of modal links between services.

According to the OAG freight forecast (2008) for the period 2008–17, the global cargo industry will be experiencing an annual traffic growth rate of 5.6 per cent by 2011. Their decennial forecast is for a slightly higher rate of 6.1 per cent. Regional business it is anticipated will be reduced to 4 per cent as security and environmental issues become more pressing. In addition they suggest that the leading edge of rapid growth will shift to the Middle East and Africa, with China reduced to third place. At the same time these latter numbers are qualified by the fact that they are projected on a very small base level of traffic.

How far these projections are still valid in the light of current events in the global money markets comes increasingly into question, as recession deepens and firms attempt to adjust their rate of expected revenue growth to the realities of falling demand? With this sobering thought in mind it is now time to turn our main attention for the rest of the chapter on the emergent role of air freight and cargo as a growth factor in China's emergent economy.

The Initial Contribution of Air Cargo to China's Economic Growth

The growth in the volume of air cargo transportation in China has tended to keep pace with the general growth of the economy, especially in the key export sector. Domestic demand together with the political determination to expand international trade were the drivers that saw an annual total of 157 thousand tonnes in 1980 become 4.5 million tonnes by 2004. In turn, China has been able to grow under market reform, as well as a high level of FDI, the production of a much broader range of completed high-technology projects.

As a working example, the supply of completely assembled computers to the United States market, China's largest customer, expanded in the period from 1995 to 2006, from 840,000 to 45 million. It is also notable that in the same period, the proportion of exports of high technology goods in aggregate rose from 38 per cent to 58 per cent.

It is very important at this juncture to be aware that there is a serious imbalance in trade between China and the United States. This is reflected in the 2006 figures which reveal China delivered goods in the order of $288 billion, while net westbound exports from the United States stood at $55 billion.

From an air cargo perspective it is clear that a great deal of the traffic is eastbound which requires carriers moving backwards and forwards between the two countries to offer a degree of subsidization on rates. This is indicated in the Booz, Allen and Hamilton study (Bliss and Haddock, 2008) which reveals a $3 per kg rate operating on board carriers from China and a $0.10 per kg prevailing return rate on the return westbound services. Further tactical responses to the effects on load manifests caused by the market imbalance include scheduled stops on westbound flights, notably to airports in Japan and Korea, and in some cases a round the world service. In addition several of the Asian hubs pool goods from multiple national sources, while in North America cargo consolidation at nominated hubs is a current practice.

It is also important at this juncture to be aware of the fact that operational changes imposed by the CAAC under the direction of the State Council have seen the progressive liberalization of the limitations on traffic between China and the United States. Between 1996 and 2003, the available number of cargo route frequencies rose from four to 20. This doubled in 2004 to 41, and then in progression to 59 in 2005, 71 in 2006 and 86 in 2007. It is now anticipated, as seen in earlier discussion, that under the prevailing China/US Air Service Agreement (ASA), commencing in 2011, all limits on the number of cargo frequencies will be formally removed.

The Important Role of the Major Chinese Airports in Air Cargo Market Growth

As a direct consequence of the historical pattern of industrial expansion since the commencement of market reform, cargo throughput has been highly concentrated in or near those major cities where the demand for passenger services has also been consistently growing. Both the rate and volume of passenger market expansion, has also been strongly influenced by government strategies aimed at increasing the productivity of both the domestic and international airport networks. As a consequence the primary focus of the market development of the air cargo sector has tended to follow the general pattern of economic expansion in China. The main airports that have led this period of cargo market growth are Beijing, Shanghai, Guangzhou on the mainland and Hong Kong, with the latter clearly established as a global hub (Table 7.1).

In the latter part of the historical period of British control before the formal handover of Hong Kong to the PRC in 1997, the decision was taken to build a new airport to replace the existing single runway site at Kai Tak on the Kowloon side of the territory. Many travellers will have memories of landing at the old airport, which could involve a carefully guided descent between high rise buildings. By contrast the new airport at Chek Lap Kok has become a positive model for multi-purpose and multifunctional aviation services, which has given the site a positive lead in cargo growth.

Table 7.1 is also reflective of the fact that Hong Kong for many years after 1980, acted as an entrepot for air cargo generated within the significantly larger area of China. Freight would be moved down to the Pearl River Delta for consolidation and the deployment of outward logistics services. With the re-designation of Beijing and Shanghai as northern and eastern centres for outbound cargo as well as for regional domestic distribution, Hong Kong has now reverted to serving south China.

Table 7.1   Comparative Rates of Air Cargo Market Growth in Key Centres: 1980–2004 (aggregate tonnes)

Year	Beijing	Shanghai	Guagzhou	Total China	Annual % Growth Rate China	Total % Hong Kong	Annual Growth Rate Hong Kong
1980	37,850	21,207	25,432	157,390	n/a	258,637	n/a
1992	187,115	186,632	171,374	998,269	26.8	989,676	14
2002	629,045	1,074,870	496,880	4,018,341	18.4	2,545,654	20.1
2004	668,690	1,936,196	506988	5,525,765	22.3	3,154,289	15.2

Note: The China aggregate covers all operational centres.

Adapted from: Fung, et al. (2005).

Table 7.2   Rankings of Chinese Cargo Airlines in the World Top 50 for 2007

Airline	Rank in Global 50	Rank in Global Domestic Category	FTKs (000)	% Change 06/07
Air China	16	3	3,586	12.3
China Eastern	23	6	2,473	2.1
China Southern	26	3	1,905	5.7
China Cargo Airlines	33	n/a	1,451	20.7
Shanghai Airlines	43	n/a	918	60.8

Note: China Cargo Airlines is a joint venture between China Eastern and the China Ocean Shipping Company (COSCO). Shanghai Airlines is the third largest domestic operator in China.

Adapted from: 'Top 50 Cargo Airlines', *Air Cargo World* (2007), pp. 26–9.

In addition the service centre of Chek Lap Kok (HKIA) which is rated as a world class international hub, accounted for 36 per cent of total cargo throughput in 2004. This aggregate grew to 3.8 million tonnes in the 2007/08 period. The full extent of the growth and development as well as the current significance of HKIA will be covered in the next chapter, when the strategic roles of the major hubs will be assessed. It remains only to note at this point that the intensity of the rate of growth of the air cargo market in China can be seen in the fact that Baiyun International Airport which formally opened in 2004, moved 653,100 tonnes of cargo in 2006, and anticipates reaching 4 million tonnes by 2020.

A further and supportive example illustrative of the growth of China's cargo traffic can be found in the rankings in Table 7.3 for the top 50 cargo airports in the world, again for 2007. Some six international locations are listed in the top 50. The balance of the Chinese airports with a ranking within the top 200 on the international list includes: Chengdu International (60), Macau International (79), Xiamen (96), Nanjing (107) and Xi'an (135). It is worth noting at this point that the places taken by Chengdu, Nanjing and X'ian on the basis of their tonnage throughput is an indicator of the further growth of regional cargo centres in central and western China.

The increasing importance of the major Chinese airports within the context of the international airport industry is further reflected in the fact that in 2007, some six places in the international top 50 list (*Air Cargo World*, 2007) were taken by the top three mega-hubs in China joined by two satellite locations in Shanghai and Beijing as well as Shenzhen.

Table 7.3   Ranking of the Chinese Cargo Airports in the Top 50 for 2007

Airport	World Rank	Tonnage	% Change 06/07	Comments
Hong Kong	2	3,608,789	5.1	Third cargo terminal due on line 2011
Shanghai Pudong	6	2,159,321	16.3	UPS China base
Beijing (Peking)	21	1,028,908	31.6	Main base Air China Cargo
Guangzhou Baiyun	25	824,906	9.9	FedEx intra-Asia hub 2008
Shenzhen	34	559,293	21.9	Home base Jade Cargo Fedex regional hub
Hong Qiao	48	363,598	1.1	Shanghai's second airport

Adapted from: Feature Focus: 'World Top 50 Cargo Airports', *Air Cargo World*, July 2007, pp. 20–22.

Some Strategic Management Problems Currently Facing the Air Cargo Industry

Despite the high growth rate of the air cargo business in China, a number of analysts have characterized the logistics industry which air cargo exists to serve as under-developed, fragmented and subject to overlapping problems. The fundamental reason for this current state of the industry is attributed to the significant imbalance suggests one of China's leading experts (Wang, 2008), between regional and highly localized administrative control at one level and the dominance of monopolistic state-owned enterprises at the other. The need to integrate the various physical aspects of operational activities, with supportive information flows between 1PL through 4PL agencies has been to date, despite a growing awareness of need, largely without much serious direction in China.

Since the entry of the PRC into the WTO in late 2001, the government of the PRC has faced a schedule of requirements for the modification of what had become conventional administrative practices. The requirements of membership included the reduction of restraints on the ability of firms located in member states to enter the Chinese economy both as joint venture partners and as stand-alone businesses. It is fair to say that since the country's entry to full status in the WTO, there has been manifest progress in China's strategic shift into the international economy, through some initiatives in market reform and liberalization.

At the same time some specific problems do arise especially for Sino–foreign joint ventures and expatriate businesses in terms of their response to bureaucratic requirements enforced at the various levels of administration from the national through the regional to the local bureaucracies. Figure 7.1 is a working attempt to illustrate some of these indigenous as well as expatriate problems.

Government motivation in sustaining such limitations are partly geopolitical since the government recognizes the need for the protection of domestic industry and the further requirement for China to develop its own multinational trade programme based on its indigenous corporate sector. It has also been influenced by the relatively slow pace of the expected efficiency outcomes that were to emerge from various domestic SOE reforms. A salutary effect has been the emergence of state-dominated monopolistic and oligopolistic firms which have tended to grow in some of the key sectors at the expense of real market competition. In addition, an acute shortage of trained human resource and skill-based managerial specialities which are required for success in international markets is found across virtually all of China's industrial sectors.

With regard to the civil aviation industry, it is also timely to remember from earlier discussions, that the initial decision to liberalize the market in the early 1990s simply failed to work effectively. The result was a return to consolidation which sees the sector dominated today by the three major state-owned carriers. The various complexities that have just been listed remain substantially in place at present, though there are some indications that centralized control is now being liberalized especially through the agency of international bilateral agreements.

Market Access and Regulatory Barriers:

Included are restrictions on the size of a total FDI investment to 49 per cent. The system also has four types of licensing ranging from A to D, with only A type allowing a full range of activities. Type A was restricted to large domestic firms, with entry by international firms restricted to joint ventures. The major integrators FedEx, DHL, UPS and TNT, were each in turn limited by this requirement.

Local Protectionism:

The decentralization of management with its location at regional and local levels, led to high degrees of protection for local operators. In turn the licensing requirements were required to be renewed if a joint venture sought to expand geographically. In addition where an inter-airline contract was planned for a given airport, the agreement would have to be negotiated as a separate document with each individual functional unit in turn such as operations, sales and interline arrangements.

Institutional Barriers:

Government involvement in air cargo logistics has been very assertive. Major airports such as Beijing and Shanghai are controlled by local government, while the major state-owned carriers, in this case Air China and China Eastern, run the terminals through their satellite companies.

Governmental Functional and Intermodal Barriers:

Problems arise due to the lack of a central authority, this means that a number of agencies have a functional interest in the air cargo business. As a working example China Cargo Airlines Ltd, is 38.36 per cent-owned by the State Council, SASAC and COSCO, China's largest shipping company. In turn the balance is held by the CAAC and the China Eastern Air Holdings Company (61.64 per cent).

Administrative Barriers:

Compliance requirements with a wide and complex range of often conflicting rules and regulations, has led to major problems with transparency and interpretation. These have been often exacerbated by the need to deal with various and varying levels of authority, as well as lack of transparency with regard to official sources of information. A notable example is customs delays, when trade facilitation calls for very time-sensitive procedures. These in turn are also affected by restrictions imposed through China's adherence to what is essentially a suboptimal network that is limiting air cargo growth.

Figure 7.1   Regulative Restraints on Foreign Businesses entering China

Adapted from: Fung, et al. (2005).

The Growing Relaxation of Control over International Airline Traffic

In the period following China's formal WTO entry in 2001, the government began a process of progressive liberalization in line with the conditional rules that had been specified in Geneva upon market entry. By the end of 2006 it had signed bilateral air service agreements with 106 countries. As a consequence 93 foreign airlines were allowed to offer 262 weekly passenger services to 31 Chinese cities. The reverse arrangement in turn, allowed 15 Chinese carriers entry to 43 countries and some 88 cities. In a real sense these developments mark a strategy that is still evolving within the somewhat limited format of what are now popularly called open skies agreements.

The US–China Air Transport Agreement, 9 July 2007

Formal bilateral agreements which permit air traffic interchange between two consenting states are, in a real sense, an operational response to the limitations imposed on global aviation since the Chicago convention of 1944. In the case of China's relationships with the United States a bilateral arrangement has been in existence since 17 September 1980. This has been subject to a major series of amendments over time that culminated with an agreement that was endorsed as a landmark event in market liberalization and signed by both countries on 9 July 2007. The current protocol calls for compliance by the parties with the three key objectives, which are listed in Figure 7.2.

The new bilateral agreement covers existing arrangements dating from 1 August 2004 and calls for further extensions of weekly services down to 25 March 2012. It is also important to note that the terms allow for the designated carriers to schedule either a combination of passenger and cargo or dedicated all-cargo flights on any route. In the matter of frequencies, the duly designated carriers of each country may, under Article 2(3) of the agreement, operate additional weekly frequencies for all-cargo services on any of the routes specified in Annex 1 of the official document.

- To increase travel and tourism between the countries and promote cultural, business and governmental exchanges.
- To promote their shared, ultimate objective of full liberalization of their bilateral air transport activities.
- To facilitate cooperative agreements between their air carriers so as to enable the mutually beneficial development of their aviation services.

Figure 7.2   The Primary Goals of the US–China Civil Aviation Agreements

Adapted from: Preamble to US–China Aviation Agreement 2007.

The agreement takes on a further geopolitical context in Article 6, with a provision for unlimited services between the PRC and Guam together with the Northern Marianas to be provided by the US carriers to three locations on the Chinese mainland. Beijing and Shanghai are excluded for this arrangement, which requires due nomination with at least 30 days of advanced notice.

It is also a matter of some moment that the government of the PRC has also allowed Chinese cargo carriers to enter into a reciprocal arrangement that will eventually see cargo hubs set up in each country. This decision clearly has some bearing on the airport building strategy that is being applied in central and western China. As discussion in an earlier chapter has revealed, there has been a substantive imbalance in the distribution of modern industrial facilities in China, which has left a conspicuous lack of fully effective logistics systems currently available in locations outside the eastern third of the country. Quite clearly investors attracted by these possibilities will need to balance the positive aspects of future lower labour market costs and the potentially negative problems created by the current degree of availability of both hub and logistical services.

It is a view commonly held by economists working in the fields of international trade and industry, that the core location at the centre of the economic evolution of the PRC is currently the expanding municipality of Shanghai. In historical terms, it has taken over this role from the Pearl River Delta the home location of Guangzhou, which has always been historically identified as the prototypical development zone. The issues raised by this significant growth in both the rate and scale of urbanization will be duly considered in a later chapter when we examine the role that civil aviation continues to play in the large economic conurbations that these famous trading cities have become since 1978.

A Selection of China's Major and Specialist Cargo Airlines

The indigenous carriers working in the domestic and international air cargo markets are led by the major airlines due to the linkage structures created by the consolidation process. It is important to remember that the big three are more than simply dedicated passenger airlines. Their roles and scope includes the ownership of hub facilities and a range of ground services. During the current decade they have also been joined by a number of secondary cargo carriers a selection of which are identified and described in more detail in Figure 7.3.

It has already been noted previously that there has been an intermittent emergence and departure from the domestic aviation market of privately owned ventures. This has been largely due, as we have seen, to the tendency for official policy to swing between a manifest degree of liberalization on the one hand and a return to consolidation on the other. In the post-consolidation period since 2002, the growth of private airlines has tended to stabilize. More recently cargo services have also become the strategic target of new private ventures in China. With this in mind, the airlines listed in Figure 7.4 have been deliberately selected as representative of this new development. They also reveal to some degree the essentially embryonic state of this sub-sector of the air cargo industry.

Air China Cargo Ltd

The carrier is an all-cargo subsidiary company of Air China and was established on 12 December 2003. It is owned by Air China (51 per cent), CITIC Pacific (25 per cent) and Beijing Capital International. Its primary base is in Beijing Capital International and it also operates from Chengdu Shuangliu International and Shanghai Pudong International. The current operational fleet comprises four Boeing 747-200Fs and five 747-400Fs. In addition the airlines have three Tupolev 204-120CEs on order.

China Southern Cargo Ltd

The parent company China Southern Airlines is the largest of China's airlines in terms of passengers carried. It is owned by China Southern Air Holdings (50.3 per cent), Hong Kong and foreign investors (H shares 26.84 per cent) and private Chinese investors (A shares 22.86 per cent). The primary base of the airline is Baiyun International in Guangzhou, and the carrier also services clients out of Beijing Capital International. The cargo services have been carried out to date by two Boeing 747-200Fs. In 2006, an order was placed for six Boeing 777-200-LRFs, with the first due for delivery in November 2008 and the balance due by 2010.

China Cargo Airlines Ltd

China Eastern, the parent company of China Cargo Airlines, is largely owned by Eastern Air Group, a government holding company. The cargo carrier in turn was established in 1998, in a joint venture with COSCO, the major seaborne carrier. It became a wholly-owned subsidiary in 2004, and now operates as an independent carrier with routes to Japan, North America and Africa. The fleet comprises three Airbus A300-600RFs, two Boeing 747-400-ERFs and six McDonnell Douglas MD-11Fs. The airline has a further order for two Tupolev Tu-204-120Cs.

Figure 7.3   The Dedicated Air Cargo Carriers of the PR's Big Three Airlines

Adapted from: Air China/China Southern/China Eastern Company Reports 2007–08.

Shanghai Airlines Cargo

The carrier was established in June 2006 as a joint venture between Shanghai Airlines and EVA Air a member of the Evergreen group. Its serves a range of clients in Asia, Europe and the United States. The fleet comprises one Boeing B747-200F on lease from Southern Air and three McDonnell Douglas MD-11Fs.

Great Wall Airlines

The company was established in 2006 under the co-ownership of China Great Wall Industry Corporation (51 per cent), Singapore Airlines Cargo (25 per cent), with the balance held by Dahlia Investments a subsidiary of Tamasek Holdings (24 per cent). The airline suspended operations on 18 August 2006, due to sanctions imposed by the US Department of the Treasury, on the grounds that the Great Wall Industry Corporation had delivered missiles to Iraq. The suspension was lifted in December of that year and service was resumed in February 2007. Its main base is Beijing International and it also operates from Shanghai Pudong International. A range of clients are served in Asia, the Middle East and Pakistan as well as the United States, the UK (Manchester and the Netherlands (Schipol)).The operational fleet now comprises three Boeing 747-400Fs.

Jade Cargo Airlines

The airline was founded in October 2004, as a joint venture between Shenzhen Airlines (51 per cent), Lufthansa Cargo AG and DEG-mbH, a leading European development bank, each with 24 per cent. After launching in 2006, the airline now serves a range of clients in Europe and Japan, as well as offering domestic services in China. It has an added advantage in the fact that its fleet currently consists of six Boeing B747-ERF freighters with considerable range and payload advantages over the conventional 400 series.

Shenzhen Donghai Airlines

Yet another of the launches of 2006, the airline is owned by Shenzhen Donggang Trade (51 per cent), Donghai United Group (25 per cent) and Yonggang (25 per cent). The inaugural service was to link Shenzhen Bao'an International Airport with Shanghai. A possible further link with Kunming is also on the schedule. The fleet comprises two Boeing 737-300SFs

Figure 7.4   Selected Private and Secondary Air Cargo Carriers

Air Hong Kong

This airline is the only dedicated freighter airline based in Hong Kong. It was created from a joint venture between Cathay Pacific and DHL express with the intention of developing an express freight service network throughout Asia. The carrier acted as the launch client for eight Airbus A300-600F freighters which came into service between September 2004 and July 2006. DHL remains the major client as the network has grown over time, with the balance of trade found through clients needing general freight services.

Figure 7.4   *Concluded*

Adapted from: Airline Cargo Management and Airline Holding Company Reports: 2002–07.

The Emergence of Air Cargo Support Services at Key Airports

The active emergence of China's air cargo sector has also witnessed the growth of the appropriate service and support systems at China's major airports. These are inevitably at various stages of development and dependent upon funding, as well as the timeframes set by strategic planners at the various locations. They also include an increasing number of specialist facilities and dedicated terminals for some of the global express carriers such as FedEx, UPS and DHL.

In order to establish where the cutting edge of airport cargo services is located in China at the current time it is necessary to pay a visit the Hong Kong International Airport Authority (HKIAA) site at Chek Lap Kok. This choice is logical since as earlier evidence has revealed, the HKIA is the market exemplar and consistently ranked at the very top of international listings. The following comments are based on the fact that the author was kindly given access to some of the following information by senior executives at HKIA, while engaged on a research and teaching assignment in Hong Kong.

HKIA International Cargo and Global Services

Terminal Services

Hong Kong International Airport (HKIA) has ranked as the busiest international airport offering cargo services since 1996. Given its location in the Pearl River Delta (PRD) it is also able to offer marine cargo services to 17 ports in the PRD, together with a bonded trucking network that can move air freight to some 57 locations in South China's industrial regions. There is currently an overlap between dedicated carriers and passenger flights belly cargo services which divides the markets into express and heavy-lift products.

The two air cargo terminal companies based at HKIA are in private ownership with Super Terminal 1 possessing a floor area of 330,000 m^2 and a design capacity for 2.6 million tonnes a year, a total that includes some 200,000 tonnes that is directed through the Express centre. In March 2007 Terminal 2 became operational featuring a four-storey warehouse area covering 130,000 m^2, two airside levels and landside access to every floor. The project represents a 30 per cent increase in handling capacity. In turn Hong Kong Air Cargo Terminal (HACTL) operates a subsidiary unit Hong Kong Air Cargo Industry Services Ltd (HACIS) in the important Shenzhen Free Trade Zone just across the bay from Lantau Island. The intention is to facilitate cargo traffic via HKIA as well as to extend the operational role of service provision into what is rapidly becoming an integrated industrial network. This is further reflected in the possibility that Hong Kong and Shenzhen will become an administrative entity in the future.

It is also developing and expanding access to alternative modes of transportation through the development of a Sky Pier at the end of Lantau Island. This will offer a high-speed ferry service for movement between the airport and some four ports located in the PRD. The developmental plan for HKIA has always included a role for bimodal interchange between marine and air transportation. Further developments are now under way, for a ferry terminal which will allow for a direct flow of passengers and cargo through to Terminal 2 of the main airport.

Base Hub Users

Some seven airlines are located at the Chek Lap Kok site as hub users. They are Cathay Pacific, Dragon Air, Air Hong Kong, Jet Aviation, Business Jets (HKG) Ltd, Hong Kong Express and CR Airways. A new international low-cost carrier, Oasis Hong Kong which was formally launched in 2005, suddenly withdrew from all services out of the airport's new Terminal 2 in early 2008.

The location of the HKIA has also proven to be strongly attractive to international carriers wishing to maximize the potential of points of entry into the mainland. A recent example of this strategy involves Air New Zealand, which now offers direct flights to Hong Kong as well as from Shanghai and Beijing under a bilateral agreement. It has also changed the route of its Auckland–London flights which used to fly through Changi in Singapore. Their one-stop destination on what is one of their most important international routes is now Hong Kong.

Services Developments

HKIA also offers clients airport management services especially in the area of air cargo. The process involves either investment in overseas sites or the provision of consultancy services. In addition it will house a new project which began in 2007 between EMC Corporation, an international leader in the provision of information infrastructure solutions, and DHL. The intention is to create the Asia–Pacific and Japan Supply Chain and Logistics Centre (APJSCLC) in Hong Kong.

Speed to the customer is the primary driver of the project, and benefits will include a paperless information system, together with assignment schedules that aim to assist DHL partners located on the mainland to deliver EMC's products within a seven-day cycle. The airport continues to maximize its geographical advantages with some 78 international carriers providing 5,300 scheduled passenger and all-cargo flights every week, to 140 destinations worldwide. Approximately 72 per cent are operated with wide-bodied jets. In addition an approximate average of some 32 non-scheduled passenger and cargo flights leave HKIA each week.

A New Mainland Venture

The HKIAA has also been successful in setting up new and strategic sites within the PRD. An important example may be found in the decision to create the Hong Kong–Zhuhai Airport Management Co. Ltd (HKZAM) together with the Zhuhai municipal government. The new company will manage Zhuhai Airport with HKIA Authority holding a 55 per cent stake in the venture for RMB198 million acquired through its wholly-owned subsidiary HKIA (China) Ltd. In turn the Zhuhai municipal government holds 45 per cent which was obtained through its own subsidiary, the Zhuhai Headway Transportation Investment Co. Ltd. The joint agreement is destined to run until 2026 and already appears to be handling increasing passenger volumes.

The fact that there are some five airports within the PRD has also led to the involvement of the HKIAA in an important collaborative agreement. The resultant consortium is seeking to achieve a degree of common practice on such matters as customs procedures. A new brand name has been developed PRD-A5 Group together with a collective website. The parties are all subject to a letter of intent on flight divisions and emergency support, which has a dual purpose: to strengthen the quality of safety standards and at the same time make the group more competitive. As a working example they seek minimum disruption caused by weather or other contingencies through the viable use of their alternative facilities.

The various developments listed in this example reveal an important role for civil aviation in China where, as in other East Asian countries, cosmopolitan centres are evolving beyond the status of cities into industrial, social and economic conurbations of considerable size and global reach. In the south and coastal regions of China this is true of important locations like Hong Kong, Guangzhou and Shanghai.

It is now time to consider the wider range of issues that are to be found on the leading edge of economic growth in China's civil aviation industry, within the operational context and perspective of its core locations. These are to be found in that area of China bounded by the capital Beijing to the north, and the industrial conurbations of the Pearl River and the Yangtze Deltas, whose influence on the shaping of the Chinese economy itself remains both seminal and consistently subject to expansion. Often referred to colloquially as the golden triangle, it remains the epicentre of both the current and future development of the civil aviation industry.

These key locations are increasingly taking the form of urban conurbations within which civil aviation facilities are embedded as a core part of the integration process. In population terms they do not represent a massive proportion of the national demographic distribution, but as further commentary will indicate, they now constitute the epicentre leading edge of China's developmental dynamic across all industrial sectors.

Chapter 8

The Golden Triangle: The Leading Edge of Chinese Aviation

It will be the primary purpose of this chapter to first identify and then consider the very important influences that have been exerted by the three great metropolitan centres of modern China on the growth of civil aviation since the commencement of market reform. Discussion will also focus on the current development of these centres as emergent forces within the larger context of China's potential role in both the domestic and international aviation markets. Attention will also be focussed on the key importance of the three regional locations as a formative influence on the liberalization and modernization of the Chinese economy.

The locational sequence will commence with the Pearl River Delta (PRD), as the prototypical special economic zone (SEZ), followed by Shanghai, as the now acknowledged leader of economic development in China. Discussion will then turn to the national capital Beijing, which is landlocked, but has very important linkages with the developments taking place in Tianjin a coastal city on Bohai bay, south of the capital. A further attempt will be made throughout the following discussion, to place the substantive roles played by the civil aviation industry, within the continually expanding economic and social growth of what Kasarda has defined as the modern aeropolis.

The Primary Role of the Eastern and Coastal Provinces in the Modernization of the Chinese Aviation Industry

The history of civil aviation development in China during the modern era has tended to be shaped by substantial decisions and events taking place largely within the eastern and coastal provinces. As earlier discussion has already revealed, three major cities have tended to develop a pivotal role in commercial aviation, most notably since the decision to consolidate China's air services with the primary hubs to be located in Beijing, Shanghai and Guangzhou. In order to fully understand the various political and economic forces that continue to shape events in these key centres we need to return in the historical sense to the opening period of market reform in China.

In the continuing history of economic reform, active and positive progress has been closely identified with the growth of SEZs which first began to take formal shape and direction in 1979. In December of that year, the People's Congress of the Guangdong Province was charged by central government with the task of creating three SEZs. These were to be located in Shenzhen, virtually just across the river from Hong Kong, at Zhuhai which is very close to the Macau SAR and at Shantou in the north of the province. A further coastal location was selected in southeast Fujian which brought the city of Xiamen into this group of what were essentially deemed to be organizational prototypes.

It was noted in earlier chapters that the strategic value of SEZs became materially evident to central government in the 1980s and 1990s as a basic tool for reforming the national economy. Given the fact that the larger plan to replace SREs by dismantling the Danwei system required that new forms of deregulation in management also be introduced, it became apparent to the central authorities that the SEZs were the logical places where managerial authority should be allowed to both devolve and develop over time. As a consequence of this change in policy direction, designated local authorities were given a comparatively wide range of discretionary powers to expand and develop the economic potential of their localities and regions. They were also later permitted to attract foreign investors through a variety of preferential policies aimed at encouraging new candidates for market entry.

In addition it was decided that SEZs could undertake their own infrastructural developments providing they were able to raise the required funding. These local administrations were also free to decide their own strategies for investment, production and marketing of the specified outputs from business. A further incentive aimed at those enterprises that had obtained FDI was to be found in various preferential tax concessions and exemptions from import licensing requirements as well as customs duties for selected imports.

While the new southern SEZs were empowered with a much higher degree of control over their decision-making powers than any other region or province in China, the relative success of the strategy especially in the PRD, triggered many further initiatives. The year 1984, for example, was to see the State Council direct action for the further promotion of FDI inflows into some 14 new city locations including Beijing's access port at Tianjin and the complex of cities that now surround Shanghai.

In the following year the tempo of reform was increased in both the Yangtze and Pearl River Deltas, with additional stress placed by government on the utilization of FDI as the means to economically develop and grow the coastal economic development zones of the southern and eastern provinces. Today, Beijing Shanghai and Guangzhou can claim with considerable justification that together they constitute the central and mega hubs of domestic aviation services on the mainland of China. They can also claim an international and growing reputation as key destinations in an increasingly global network of ultra-long-haul international air services

Their continuing and dramatic evolution of what, according to Ning (2007), are now known as metropolitan interlocking regions (MIRs) also tended to depart somewhat radically from conventional descriptions of evolutionary and urbanized market growth over the medium to long term. This process can be identified from a civil aviation perspective through the growth of what are now becoming known in the term coined by Kasarda (2004) as the modern urban areopolis. From an operational perspective they literally constitute industrial cities in which large-scale and multi-functional airports act as the core operational sites in the domestic and international value and supply chains of a given country. In the Chinese case such locational growth is increasingly driven by demographic and social factors, as well as the ubiquitous processes of urbanization. As a direct consequence modern transportation systems now evolve and link not single, but networks of cities into MIRs.

These trends also reflect, as noted again in earlier examples, the fact that a major source of urban population growth reflects the persistent consequences of a growing rural urban migration. In fact this form of migration has been defined in demographic terms by some Chinese scholars as the major positive force now shaping city-based urbanization as people continue to leave the countryside, initially in search of work opportunities

By contrast the impact of the one child policy that commenced in the 1980s has seen a significant negative natural growth rate in existing urban populations. A fuller exploration of this topic really lies outside the context of the current discussion. It is worth noting however as a final comment on this important demographic signal, that the available data on the distribution of China's general population indicates, in common with many other countries, a significant decline in population growth over time leading to the inevitable expansion of an ageing labour force.

We will now commence a more detailed discussion of the key issues with a review of the current stage of aviation industry development in the Greater PRD. Consideration will then shift to the events that have shaped the Yangtze River Delta, now universally recognized as the economic power house of China, that has superseded the PRD. Finally discussion will centre on the emergence of Tianjin as a major new locale for aviation development within the larger political geography of Beijing's regional strategy.

The Pearl River Delta in its Geographical Context

The PRD differs from the other two major regions of China which are the combined focus of this chapter in the geopolitical sense of the term. This is because the former colonial territories of both Hong Kong and Macau through their proximate location in the PRD estuary are really a natural geographical extension of the national mainland. The prescribed dimensions of the official SEZ are contained within the provincial borders of Guangdong, and the province constitutes some nine cities with Guangzhou as the provincial capital. They include in turn the four districts and counties of Huizhou in the eastern sub-region, and the same administrative distribution in Zhaoqing on the western side of Guangdong. Both the latter areas have enjoyed significant development as highly diversified new urban centres. The effects of these structural changes are also to be found in the percentage distribution of the various categories of industrial production to be found in the cities of Guangdong province as is indicated in the Table 8.1.

The period from 1997 through 2000, was to see the political identity of both Hong Kong and Macau undergo a fundamental structural change. Both now enjoy a special political status as part of the mainland, but in the form of strategic autonomous regions (SARs). This is because under the terms of their return to China by the British and Portuguese governments, they were allowed to continue for a further and considerable statutory period what had become their traditional administrative and functional roles. This permits the SARs to continue their economic development, with a significant degree of geopolitical independence. In the case of Hong Kong post-1997 (according to Abbas, 1997) the city has seen the expansion of its major role as both a global airport city and as a very important international financial centre, while Macau has superseded Las Vegas as the world's largest centre for public gambling.

The Processes of Industrial Evolution in the PRD

The early period of provincial development in the PRD, dating back over a very long time, was driven by highly labour-intensive light industries. This has now given way in the twenty-first century to both the growth of heavy industry and the rapid expansion of high technology-based production. It is also further illustrated by the following indicators of changing growth trends. In 1979 light industry accounted for 55.6 per cent of industrial production in the SEZ as against 43.3 per cent for heavy industry. By 2004 the ratios had undergone a virtual replacement effect, since the figure for heavy industry now stood at 55.5 per cent, while light industry was down to 44.5 per cent.

Table 8.1   Selected Economic Indicators of Eight Key PRD Cities in 2006

City Locations	% Primary Industry	% Secondary Industry	% Tertiary Industry	% of SEZ Total Output
Shenzhen	0.4	61.6	38.0	23.8
Guangzhou	2.8	44.2	53.0	18.4
Dongguan	2.4	55.4	42.2	9.4
Zhuhai	3.4	57.0	39.6	4.6
Foshan	5.0	57.8	37.2	12.2
Zhongshan	5.0	65.0	30.0	6.2
Jiangmen	8.9	49.5	41.5	4.8
Huizhou	12.1	57.1	30.8	4.1

Adapted from: Li and Fung Research Centre CUHK, Industrial Cluster Series, May 2006, Issue 2, p. 19.

The more fundamental proportional changes between primary, secondary and tertiary industries can be found across the same time series. In 1978, the figure for primary industry stood at 29.8 per cent, heavy industry at 46.6 per cent and tertiary industry at 23.6 per cent. By 2004, primary production had fallen to 7.8 per cent, heavy industry stood at 55.4 per cent and the tertiary sector at 36.8 per cent. The relevant changes are reflected in the following results for the period 1978–2004: primary industry = −22 per cent; heavy industry = +8.8 per cent; and tertiary industry = +13.2 per cent. These indicate that there has been a significant fall in the concentration on primary industry as it existed before the PRD was nominated as the prototypical SEZ by Deng Xiaoping in 1992.

The Significance of Industrial Clusters and City Locations in the PRD

In keeping with the strategies deployed by other regional economies, industrial production is clustered in what are now called specialized towns. Most of these are geographically located in the western sub-region with significant activity to be found in Foshan, Jiangmen and Zhongshan. The development of this strategy over time has led to some significant problems which have emerged as the various clusters have tended to grow exponentially and over time. This has been partially caused by the fact that Guangzhou as the primary city of the provinces sustains its historical role as a centre of conventional trade. A very cosmopolitan population with significant ethnic minorities are engaged in a consistent sequence of trade fairs which, at the peak of the season, brings in over 250,000 business visitors to the world famous Canton Trade Fair. In a sense the fairs are really at the end of the supply chain, which extends in role and scope and range of products beyond the goods supplied by local clusters, as Figure 8.1 seems to indicate.

The introduction by government of a new labour contract law which came into force in January 2008 and which introduces a new range of employment rights for all immigrant labour, has also led to a significant negative response from PRD employers. Many have as an initial reply to what is perceived to be higher labour costs, signalled their intention to relocate in locations such as northern Vietnam if their operational costs rise due to the new law.

Under the current 11th FYP for the region, the focus has been placed on the creation of a large-scale enterprise development strategy that would encourage innovative branding. The aim is to build a strong regional image for these firms with greater specialization and high quality operational management, especially in R&D, Logistics, Quality Control and other managerial improvements. This objective has led to the development of a regional cooperation and development forum which aims at the coordination of the further development of a Greater PRD.

Low Profit Margins and High Operating Costs

Economies of scale in operations are offset by low profit margins, which can be as low as 3 per cent to 1 per cent.

Replication and Severe Competition

Caused mainly by too many small to medium firms competing for the same FDI contracts.

Bottlenecks in Land, Labour and Energy Supply

This is driving a movement away from eastern cities to western locations with some firms moving out of the province. Transportation issues and reliance on high levels of component importing also contribute to these problems.

Weak Vertical Linkages

Inter-enterprise relationship tends to be weak with a resultant limitation on effective supply-chain collaboration.

Lack of Innovation Capability

The principal driver within clusters is price competition, rather than product innovation. Low value added products also result in the lack of an identifiable local branding able to compete in international markets.

Lack of Local Industry Culture

Many of the export-oriented clusters are foreign owned. Their basic motivation for market entry is found in cheap labour and location costs. This tends to reduce the potential for cluster-based strategies to develop.

Figure 8.1   Some Economic Problems Being Experienced by the PRD Clusters

Adapted from: Hong Kong Trade Development Council, February 2007.

The Role of the Closer Economic Partnership Arrangement (CEPA)

The formal return of the territorial area of Hong Kong to the PRC in 1997 raised important questions with regard to future relationships between the newly designated SAR and what is popularly called the mainland. As a consequence the main text of the CEPA was formally signed in 2003. The agreement calls for the parties to allow for the continuing introduction of services liberalization and other measures for deepening economic and trade cooperation between the former colony and the Guangdong province. The result has been a continuing programme of modification with further annual endorsements from 2004 to 2008.

In addition to Hong Kong International Airport, the Greater PRD has no less than three other major airports within its borders: Guangzhou's Baiyun International, Shenzhen's Bao-An International and Macau International. Zhuhai International on the western arm of the PRD, after a long period of very slow growth, also currently provides services, as was observed earlier under the management of the HKIA Authority. An indication of their aggregate services capacity is provided in Table 8.2, which is also reflective of the very significant market advantages enjoyed by the HKIA.

It is clear that the HKIA has a leading role in the continuing expansion of civil aviation in the Greater PRD, based on its experience and status as a leading global airport. This is reflected in the liberalization strategy agreed with the PRC that is directed toward the integration of both primary and secondary aviation services. Growing access allows not only for the transfer of relevant expertise, but for Hong Kong to maximize its international role as a financial centre, through the continuing establishment of wholly-owned enterprises, equity joint ventures as well as other forms of contractual arrangements.

HKIA's importance for civil aviation in the Greater PRD is also reflected in the fact that local suppliers are able to lodge project applications directly with resident bodies such as the China Air Transport Association. From a Hong Kong perspective the dual policy targets suggested by Fung (HKIA Press release, 21 December 2006) of medium to long-term sustainable growth coupled to evolving integration within the geopolitical framework of the PRC is now clearly the SAR's primary aim.

Evidence of further movements toward both the liberalization and integration of Hong Kong with the mainland can be found in the significant and new memorandum of understanding announced in December 2007. Its primary concern relates to new arrangements for the granting of operational rights on most domestic routes. Commencing in March 2008, restrictions on the number of designated airlines on

Table 8.2   Air Traffic in the Greater PRD Region in 2006

Airport	Passengers (millions)	Cargo (000 tonnes)
Hong Kong	43.27	3,580.35
Guangzhou	26.22	653.26
Shenzhen	18.36	559.24
Macau	4.98	220.57
Total	56.56	5,013.42

Adapted from: Enright and Scott (2007), p. 52.

most of the individual routes were scheduled to be removed. In the case of routes for services to Beijing, Shanghai, Guangzhou, Shenzhen, Kunming, Dalian and Chengdu, each side was to nominate three designated airlines to fly passenger or all-cargo services as well as two further all-cargo services from mid to late 2008. A decision was also tabled that would eliminate capacity restrictions. From mid 2008, there would be no restrictions on 49 routes for both Hong Kong and mainland carriers. In turn the full liberalization of all cargo services was anticipated to be operational by December 2008.

It is now time to consider the eastern regions and notably the Yangtze delta system which Deng Xiaoping referred to as the dragon's head. The estuary of the Yangtze river system has already been noted as the region that now leads China's advancement as both a national and international economy. It is clear from the evidence shown below that its future has a degree of role, scope and magnitude that presents a new order of strategic planning needs to be instigated by the PRC.

Shanghai and the Emergence of the Yangtze Delta Megalopolis

The concept of a megalopolis is in a very real sense a logical expansion of the idea of a metropolitan centre. In other words it is really the total sum of the expansion of a number of metropolitan regions into an even larger and unified conurbation. While it is important at this point in the discussion to be aware that Shanghai has always been the most prominent city in the Yangtze River Delta (YRD), politically, historically and economically, its future is now further embedded within the larger spatial strategies that are shaping development plans for the whole of the region and even beyond its boundaries.

The development of a network of multimodal transportation systems is well advanced and includes a future role for an international aviation location in Shanghai that will be developed to serve as a mega-hub for western Pacific aviation services. In addition the proposed spatial strategy is intended to contain not one, but a number of the existing metropolitan regions. At the current core of the megalopolis we can find two city growth triangles, each with Shanghai as its anchor point, based on its identity as China's mega city, which makes it the logical development pole around which economic growth and expansion of the YRD will swing.

The proposed organizational form for further amalgamations with the urban centres of Suzhou, Wuxi and Jianxing linked to Shanghai as the primary centre are shown diagrammatically in Figure 8.2.

The developmental plan calls for the full integration of the three urban centres into the metropolitan city of Shanghai. The growth trend is expected to continue across provincial boundaries so that Nanjing and Hangzhou, in turn, become metropolitan centres in their own right within the total megalopolis.

It is anticipated that these existing developments, which replicate on a much larger and more complex scale the cluster arrangements already found in the PRD, will develop over time into no less than three metropolitan regions with Nanjing and Hangzhou–Ningbo forming two further groupings, based on their identities as important provincial capitals. In effect this creates a megalopolis within the YRD which allows for networking and integration at three distinct levels of role, scope and function. Given the flexibility of economic expansion across administrative boundaries it is also likely that the border of the YRD megalopolis will expand over time north into the Jiangsu, south into the Zhejiang and east into the Anhui provinces.

Current Aviation Services in the YRD Area: Airports and Airlines

The YRD bears close comparison with the PRD, since there are some five major international airports whose areas of coverage are generally found to be within one hour's drive from any point within the delta. The five airports are listed in Figure 8.3.

The two Shanghai airports in combination serve the heaviest traffic flows within the national system. Hongqiao is physically situated in the city itself, while Pudong has the status of a sub-province. Within the overall process of development these locations constitute what can be called the tip of a very large developmental

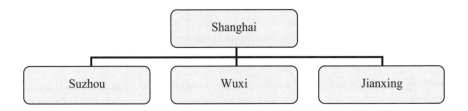

Figure 8.2   The Future Shanghai Megalopoli

Adapted from: Williams, A. and Williams, B.A. (2008). Williams and Partners NZ Ltd. Management Education Consultants.

- Shanghai Pudong International;
- Shanghai Hongqiao;
- Nanjing Lukou International (Jiangsu);
- Hangzhou Xiaishan International (Zhejiang);
- Ningbo Lishe International (Zhejiang).

Figure 8.3   The Major Airports of the YRD

Adapted from: Pudong.govt.cn.

iceberg. According to the aviation industry survey appended to the 10th FYP (2000–05) the number of airports in civil use in East China was supposed to reach 36 by 2005, with an increase to 48 by 2020. On average there are some eight airports per 100,000 k^2 in the YRD. This is a larger proportion than can be found in the United States within the same land area parameters.

The various strategic complexities that will inevitably arise over the relative roles of the different airports located in the YRD are far too large to discuss here in more detail, save to comment that there is a recognizable need to identify the various operational activities that airports will be required to carry in the evolving system of complex levels of administrative structure that the current growth models are proposing. With this in mind we can now turn to the key role played by Pudong International as a recognized major national and international hub both in China and in Asia.

Pudong International: One Airport with Multiple Roles

Shanghai Airport Authority which manages both Pudong and Hongqiao Airports reported that the two sites handled a combined 51.6 million passengers in 2007 which reflected an 11.8 per cent increase year on year. At the same time aircraft movements rose 7.6 per cent to 440,809; of these, Pudong handled 58 per cent (253,671) and Hongqiao the balance (187,138). At the current time some 71 domestic and foreign airlines operate scheduled services in and out of both airports, which effectively link Shanghai as China's financial and commercial hub to some 179 cities worldwide.

Unlike the PRD, the YRD has always been a primary location for heavy industry, which today sustains a thriving aerospace and high technology network operating throughout the region. It is also worth bearing in mind the fact that Pudong International occupies a 40 km^2 site located some 30 km from the Bund in Shanghai city, and is already fully integrated into a multi-modal regional transportation system. This offers passengers and freight alike a highly developed transportation corridor, in which road expressways go to, and metro systems literally run into stations within, the airport itself.

Multi-system transport integration will be developed even further, when the proposed introduction of a Maglev high technology express rail service linking Shanghai to Beijing comes on line. Some indication of the effect of this technology is already evident with the current city–airport Maglev service covering the 31 km between the two centres while completing each journey in seven minutes at a maximum speed of 430 kilometres per hour. On the other hand according to popular local belief, the primary revenue produced by this state of the art technology comes from tourism interest, rather than regular and local commuter usage.

Passenger Services   Pudong International is the base location for China Eastern Airlines as well as the home location for Shanghai Airlines and also serves as a major international hub for Air China. Some 28.92 million passengers passed through the airport in 2007, a number which was actually 45 per cent higher than the capacity limit of 20 million imposed by the fact that only the first terminal was operative during that period. Incidentally, this result also makes Pudong the third busiest passenger airport in the PRC. In fact its total of international passengers with some 17,52 million moving through the airport, actually exceeding the level of international traffic through Beijing Capital, China's overall champion.

With the opening of Terminal 2 on 26 March 2008, the new facility added a further 40 million passengers per year to the airport's capacity. This will be extended to 60 million when the second phase of the new terminal is brought on line. The terminal is also now home to some 33 airlines, a significant proportion of these are international of which there is a significant group from Star Alliance including Lufthansa, ANA, Air NZ, SIA, Thai and United.

The Air Cargo Dimension   It is perhaps not surprising that Pudong has seen a significant growth of on-site services by global express parcel firms who have chosen to locate dedicated operational facilities at the airport. These include Fedex and UPS who will be joined by TNT. DHL has also signalled its intention to invest some US$175 million in a new 55,000 m^2 complex that will serve as a North Asia hub, servicing this region as well as the United States and Europe. With DHL proposing in late 2008 to withdraw services from the United States, it will be interesting to see how this decision will impact on the range of services now targeting China and East Asia.

In addition dedicated freight carriers such as Atlas, Polar Air, Eva Air and Cargolux, operate regular scheduled routes out of the Pudong location. They are joined in this activity by major international airlines operating both specialized and belly-loading related services. The airport has experienced a continuous growth rate in cargo handling since 2002. In fact the cumulative rate of growth in the period up to 2006 reached an aggregate 87.3 per cent. As a contributive example, in 2007 the combined weight of cargo handled by both Shanghai airports was of the order of 2.9 million tonnes or 14.6 per cent year on year.

The Future Plans for Continued Growth   On 7 September 2007, Shanghai International Airport Co. Ltd (SIACL) in which, the Shanghai Airport Authority has a controlling interest, obtained regulatory authority to issue a total of RMB2.5 billion in ten-year corporate bonds. This followed the decision to fund expansions at Hongqiao by raising some RMB15.3 billion for a new runway and the modernization of the current airport. The purpose of the capital raising initiative was to provide, in turn, funds for the ongoing expansion of Pudong as shown in Figure 8.4.

In sum the intention is to make Pudong one of the largest airports in the world in direct competition with aeropolis locations such as Incheon in Korea and Narita in Japan. It is now time to consider, albeit briefly, the important role that is being played in the YRD region by China's burgeoning aerospace industry, a theme that will be covered on more specific detail in a later chapter.

- The addition of a fourth and fifth runway.
- A satellite concourse bigger than Terminals 1 and 2.
- Additional and dedicated cargo terminals.
- Land reclamation to support the fifth runway.

Figure 8.4   Developmental Planning for Pudong International Airport to 2015

Adapted from: Pudong.gov.cn.

Shanghai as a Key Aerospace Industry Location   The evolving presence of a significant element of China's aerospace production has been a notable aspect of industrial growth in the Shanghai region since the 1970s. Under the state control of China's Aviation Industry Corporation (AVIC 1), the Shanghai Aviation Industrial Group Ltd (SAIC) is the holding entity for a number of important subsidiaries that include:

- Shanghai Aircraft Manufacturing Factory;
- Shanghai Aeroengine Manufacturing Factory;
- Shanghai International Aerotechnology Trade Company;
- Shanghai Aircraft Research Institute.

The group's activities have ranged over specific joint-venture production contracts, notably for the co-production of the McDonnell Douglas MD80 series, which ended in 1999. In addition many of the intermediate components for the series were produced in China. The merger with Boeing in 1996 effectively saw the end of commercial aircraft production under the McDonnell Douglas marque, which was in any case experiencing a terminal decline symbolized in the falling demand for its MD models.

This event however did not disturb the continuity of Chinese aviation's relationship with Boeing which in the Shanghai context continues to grow in importance. The decision to return to the production of a domestic wide-bodied jet in collaboration with Boeing will be discussed in more detail in a later chapter, since the proposal will involve potential joint-venture production in both Shanghai and X'ian. To conclude this discussion on developments, in Pudong's role, a current example will now be given from a new venture now getting under way.

Pudong International's New MRO Joint Venture   On 24 October 2006, it was announced that a new services project was to commence development which would incorporate a dedicated MRO operation. The controlling partners would be three in number: Boeing, the Shanghai Airport Group (SIACL) and Shanghai Airlines. The completed project, Boeing Shanghai Airport Services, represented an investment of US$85 million, what is significant however is the fact that the equity share gives Boeing a 60 per cent holding with the Shanghai Airport Authority, the parent of SIACL and the airline holding 25 per cent and 15 per cent respectively.

The equity distribution is a very significant shift in policy terms since it allows a foreign company to exceed the 49 per cent equity limit. As later discussion on developments in the north will indicate, the location of a new offshore Airbus A320 assembly line in Tianjin, the first outside Europe, has also permitted the same equity distribution to be put in place. The new company has received a licence to conduct business issued by the Shanghai Bureau of Industry and Commerce. It is also very significant that on 15 October 2008, the US FAA issued to the new venture its Repair Station Certification under the US Federal Aviation Code, Part 145. The decision to do so reflects a major international step forward for Pudong International in terms of its future general importance as a mega-hub in the western Pacific.

The initial role of the service will cover heavy maintenance for the Boeing Next Generation series which has some 235 aircraft currently flying in the East Asia region and some 260, including the 900ER, on order. Further developments will include expansion into twin-aisle services commencing with the 767-300 series. Expansion is also projected into services for regional and international airlines as well as for domestic carriers.

It is now time to shift the focus of discussion yet again to the northeast where the pattern of strategic developments shaping both the Greater PRD and the Shanghai–YRD are repeated but with a localized set of characteristics the influence of which we can now begin the examine in more detail.

The Beijing–Tianjin Search for an Integrative Economic Balance

Through an accident of geography strongly influenced by China's political history, Beijing does not possess a coastal or delta region of its own. Its closest connection to the sea, in fact, lies to the south of the national capital in Tianjin, which is located on the lower coastal reaches of the Haihe river. The city is an important seaport location with a growing industrial complex on its eastern coastal plain now known as the Binhai New Area of Tianjin (BNAT).

Under the developmental specifications for the current Tianjin FYP, the intention is to develop the new area both as an international port and also as the northern economic hub of China. This strategic objective has also gained support from the State Council, which has proposed that Beijing relinquish its existing role as the economic centre of activity in northern China to Tianjin. The proposal has generated a serious debate involving both pro and con issues, which continues to grow in terms of range, content and sometimes controversy. What is important for the purposes of discussion here however is the fact that there have been some major developments in the BNAT with regard to the creation of a major industry development zone expressly aimed at making the SEZ a major centre for civil aviation development. The developmental plan is described in some detail below.

The Creation of Tianjin–Binhai New Area Aviation Industry Park

The decision to create what is an aviation technology platform, popularly known as Aviation City, includes a wide variety of activities to be located in a planned area of 102 km². In the macro-sense, its mandate will cover aviation ecology, logistics, the civil aviation industry, scientific training for aviation industry specialists and aeronautical fairs and expos. More specifically the operational activities of the new city will include the locational activities shown in Figure 8.5.

The educational functions and research programmes to be carried out within the various locations of the industry park will be technically supported by staff from the Civil Aviation University of China, which is located in Tianjin. The institution has both national and international status and offers teaching and research programmes in a broad range of relevant industrial disciplines. This strategic game plan has been materially aided by the arrival in Tianjin, as noted earlier, of an Airbus A320 general assembly line, which is currently building up its operational momentum. The development of this important project from the Chinese point of view, is described below in some detail.

The Airbus 320 Project

In October 2006, AVIC 1 and AVIC 2 signed a framework agreement with Airbus Industrie, with the intention of setting up a general assembly line for the A320 in Tianjin. The project was the first to be located outside Europe by Airbus and was officially opened on 28 September 2008 as the A320 Family Final Assembly Line (FALC). Airbus has the controlling equity interest set at 51 per cent and the process of sub-contracting for components to Chinese firms began in 2007. The ceremony at the opening also included a memorandum of understanding between the parties which will cover managerial training for staff of aviation authorities, technical maintenance support for airlines, ATM technologies development and training for both university and industrial training personnel.

- Area 1: Airport operations and quality assurance.
- Area 2: Aeronautics training and research.
- Area 3: Civil aviation technology industrialization base.
- Area 4: Airport operations management park.
- Area 5: Airport logistics park.
- Area 6: Aircraft MRO area.

Figure 8.5   The Proposed Operational Functions of the Tianjin Aviation City

Adapted from: Tianjin Planning and Development Commission 2007.

The medium to longer term projections for sales, foresees the completion and delivery of some 247 A320s to Chinese airlines by 2015. Further expectations envisage post-2015 production to be sold both in the larger region and internationally to other countries. It is also anticipated that by 2011, the FALC production flow will reach a rate of four aircraft a month. The first off-line delivery to Sichuan Airlines is expected to be made through Dragon Aviation Leasing in mid 2009.

Developments at Beijing Capital International and Tianjin Binhai International Airports

Commencing in 2008, the Capital Airport Holding Company (CAHC) as parent agency for the Beijing Capital International Airport Company Ltd (BCIAC) plans to both revise its development strategy and to proceed with some appropriate attempts to attract key investors. Further proposals for change include the need to give increased attention to the greater integration of its member firms' core businesses. This is because the CAHC holds equity shares in over 30 airports located across nine provinces, municipalities and SARs.

Particular attention is also being given to attempts to increase non-aeronautical revenues by introducing a franchise business model in its new Terminal 3. While these activities signal an expansion of developments in a very specific direction the firm's strategic intention to also make a significant operational return to its core business is indicated by its further decision to withdraw from its investments in travel insurance and air cargo transportation. This will involve withdrawal of its equity in Metlife, and the probable sale of its shares in Air China Cargo back to that airline.

At the end of 2007, BCIAC ranked first in the list of China's busiest airports, with a total of 56.6 million passengers passing through, a percentage increase of 10 per cent per year since 2006. It was also second to Pudong International in the rating for air cargo. With the third and truly massive terminal now fully in place, strategic projections by management have anticipated that by 2015, passenger movements will exceed 76 million with aircraft movements predicted to reach 500,000.

A Tianjin–Binhai Air Cargo Development Overview

At this stage of its development the Tianjin airport is experiencing a healthy growth in its cargo throughput. In 2007 it processed over 125,000 metric tonnes, a net growth of 29.3 per cent year on year. This achievement placed it at number 12 in the ranking list of China's airports. In January 2008 Lufthansa Cargo announced a new joint venture which will see the construction of the Hua Yu Air Cargo terminal on the airport site. The agreement joins together Lufthansa Cargo (46 per cent) with Taiwan's Hwa-Hsia International Holdings (49 per cent), which leaves the Tianjin Airport International Logistics Company holding 5 per cent. When it is finally operative the project will involve a 90,000 m² freight terminal with a 360 tonnes capacity, a specification which will triple the airport's current cargo volume.

The same month saw the establishment of the Tianjin Cargo Transportation Cooperative which will be the operator of one of the major new terminals planned for the airport. The investing partners in the project are Korean Air (47 per cent), Sinotrans Air Transportation Development (20 per cent), and Hanjin Transportation (10 per cent), Korean Airport Services (15 per cent) and the Tianjin-Dongfang Credit Investment Company (8 per cent). The project involves an investment of US$43.7 million and it will be managed by Korean Air staff. The new joint venture has also contracted to rent a further 128,000 m² space on which an air terminal will be constructed in two phases.

These developments signal an important growth phase in the role of the airport, which incidentally was scheduled to handle the bulk of air cargo operations for the Olympic Games, as well as serving as an alternative destination for incoming traffic, should congestion at BCIA have required it to play that role. In addition to these major projects, work on the second runway for Tianjin International was scheduled to begin in March 2008, accompanied by a proposed extension to the existing runway to be completed by June. The growing optimism that encompasses all of these developments is reflected in the fact that at the time of writing, Tianjin International serves 48 domestic routes in China and a further 18 international routes linking with 59 cities. It is expected that both capacity and client usage will increase as international knowledge grows with regard to the key role that civil aviation plays in the Tianjin–Binhai region.

Summary

It has been the purpose of this chapter to examine the role of the three major metropolitan regions that constitute the core locations than have both shaped and continue to drive the development of civil aviation in China. This view will be reinforced by further and later commentary and discussion. It remains at this point only to observe that the four major hubs we have been discussing, are also strategically possessed, each in turn, with a larger vision of future civil aviation development in both China and the states that are to be found in the proximate and international region.

There remains as a final comment the need to be aware that Hong Kong International, Baiyun International, Pudong International and Beijing International have another conjoint set of expectations that flow from the fact that they are all members of the East Asia Airport Alliance (EAAA). As a consequence of this affiliation they are able to develop important relationships with some key Korean and Japanese hubs particularly with regard to important matters of common concern.

The range of major projects that have been discussed in some detail above, indicate the growing interest of China in the development of a viable and competitive aerospace industry, in which aircraft manufacturing plays an increasingly important role. The next chapter will examine what appears to be an emerging game plan to develop a greater degree of independence and control over such important possibilities as the emergence of an indigenous series of jet transport aircraft.

The plan for which target dates for final production have already been mooted, anticipates a dual outcome. The reduction of dependence on international suppliers for both fleet purchase and replacement, and the development of a range of aircraft that may be offered on the international market in direct competition initially with Embraer and Bombardier and ultimately with Boeing and Airbus. Consideration of the game plan will be followed in Chapter 10 by a review of the problems that the game plan faces in a highly competitive and specialized market.

Chapter 9

The National Quest for a Viable Broad Spectrum Aerospace Industry

Some of the earlier discussions with regard to the development of civil aviation in China located the history of the modern industry initially within the operational context of military aerospace requirements as specified by the People's Liberation Army (PLA). What became after 1949 the national defence industry, took as its working model the Soviet style of centralized planning, which saw a high degree of priority production of military technology, based upon what was essentially a very weak economic base. It was also, as already described in Chapter 4, a period in which the aviation industry as a totality, which included aerospace, was dominated by the strategic priorities and imperatives of the PLA.

The result of this approach produced a very fragmented defence industry in which the state had total control over the all matters from technology choices and product designs through to the management of costs and profits. This was further exacerbated by the need to prepare technological inputs, solely on the basis of preparation for a possible defensive future war. As a direct consequence the possibilities that, over time, there would emerge the kinds of military–commercial technological linkages that are found in the aerospace industries of Western countries simply did not eventuate. The need to revise this policy overview however in the interests of such possibilities appears to have been fully understood by the post-1978 reformist administrations.

From a military perspective, in more recent times, there has been an attempt to maximize potential benefits in the development of non-military aerospace technology intended for commercial use with a strategy based on the principles of civil–military integration (CMI). In general terms this approach allows for the development of technology with military applications to be carried on in parallel with a more commercially orientated programme, with the further anticipation that there will be material benefits and outcomes forthcoming for both sectors in the aerospace industry.

This chapter will review selected and important developments currently taking place in the civil aviation sector beginning against the CMI background. It will do so while keeping in mind the dominant and current ideological concept of economic progress based on the principles of Scientific Development as defined the fourth generation of CPC leadership.

Introducing the Concept of Civilian–Military Integration (CMI)

The process of civil–military integration or CMI involves a deliberate intention on the part of those in authority, it is suggested by Bitzinger (2004), to combine military and commercial production activities so that common technologies, manufacturing agents, equipment, facilities and technically qualified human resources can produce items that meet the needs of both defence requirements and commercial markets.

Commencing with research and development, economic efficiencies can be maximized such that final end products for both may well be produced on a single production line or by a single firm or in a given location. The functional distribution of activities may under such circumstances give rise, as is not uncommon in the world's more advanced economies, to outputs that somewhat blur the distinctions between a given completed item and its range of possible final uses.

From a military perspective, China shares with many countries a strong awareness of the benefits which would accrue from greater self-sufficiency in arms procurement. Such a goal could a major factor in both the modernization of weaponry within changing international strategic parameters, and at the same time could lead to the maximization and accrual of the dual-use benefits of specific technologies for national security and defence. It would appear that to some extent current thinking in Beijing, tends to see the major aim of Chinese strategy as a form of conversion from a defence specific sector in which only military aerospace requirements reside, toward a national network of military/commercial enterprises. Quite clearly this model fits into the current trend where multinational aerospace firms are able to expand and link civilian research to technological developments so that they can develop important and commercial/military potentials.

It has been suggested by Chueng (2007) that this strategy can be described as a two-pronged approach to the reform of the defence industry. The first objective is to internally re-engineer activities with the intention of developing an industrial culture that will be less subject to direction by the state. From these changes it is hoped that a competively minded and entrepreneurial sector will emerge that will nurture the advancement of both production technologies and scientific knowledge.

The second objective as already described above calls for the CMI process to be developed in China, so that the successful integration of dual functions can be the future driver of developmental programmes in the aviation industry. This calls for a seamless system and an operational culture, where indigenous research and planning is ultimately incorporated as the first step in the final production process.

The introduction of the programme comprised the normative public announcement of the directions that should be taken in very general terms and in the conventional form of what can best be described as a wish list. This approach is described in Figure 9.1.

- Expansion of defence industry priorities to include commercial activities for national economic construction
- Extension of production methods and system for dual production military and commercial usage.
- Increased cooperation in technology and economics across all industrial sectors
- Quality changes to replace general production with high technology, intensive technology production for export as well as domestic markets
- Military enterprises should expand their roles to include research and development, technical training, marketing and maintenance and repair services.

Figure 9.1   China's Five General Policies for Conversion from Defence to CMI Joint Enterprises

Adapted from: S. Zhenhuan (PRC State Planning Commission) Reform of China's Defence Industry. gov.China.

The rise and growth of what can be described as the search for CMI can be located in the late 1970s within the broader context of government's move toward economic reform. It was from the mid-1980s however that the pace of growth really accelerated. Estimates suggest that the number of military affiliated firms grew from 10,000 in 1985 to 20,000 three years later. They were particularly active in the services sector with a growth surge of from 50 to 5,000 between 1978 and 1992.

The rate of growth was accompanied by increasing industrial diversity, with the introduction of service industry activities located in shipping, pharmaceuticals, motor vehicle production, electronics, satellites, telecommunications and real estate, and the list continues to expand. An important macro-driver for change can be attributed to the period of the breaking of the iron rice bowl. Economic reforms by definition called for serious budget cuts to be made in sectors that were contributing to a grossly unproductive economy. The PLA alongside other public agencies as well as local governments thus became a candidate for productivity reforms.

It is a matter of some strategic ambiguity that despite the fact that the military were clearly listed as key agencies in the Four Modernizations, there was clear evidence of a steady decline in the military defence budget recorded at a rate of 5.8 per cent per annum for the period of the 1980s. This had the consequential effect of reducing the figure for defence expenditure from 16 per cent in 1980 to 7.52 per cent in 1992. It seems that in that period the government's decision to reduce the defence budget simply extended the same process that was being experienced in other SRE sectors of the national economy to the military.

The intention was, it seems, to push industrial production as well as services toward profit-orientated activities and in this specific case to make military specific technologies develop applications with a much wider operational context. It is worth noting here, that the creation of an integrative and dynamic link between military and civil aviation was clearly in the minds of the planners.

This became transparently so with the official statement that the purpose of government was to reform and convert the past unified military production system into an integrated military–civilian national defence scientific research programme connected to a consequential military–industrial production system.

It is also timely at this point to make the comment that service to the greater good implicit in the principles driving the macro-strategy had had untoward and ambivalent results at the micro-level. Given the new market opportunities, both organizations and individuals have frequently acted to enrich themselves, a corrupting motivation that really does not do much for basic institutional survival.

The Post-reform Development of the Chinese Aerospace Industry

China's strategic objective from an industrial production point of view has two major goals. The first was to develop a modern and indigenous aircraft manufacturing sector which would supply both the domestic demand for new aircraft and, ultimately, offer very competitive models and outputs to buyers in the international market for primary fleet purchase and subsequent replacements.

The second would seek the development of a modern air traffic management system which would offer an effective and comprehensive national system for air space management. The latter objective has ramifications for government's plan to locate Chinese aviation in the mainstream of international air safety and development, and will be dealt with in more detail in the next chapter. The balance of discussion here will therefore concentrate on the first objective.

Developing a Civil Aviation Industry with Chinese Characteristics

By its nature the evolution of an international aerospace industry presented generations of manufacturers with a highly complex set of supply-chain requirements, which required in turn the ability to manage risk, time, finance and often long drawn out learning curves. In more recent times effective production strategies have tended to become subject to the consolidation of major specialized production, requiring in turn, a veritable multitude of sub-contractors and product outsourcing on a global scale. This then leads progressively toward final assembly, which increasingly may not be carried out in the parent firm's country of origin, as the Airbus decision to move its A320 line to China indicates.

During the 1980s the idea took root, that China should attempt to build an industrial capacity that would lead, as analysed by Nolan and Zhang (2003) and Goldstein (2005), to the emergence of a successful indigenous aircraft manufacturing sector. The result after a preliminary programme of reverse engineering using the Boeing 707 as the template model saw the creation of the Y-10 developed by the Ministry of Aerospace Industries. In turn, the X'ian Aircraft Corporation (XAC) developed the Y-7 a 60-seat turbo-prop regional carrier.

Both ventures proved to be failures, though a number of managerial ambiguities in decision making surrounded the halting of the Y-10 programme in 1985. Given the range and diversity of international aircraft available to airlines seeking fleet replacements at that time, economic logic, as clearly specified by Nolan (2001), suggests that for the Y-10 to be a success there would have been the need for government protection in the form of subsidies within the domestic market for the model to overcome the domestic airline preferences for the range of international alternatives.

The development of an indigenous and efficient aviation industry in China forms a part of a much larger ambition as described by Shenkar (2006) in which foreign firms as well as international research and new technologies currently continue to play a major part. This is strongly reflected, as discovered by Sigurdson (2004), in the year on year comparison of the export and import of aircraft, parts and accessories, for the period 2002–03. The figures for 2002–03 exports are static at 4.39 per cent; by contrast foreign imports of components in the same period rose from 40.52 per cent to 44.61 per cent.

This substantive imbalance has been fully recognized by the PRC which anticipates a considerable expansion of both domestic and international activities as earlier discussions have already indicated. What has emerged is another form of a dual strategy in which existing industrial plants are being rejuvenated and projects are being supported by a growing number of joint ventures and other forms of agreements with foreign players.

Mapping the Political, Organizational and Company Responses to the Demand for Strategic Change

It has already been noted that the CAAC is now located within the newly created super Ministry of Transport as a Civil Aviation Bureau, the precise roles and functions of which are yet to be fully defined. It can be assumed in the interim that the effective management of the civil aviation industry will continue to be a major activity of the new body, within the operational context of responsibilities for urban, road and maritime services.

In matters relating to actual policy setting for the industry at large, the State Commission of Science, Technology and Industry (COSTIND) will remain as the lead authority with retention of control over the existing roles of the China Aviation Industry Corporations (AVIC I and AVIC II). Before commenting on the activities of what currently constitutes two industrial conurbations, it is important to make the further observation that COSTIND may, as proposed by Air TN-EU (2007), also be responsible for the technology policies that will drive the development of nuclear, aerospace, aviation, shipbuilding and weaponry industries.

In addition it will also have to carry out the management of foreign cooperation and acquisitions, especially for military hardware, the additional management of sensitive military technologies and the project management of weapons projects and defence conversion. On the other hand, given the current focus by the CCP on structural changes in administration, the possibility still exists that both its title and its current role and functions might continue to undergo change.

The Operational Dimensions of AVIC I and AVIC II

The conjoint organizations employ a labour force in excess of more than 450,000, of which approximately 50 per cent are employed in the aerospace programme. It consists of over 100 large and medium-size firms, 31 applied research institutions and three scientific research centres. Currently production involves the building of military aircraft to both Chinese and Russian specifications as well as a range of smaller aircraft and helicopters. In addition, work on the production of commercial components under international contract, has a client list which includes Boeing, Airbus, Rolls-Royce and Pratt and Whitney, GE, SNECMA, Honeywell, and Rockwell-Collins. It also produces a wide range of weaponry, fire-control systems and includes ground support equipment.

The Central Role of the China National Aero-Technology Import and Export Corporation (CATIC)

CATIC was created in 1979 under the joint ownership of AVIC I and II each of which holds 50 per cent of the company's equity. It has been officially described as a large-scale state-owned conglomerate with a core business based on the import and export of aviation products and technology. The organizational structure of CATIC ranges from seven specialized firms and ten regional subsidiaries located on the mainland, with some 56 subsidiaries located worldwide. The corporation has a total equity in the range of RMB24 billion and an accumulated volume of earnings with a net worth US$24 billion since it opened for business. This gives CATIC a consistent ranking position in the top 20 import–export firms in China.

The active role of CATIC as a multi-market conglomerate is reflected in the range of activities carried out by its various specialized companies and regional subsidiaries. These include shipping services, civil engineering, food processing, medical equipment, container inspection systems, automobiles, in which the conglomerate is China's largest player, motorcycles and bicycles. The group is also active in the international construction industry with projects located in Asia, Africa and the Middle East. Such activities reflect a larger and older history of Chinese business that predates the modern period and reflects a tradition of responding to many and various business opportunities as they arise.

This seems to have been the strategy of CATIC which has become known as a famous brand owner, the possessor of a range of interests in commercial real estate and for the further ownership of five public companies which are listed on the Shanghai, Shenzhen and Hong Kong stock markets. These developments, it seems, are a reflection of CATIC's determination to be duly recognized as a major multinational. In the meantime, it continues to develop its primary role as the major broker straddling the aviation import and export business.

The Proposal to Integrate AVIC I and AVIC II

It has already been noted in earlier discussions that one of the final goals of market reform in the PRC plans for a total of up to 100 large firms to be permanently active on a global basis. There is however an element of history repeating itself in the government's decision, taken early in 2008, to merge AVIC I and II. This is because the two dominant players in the Chinese aerospace industry were in fact an earlier and organizational product of the government's decision in 1999 to split the then existing China Aviation Industry Corporation (CAIC) into two.

The current intention it seems is to create a conglomerate which will unify the development of a viable large aircraft programme. The date of the actual formal launch of what has been popularly called AVIC III remains uncertain at the time of writing. The primary goal of the amalgamation it seems is to develop a new and indigenous sector of the aircraft industry that will produce a range of wide-bodied large jet carriers, able to compete on international terms with the current manufacturing oligopoly that is dominating the market. The revived China Aviation Industry Corporation Group (CAIC Group) will have total oversight over aircraft manufacture in China, with 2020 set as the goal for the launch of a new indigenous wide-bodied passenger jet. The ensuing period would then see the production of further indigenous models that will then be designed to compete directly with the B737 and A320 as well as their successors.

The CAIC Group will have 14 departments based at corporate headquarters in Beijing and will own a total of ten subsidiaries. Authority will also be extended to cover the management of the Commercial Aircraft Corporation of China (CACC), which has been charged, as discussion below will reveal, with the task of developing the much publicized 90-seat ARJ 21-900 regional jet, an anticipated forerunner of a new generation of a much-needed domestic type. In addition it will be charged with the development of an indigenous series of large wide-bodied long-haul jet aircraft.

From an operational perspective, the strategic intention is to develop a Chinese version of the conventional main manufacturer-multiple supplier system, with a group of operational divisions that cover the total range of activities from research and conception to flight testing, certification and sale. Such an approach signals the fact that the conventional policy for civil aviation development remains based on the incorporation of not simply corporate foreign investment, but also the technical know how and experience of the world's largest players in aircraft manufacturing.

The implications of what can only be called this vitally important limitation on innovative capacity will be considered in much more depth and detail in a later chapter. At this point in the discussion attention will be turned to the roles that major producers have played to date in shaping the Chinese aerospace industry.

The Impact of Foreign Manufacturers on the Growth of the Domestic Aircraft Industry

It is clear that the growth of China's aircraft manufacturing sector has materially benefited from the willingness of some of the world's leading players to subcontract component manufacture to Chinese firms located on the mainland. For example Airbus produced a number of technical components for the A320 in X'ian, Chengdu and Shenyang, prior to its recent decision, discussed in Chapter 8, to move its first assembly line to be located out of Europe into China.

In turn Boeing reports that it has purchased over US$1 billion of hardware and services since the 1980s, with existing contracts signed by both the company and its partners possessing a value of well over US$2.5 billion. The willingness of the major international companies to relocate operations from their home country and subcontract for a wide range of aircraft components and sub-assemblies, has given rise to a growing number of domestic operators in China. The leading group of firms is listed in Table 9.1.

The continued presence of international players within the Chinese domestic market both as investors and as operational companies is also reflected in the tendency for a quasi-permanent location in China to be embodied within the larger strategic context of their international operations. Boeing, for example, claims with some justification that they have been busy and active in modern China since 1972, but have a history of business in the country dating back to quite early in the twentieth century.

Table 9.1   A Selection of China's Leading-edge Aircraft Manufacturers

Leading Aircraft Manufacturers	Leading Engine Manufacturers
Shenyang Aircraft Co. (SAC)	X'ian Aero Engine Corp. (XAE)
Shanghai Aircraft Industry Co (SAIC)	Liming Engine Man. Corp. (LM)
X'ian Aircraft Industries Group (XAC)	Dongan Engine Man. Co. (DAE)
Chengdu Aircraft Co. (CAC)	CAE–Chengdu Aero Engine Co. (CAE)
Harbin Aircraft Co. (HAC)	South Aero Engine Co. (SAEC)
Hongdu Aviation Industry Group (HAIG)	
Hafei Aviation Industry Co. (HAI)	

Adapted from: AirTN Web www.airtn.eu.

Today Boeing China Inc. has its head office in Beijing and an office in Hong Kong. It employs a staff of 160, with some 5,800 employees located in their subsidiary and joint-venture businesses. In addition the world's largest aircraft manufacturer's public relations department has been signalling a corporate willingness to remain in China for the foreseeable future. A working example of international integration can be found in the small aircraft manufacturer, Bombardier of Canada. The company has a dual role in China as a leading provider of railway equipment, systems and services in one domain, and as the number one foreign provider of regional jets in the other. Some 34 aircraft in their CRJ series are currently operated commercially by six domestic carriers. In addition 2007 saw the company sign a strategic cooperation agreement with AVIC I to assist in the development of a 90- to 145-seat range of jet aircraft. The prototype specification calls for a 150-seat aircraft with a take-off weight of 100 metric tonnes. By implication this would, in terms of size, be in the B757-767 or Airbus A310 categories.

What is interesting at this point, given that the anticipated demand for an aircraft of this type calls for over 1,700 new aircraft to be in service over the next 20 years, is the often expressed unanimity of the various parties with regard to their individual, as opposed to, mutual self interest. This is reflected in the fact that Airbus, Boeing, Bombardier on the foreign side, and the domestic firm CACC, which was created for this project, have consistently discounted any potential conflict that might arise over the delicate question of future market share.

They have done so on the expatriate side on the grounds that China will not really be a viable competitor in the development of an indigenous large jet series for some considerable time to come. We shall return to these somewhat ambiguous expectations of the foreign partners in more detail and in Chapter 10. It is now time to examine some case examples of current projects being advanced by indigenous firms.

First Project: The XAC Modern Ark MA60 and MA600 Short- and Medium-range Commuter Series

The MA60 is a short- to medium-range commuter turbo-prop with seating capacity in the 48–60 range. Designed and built by the X'ian Aircraft Corporation, it began testing in 1993 and was granted official permission to enter commercial service in 2000. The aircraft has a short runway capability and has been deliberately designed for heavy-duty services with a take-off weight of 21,800 kg and with further specifications that are aimed at offering buyers competitive and low operational costs, a fact that has attracted some positive attention outside China. The reason for this can be found in Chinese media reports that foresee a large and growing demand for regional turbo-props, due to a rising international demand for commuter services.

In China itself commuter routes are frequently being flown at the current time by often unsuitable larger aircraft with significantly high operational costs which logically, and in turn, are having a negative effect on revenue flows. The MA60 made its maiden commercial flight on 19 October 2008, for OK Air, which has placed an order for ten MA60s. The XAC management has also reported orders to date both in China and overseas for some 122 aircraft.

From a purchaser's perspective supply side information for this aircraft is becoming somewhat ambiguous as well as confused. This is because on 29 June 2008 it was publically announced by the X'ian Aircraft Industry Group that, after three years, developmental work had been completed on an 'improved' version of the original model, namely the MA600, which was 300 kg lighter than the MA60, a fact that made it 40 per cent more fuel efficient than the older aircraft. In addition, the public statement noted a sequence of improvements had been made to the power systems, cabin design and flight capabilities of the new model, which is scheduled to go into production in 2009.

Plans were also announced for a further new aircraft, an MA700 which would add ten further seats to the carrying capacity of the original model. The strategic intention according to a senior XAC official is to develop the MA type as a series of models during the next five years. In turn the market intention is to challenge both Bombardier's CRJ series and the Aerospatiale ATR 500s in order to obtain a larger market share. The anticipated growth of the MA60 series raises yet again the further question, frequently asked by scholars and technical experts, as to the degree and extent of subsidies that will be needed to make sure that the proposed output targets, implicit in every stage of the proposed production cycle, are reached efficiently and on time.

The confusion is further deepened in the marketing sense by the fact that potential buyers for the initial XAC series are going to be faced with a range of choices between the current model in production and those proposed for further development as more advanced models. In terms of market competition the Chinese company is effectively putting its MA60 aircraft, currently in the early stages of its production cycle up against the new and more advanced model it intends to bring on line, with another and further version in the pipeline. As a result prospective buyers may want to wait for the specific model that meets its defined operational needs, at the cost of some delay in the matter of sales.

In doing so XAC is also offering competitive companies, especially foreign firms, a considerable degree of market advantage. One senses also that a key driver in the XAC approach to business can be found in the old pre-reform tradition that sees the maximization of production goals through size of output as the final purpose of the whole exercise. If the XAC project does wish to meet all of its targeted goals for what is rapidly become a series, with each model exhibiting improved technologies, then it is essential that planned marketing requirements should shape the production schedule for each model in a clearly stepped sequence. In other words, the XAC sales strategy must replace its seeming fixation with production schedules as the manufacturer's primary strategic goal.

Second Project: The ARJ21 Regional Jetliner

The project name of what is intended to be a pure jet regional airliner can be translated as Advanced Regional Jetliner for the Twenty-first Century. This is a fitting title perhaps for what is being publically identified as China's first move toward the production of its own indigenous commercial jet aircraft. The project was put in train formally in 2002, after State Council approval, which led AVIC I to create a consortium of five major industry groups, namely, Harbin, Shaanzi, Chengdu, Shenyang and Xi'an as the primary contractors. Shanghai was nominated as the location for research and development as well as final assembly and final testing, which will take place at Pudong International Airport.

The project consortium is clearly initially targeting the demand in domestic market for a wide-bodied medium-range aircraft that will carry up to 85 passengers, especially on routes that are being currently serviced, as we have seen, by larger aircraft at some excessive operational cost. This is incidentally a market that has also been targeted by China's embryonic LCC carriers. Table 9.2 provides the specification data for the ARJ21-700 prototype.

Table 9.2   Specification Data for the ARJ21-700 Prototype

Key Data	Specifications by Category
Passenger Seats	78–85 in 4 (first class) and 5 (economy class) row configurations
Wingspan plus Winglets	27.448m
Fuselage Length	29.464m
Cabin Volume	117.101m2
Cabin Length	18.426m
Maximum Take-off Weight	37,648kg
Maximum Payload	8,935kg
Maximum Fuel	10,386kg
Engines (2)	CF344-10A
Take-off Field Length	1,472m
Landing Field length	1,436m
Maximum Operating Speed Vmo	Mach 0.32
Cruise Speed	Mach 0.78
Maximum Altitude	12,000m
Range – standard version	2,225km
Range – extended range version	3,704km

Adapted from: Aerospace Technology.com-SPG Media.

The concept of an indigenous wide-bodied jet has its origins in 1970, as a spin-off from the development of a military transport model. The resultant Yun-10, reached the test flying stage, when lack of funds and a change in strategic direction toward the adoption of a market for technology policy, plus the technical problems that emerged after a test model crashed, saw the idea abandoned until the emergence of the current project. The new aircraft will be produced in commercial, executive and freight formats, at the same time. Despite its indigenous development from the conceptual stage, some 50 per cent of production components are in fact of foreign origin.

The inaugural flight was scheduled to take place early in 2008. In fact it has been postponed several times. On 10 October of that year it was further announced that the delay would be extended into November. This means that the scheduled first orders which were expected to be delivered in 2009, will not now be available until 2010. The aircraft will also be subject to a certification process extending up to 18 months, and CACC is hoping this will be reduced to 12. Unfortunately the process of certification is not only subject to the conventional internal procedures, in the case of the ARJ21 the entire activity is subject to due examination by the US FAA, which has the task of evaluating and ensuring that all certification procedures meet prescribed international standards.

The need for the FAA to carry out this task appears to have developed as a consequence of the fact that Beijing has sought the required certification for the potential sale of the ARJ21 in the United States. While, as one analyst has observed, US sales are unlikely given the market competition, he goes on to suggest that the Chinese motive is to inaugurate due certification process in order to gain as much insight as possible into the quality control standards and procedures employed by the US aviation industry.

This immediately raises an ongoing problem with the constantly vexed question of intellectual property rights that has long bedevilled Chinese businesses in their relationships with foreign firms particularly in joint-venture projects. We can now turn the focus of discussion to the next major question. What plans are there being made to advance both the development of the current aircraft and their possible progeny?

Cooperative Efforts to Use the ARJ21 as a Developmental Platform

It was reported on 18 June 2007 that AVIC I had reached agreement with Bombardier Aerospace to collaborate on the development of an aircraft series ranging from 90 to 100 seats. The deal aimed at combining the development programmes of both the projected ARJ-900 series and the proposed further development of the Canadian company's C-series of passenger jets. AVIC I has advised that it planned to invest US$400 million for research and development and the construction of new facilities and equipment should the C-series aircraft programme be launched. In turn Bombardier saw their financial contribution in the range of US$100 million with the addition of technical assistance for the development of the ARJ21-900. The firm's expectations included efforts to enhance the competitiveness of the Chinese aircraft, while also exploring potential communality between the two programmes.

Both parties also advised that outcomes from collaboration would include mutual cost reductions as well as production efficiencies. Such projects bring with them steep learning curves if China is to become a serious international competitor. They also raise very large questions with regard to human resource needs and the availability of indigenous managerial capacity of the high professional calibre that projects of this scope and scale demand. With these uncertainties in mind the direction of discussion can now return to the issues of viability that surround the possible successful operationalization of CMI within what has been called the building of a dual-use economy.

CMI and the Need to Develop Dual-use Economic Outcomes

Government has signalled that a key task in the period from 2006 to 2020 will be the creation of a Yujun Yumin system. This requires that China speed up the operational development of the military use of civilian products in defence construction. The resultant attempt to build a dual-use aircraft manufacturing industry brings together a significant number of high technology civilian firms who are engaged in industries with a strong research and development culture, which in turn is embedded in advanced scientific research on new product applications.

What might be described as the other half of the dual-use equation will involve legacy firms within the state-owned defence industries, who are seeking to transform themselves into military technology entities that can meet all of the necessary information needs of a modern military production system. This raises inevitable and serious questions with regard to how successful fusion can be achieved.

One major issue will involve the question of what dominant organizational culture and values will emerge from the merger? It is necessary to ask at this point, will civilian values in the matter of transparency and market-based commercially acceptable business practices prevail? Uncertainty takes over here, since many of the concepts and practices that are commonplace in civilian enterprise are also alien in terms of current military perceptions, with its traditional working stress on project security, based on the limitation of the need to know to be limited to very specific and designated staff.

A second important issue arises from the obvious need to build the new dual system on the foundations of the existing military production arrangements. The raises the immediate question as to how and how fast total reform and restructuring can proceed to its successful and targeted completion. Unfortunately, the initiatives undertaken in the 1980s and 1990s were to say the least haphazard and at best not stellar as one critic has put it. The result produced a poorly structured and uncoordinated system, in which a significant gap emerged between civilian production on one hand and military expectations on the other.

It has been suggested by some military planners, according to Fan Xiehong (2004), that China should speed up the advance of modernization in the defence industry, by skipping some developmental stages in a transformational process and moving straight into the frontiers of knowledge areas of information-related technologies. The problem of course with this approach lies in the fact that much of the frontier technology that is being sought is overwhelmingly in the civilian and existing dual-use sectors, which returns the argument in a circle back to the need for an effective dual-use system.

Finally, the need for a much larger budget for the defence industry comes to the fore. In the late 1990s, China's defence research budget was about 5 per cent of that of the United States. While the numbers have improved in the last decade, it is clear that even under the present allocations this aviation-based version of the Great Leap Forward would fall short of the comparative and expected technological standards enjoyed by the leading international states. It is clear that a more effective strategy might require China to go with a selection of projects where the opportunities to actually narrow the technological gap are the greatest.

The Emerging Problems of Environmental Change Confronting Industrial Production Planning in China

The question of the effects of China's industrial growth strategies on the both the indigenous and international environments has emerged with some force especially with regard to climate change issues. When compared with the United States the dimensions of the PRC's carbon footprint becomes vividly apparent. According to Houser (2008), more than 70 per cent of CO_2 emissions in the United States comes from the public consumption of goods and services, while in the Chinese case the main cause is found within industry. In the case of steel alone the energy consumption currently stands at 18 per cent, which is approximately nearly twice the rate of all Chinese households. In turn the chemical sector consumes more energy than all forms of private transportation.

There can be no doubt that Beijing is fully cognizant of the need to enforce controls over the major contributors to what is an increasingly massive problem. The energy-intensive footprint created by the production of steel, cement, chemicals, paper and aluminium alone account for nearly half China's energy needs while contributing, it is estimated, through pollution to the deaths of some 300,000 citizens on a yearly basis, at an estimated social and economic cost of RMB100 billion.

Ironically the five industries at the centre of the problem (Houser, 2008) make only a modest contribution to the general level of employment, with some 14 million at work in a national total of 770 million. This number in fact is lower than it was a decade ago, a situation which places China in an invidious position, since investment in high energy production does little to improve the constant problem of high unemployment.

Any potential response by the government of the PRC with regard to a strategy to offset the effects of pollution intensity on a national basis will need to balance macro-initiatives across industry in general with the more specific requirements needed in certain sectors. The CAAC is well aware of the fact that international civil aviation has been widely identified as a target industry for a specific programme of pollution controls, which has led to increasing controversy over the actual degree and extent to which civil aviation is a major polluter. From an international perspective as reflected in comments and statements by both ICAO and IATA, how the Chinese government will respond in strategic terms to the need for environmental reform is a very significant issue, given the relative size and growing importance of its national aviation industry.

These many uncertainties underlie the larger question as to the operational and organizational dynamics that currently drive the international aerospace industry today. It arises from the fact that any serious development of an efficient, indigenous and competitive Chinese aviation industry must take into consideration the major structural shifts that continue to shape and re-shape the international market as the dominant context within which there is an urgent need to become seriously competitive.

The key organizational issues which require a significant response from those charged with the strategic direction of China's civil aviation development programme will now become the primary focus of the next phase of discussion. It is time therefore to focus attention more closely on the larger organizational and administrative questions facing the planners who are charged with the task of translating plans for an indigenous aerospace construction industry into a viable and efficient operational reality. As a consequence the next chapter will attempt to look somewhat critically at the substantive and important uncertainties that surround the future of what can be described as a brave new venture. In doing so due attention will be paid to the degree and extent of international competition that currently exists within this increasingly complex and diverse industry.

Chapter 10
Some Organizational Problems and Competitive Market Uncertainties

The previous chapter explored the various strategic contexts in which China's aerospace industry finds itself in the first decade of the twenty-first century. In doing so it traced the evolution of what has consistently been an essentially dualist process. The country's emergence as a super power and a major force in the global economy is under way and still gathering momentum, a fact that is generally recognized by those developed countries that have been at the forefront of internationalization thus far. But it is also necessary to recognize that economic progress in China is also directly related to a deliberate geopolitical strategy driven by successive governments of the PRC.

This has been based on the government planning imperative that the national economy be opened to very large components of foreign capital investment, technological know how and professional expertise. In order to gain a degree of operational advantage in both aspects of this strategy, government policy has progressively advanced the further development of market entry by foreign firms either as individual businesses or through a range of Sino–foreign joint ventures.

It is also clear that when the future of China's aerospace industry becomes the subject of discussion that the government in Beijing perceives the current operational status quo in, for example, aircraft design and manufacturing, as an intermediate phase in the industry's development. It assumes somewhat simplistically that the current processes of market development will give way, over some period of perceived time, to an efficient indigenous industry able to compete in both domestic and international markets for the effective supply of airline orders for initial fleet planning as well as the cyclical need for aircraft replacement.

Some large questions remain however in regard to China's ability to attain this objective in an industry which internationally is no longer constrained by national boundaries or, latterly, given the existence of the relatively small number of leading players, by the tradition of national ownership. It will be the primary purpose of this chapter to explore both the dimensions of the current dynamics driving international aircraft production and to identify the complexities and problems that China will face as it attempts to join the market leaders. The course of discussion will cover both the financial and managerial dimensions of the current strategy as well as the limitations and problems it currently poses for aerospace industry planners.

It will begin with a consideration of the primary role of overseas direct investment (ODI) which to an extent reverses the traditional mode of analysis. It does so by attempting the identification of investment outflows from China. The purpose is to indicate the important fact that the PRC's bigger firms are very active outside the parameters of the national economy. As ongoing discussion will reveal the ODI programme is fraught with serious ambiguities in which a very significant number of strategies other than those relating to the aviation industry are involved. This will precede further discussion that will then focus on an extended analysis of the international and internal dynamics of the global aviation industry.

The subsequent balance of the chapter will have a dual purpose. The first task will be to identify the major structural changes that have occurred in the global industry which has produced fewer but very much larger operational firms whose activities are increasingly found within cross-border production networks. The second will then attempt to locate the present stage of development in China's aerospace industry, against the very high competitive standards of the global industry. A concluding section of the chapter will go on to review and comment on the potential need for a new strategic approach that needs to be developed, if China is to maximize its real potential in both the domestic and international aspects of its current policy.

Applying the Principles of both Bringing In and Going Out

There is a need at the commencement of discussion to distinguish by precise definition investment into and out of China. Foreign direct investment (FDI) is the flow of international capital into Chinese markets. This has been conventionally obtained either through mergers and acquisitions (M&A), joint ventures with indigenous firms, or medium to longer term greenfield investment undertaken by overseas companies with the intention of establishing new operational or service activities. By contrast, the flow of investment out of China will be represented here by the distinguishing term, overseas direct investment (ODI), which is synonymous with FDI, but will be used in this context as a more precise indicator.

The origins and current purpose of this strategy are to be found at the beginning of the current decade. Beijing's intention it seems, has been to encourage the international expansion of China's champion multinational enterprises (MNEs) (which include AVIC I and II) with a view to the acquisition of further strategic resources, the active expansion of business activities into foreign markets and as a response to the need to reduce market restraints at home. The trends in aggregate growth rates shown in Table 10.1 offer evidence collated by a major international agency for inward FDI, outward ODI and M&As in the current decennial period, 2000–07.

Table 10.1   Inward FDI, Outward ODI and Cross-border Mergers and Acquisitions 2000–07 (US$ millions)

Fiscal Year	Inward FDI	Outward ODI	Cross-border M&As
2000	40,715	916	470
2001	46,878	6,884	452
2002	52,743	2,518	1,047
2003	53,505	1,800	1,647
2004	60,630	5,498	1,125
2005	72,406	12,261	5,279
2006	72,715	21,160	14,904
2007	83,521	22,469	4,452

Adapted from: Fudan-VCC 2007 Survey UNCTAD World Investment Report, 2008.

The momentum of the growth in ODI has clearly accelerated since 2005. There are however serious problems with data relevance due to the fact that the dominant players are primarily to be found in the SOE sector. These in turn tend to be officially sanctioned monopolies in some major industry, for example, natural resources or IT. This means that the largest ODI players tend to functionally overlap to a considerable extent with the most profitable of China's SOEs. The civil aviation industry is inevitably represented by the China Aviation Group (AVIC I and II), which ranked number 11 in the 2005 list of the country's 30 largest companies.

It is also important to be aware that when the distribution of ODI by country location is brought into focus, it does not indicate a heavy concentration in the key Western countries. In fact as the 2006 figures indicate there is a significant skewed distribution toward developing as opposed to developed countries, with the Southern and Southeast Asian countries well in the lead (Figure 10.1). How far this indicates the movement of production to strategic locations within the larger and proximate region offers some interesting possibilities too complex to be considered here.

As Figure 10.1 indicates the primary focus of China's ODI strategy is geographically concentrated in Eastern and Southeast Asia and to a smaller extent Africa. In the latter case it is worthy of note that China imports over 25 per cent of its oil from Africa and has a significant industrial presence as a client in the mineral markets of Algeria, Angola, Sudan and Niger. In fact it is the second largest buyer after the United States. It has also developed a strong presence in the mining industries, both in Africa and Latin America.

South and Southeast Asia	41
Africa	26
Western Europe	17
North America	10
Western Europe	9
Latin America	8
Japan, HK, S. Korea	6
Middle East	3
North Korea	3
Australasia	2

Figure 10.1   Number of Planned ODI Projects by Destination in 2006

Adapted from: Morck, et al. (2008).

The Ambiguous Role of Tax Havens in China's ODI Strategy

When the individual host country locations are brought more precisely into the discussion, it is interesting to find that the top destinations for ODI flows are to Hong Kong, and the various Caribbean tax havens located in the Cayman and the British Virgin Islands, which collectively in 2005, accounted for about 70 per cent of the total ODI movement. The locations selected are in effect part of a quite rapid equity flow out from and back into China, a process that is popularly referred to as round tripping.

The intent and purpose of the exercise is to ensure that domestic capital flowing out of China can be returned to the home economy as foreign capital. It needs to be observed that in the Western business world the use of tax havens as an international practice often reflects their value as repositories for MNEs and other investors to store wealth outside the formal gaze of their national taxation authorities. The depositing firm can then if it so wishes use subsidiaries located in the havens either as a place to set up an operative presence with the aim of gaining access to trading or as a place offering further investment opportunities.

As an alternative ploy, especially in Hong Kong, a capital round trip back into China can be planned on the basis of a subsidiary acquiring the formal status of a foreign-owned enterprise (FOE) on the mainland. The underlying purposes of such actions remain complex and subject to a number of interpretations. The possibility arises for example that strategically placed subsidiaries may well fit the definition of what has been called a form of spontaneous privatization, in which the motivation driving capital flows into tax havens is insider personal control.

Unfortunately, the full degree and extent of these activities, especially with regard to Hong Kong is unclear, given the ambiguities present in the available published data. What is clear however is the fact that the main players still tend to be the large profitable SOEs which control what have become lucrative state-enforced monopolies. The fact that these players tend to hold on to retained savings, rather than distribute them on a shareholder basis, is also further reinforced by the retained control of capital allocation by the major banks. These, in their turn, transfer savings disproportionately to the SOEs.

The fundamental emphasis on control is perhaps reflective of China's relatively slow abandonment of the traditional operational rules of the command economy. It is also compounded by the fact that bureaucratic devolution has created various levels of authority, in which the parameters of control are often not clear. These issues lie outside the range of topics under immediate discussion, but will re-emerge again in the final chapter.

In order to advance the current discussion further it is necessary first to examine what are in effect alternative views of the nature of market competition. The intention is to establish an operational view of current structural changes that have tended to re-shape the global aerospace markets, against which, the current competitive position of China as a small player trying to learn from the leading-edge corporations can be better assessed.

The Global Business Revolution in the Aerospace Industry

The conventional neo-classical view of market competition in capitalist society presumes that when a firm reaches a specific size, diseconomies of scale tend to exert a delimiting effect on further growth, with an attendant loss of market share over time. Supporters of these assumptions tend to argue that while globalization, and mergers and acquisitions have increased very significantly over the 1990s and into the current decade, the actual levels of global concentration have not really increased in any real sense. As Peter Nolan, a world expert on Chinese business, has consistently pointed out, these views have tended to largely rely for their evidence on the analysis of the consequences of mergers and acquisitions on the effects for shareholder value in the short run. By contrast when the focus shifts to business survival and growth, based on clear strategic intentions, business capabilities can be effectively increased through a wide range of consequential and incremental gains.

These can include access to geographical locations and technological benefits, scarce human resources, additional and valuable brands, research and development and economies of scale and scope in procurement. Subsequent discussion for the balance of this chapter will adopt the conceptual model proposed by Nolan, *et al.* (2007), that for firms from low-income countries, access to developed country markets has become increasingly dependent upon the ability to enter into the global community supply and production chains of core firms based in such high income countries. Quite clearly the strategic intention of China's embryonic aircraft manufacturing industry as noted in the last chapter offers an emergent model of such an approach.

Structural Change in the Global Aerospace Industry

After 1978 the privatization of the world's major airline, as well as the growth of international alliances, placed great pressure on aircraft suppliers to reduce cost. This pressure was replicated in the defence aerospace sector by the drastic fall in national defence sector budgets both in the United States and Europe. The end result was a significant tendency for procurement techniques in the two sectors to become increasingly aligned over time.

The modern international firm enjoys large economies of scale in the assembly process. These emerge through various learning effects as production runs of specific aircraft types move sequentially through their scheduled time cycles. The fact that a family of models such as the B737-200-900 series can be grown off a basic platform that allows for further economies of scale in, for example, component acquisition, can mean significant benefits then accrue to Boeing's customer airlines. In turn reputable branding is a critical factor as many of the foreign aircraft purchases made by Chinese airlines during their experiences of market growth will attest.

Contrary to the neo-classical perception of the relative failure of mergers and acquisitions, the international world of the aircraft manufacturing industry can offer countervailing empirical evidence that contradicts this generalization. The leading example of the United States industry offers a useful working example of the benefits of a positive structural shift through mergers and acquisitions (Figure 10.2).

During the 1990s more than 50 American firms were consolidated into the Big Five, namely Boeing, Lockheed Martin, Northrop, Grumman, Raytheon and General Dynamics. From a civil aviation perspective, this left Boeing as the only airline manufacturer left in the United States with some 84 per cent of the world's total aircraft in service in 1987. Events in Europe were in turn shaped by the need to reform a smaller and more fragmented defence industry in the wake of the United States decision. The result saw in 1999, the emergence of the European Aircraft and Space Company (EADS).

- Fixed wing firms reduced from 8 to 3.
- Rotary wing firms reduced from 4 to 3.
- Tactical missiles firms reduced from 13 to 4.
- Expendable launch vehicle firms reduced from 6 to 2.
- Satellites building firms reduced from 8 to 5.
- Strategic missile firms reduced from 3 to 2.

Figure 10.2   Mergers and Acquisitions between Aerospace Firms in the United States between 1990 and 1998

Adapted from: Nolan (2003).

The subsequent and serious managerial difficulties experienced by EADS has led in turn to firms like Britain's BAe Systems making the decision to enter into a full partner contract with Lockheed Martin in the Joint Strike Fighter (JSF), while both France and Italy are engaged on their own military ventures independently from designated European projects. In the case of Russia the abandonment of the command economy market system and adoption of geopolitical reforms based on neo-classical and free market-driven assumptions has left what was a highly successful and competitive industry, struggling to obtain a foothold in the modern global market.

The Organizational Complexities of the Modern International Aerospace Industry

Today's global aerospace industry embodies advanced technologies, and very powerful operational economies of scale and scope. In addition the scale of investment in a given model is enormous, with very significant front-end costs at the launch stage. The end product can be a major success, coupled to the ability to lock up a chosen market segment for a long time as exemplified by Boeing's 737 series. By contrast the cost of failure is equally high which then tends to turn survival in the industry into a win–lose game. Some idea of the size of the cost factor may be found in the fact that a modern high technology airliner may have a market price of up to or even well over $200 million. The steady rise in final unit prices has done more than anything to advance the consequential growth of aircraft leasing systems by airlines.

In terms of market size and volume, Boeing and the EADS civil aviation arm, Airbus Industrie, are currently engaged in a competitive duopoly, with Airbus placing its primary emphasis on a mega-ultra-long-haul carrier, the A380, which has just begun to supply the first orders to their original clients such as SIA and Qantas and Emirates. By contrast, Boeing after a long and interesting debate as to the actual size of the market for the A380, decided to use its long-range twin-engine platform which has proven successful in the earlier 767 as well as the 777-200 series, to both expand the capacity and range of the ETOPS family. Their success is reflected in the decision taken by ICAO, to introduce LROPS standards, which will accommodate the ultra-long-haul capacities currently found in the Boeing 777 and subsequent 787 series.

In addition global attention has been drawn to the new 787-800 Dreamliner, which is designed to incorporate both new technologies and a revolutionary ultra-long-haul passenger environment. As an indicator of the pre-launch success of this decision by Boeing, the current waiting list of orders for the new model, according to a recent New Zealand university address by the President of the Australasia–South Pacific Division of Boeing International, will not be completed until the year 2016. How far this target date is viable now remains a matter of speculation given the fact that Boeing has recently (December 2008) advised, for the fifth time, that the launch of the first off-line aircraft has been delayed.

We can now turn attention to a more detailed and descriptive review of the core dynamics that are currently driving Airbus with its sub-assembly system, and Boeing which in 2000, replaced its reliance on batch processing with one of the industrial world's most famous innovative methodologies, namely the classic Toyota Production System (TPS). In doing so Boeing radically changed its inventory control system, to include the now universal Just-in-Time (JIT) arrangement which has become a core supply-chain practice across most of the global industries.

The introduction of JIT and the effective centralization of the procurement system, saw between 2000 and 2005, the number of direct suppliers servicing the production system reduced from 3,600 to 1,200. In the current example of the B787, Boeing deals very directly with some seven or eight first-tier suppliers, which allows them to maintain closer collaboration and a strong control over design and assembly, as supply-chain and technology costs tend to rise over the production cycle.

The Emergence of System Integration as an Effective Production System

As the world's leading manufacturers both Airbus and Boeing have become primary system integrators. This means in effect that design and development activities are now pushed down the supply chain, where first tier sub-system integrators are located across the entire complex of capital investment, research and development and on through sub-assembly into final assembly (see Table 10.2). It is important to be aware that under this type of system contributing firms are not sub-contractors in the traditional sense but rather actual investors and risk-sharing partners. They also tend to be major global firms, giants in their own right, all of whom have engaged in serious programmes of merger and acquisition in order to strengthen their roles as global key players, able to meet the needs of both Airbus and Boeing when required and if necessary at the same time.

It is important to be aware that the supply-chain system adopted by Airbus and Boeing is in fact driven by an extensive external network of independent companies, each with their own subsidiaries and all with numerous cross-border locations (see Table 10.3). They are also by definition investors in key areas such as research and development, which means that they have a significant return on a successful project from intellectual capital rights. It is further estimated that between 60 per cent and 80 per cent of the end product value of aerospace products is now produced by the external supply-chain system.

Table 10.2   System Integration in the Global Aerospace Industry

Operational Level	Identity Roles and Functions
Primary Integrators Located at the Cusp of Vertically Integrated Supply Chains Focus on planning and supply-chain coordination rather than production.	Airbus and Boeing owners of Key Brands and Market Supply Leaders
First-tier Subsystem Integrators	Sub-Assembly Management brought in as Investors and External Independent Partners running External Supply networks
Second-tier Suppliers	Specialist Component Firms owned or merged with the Sub-assembly Integrators
Independent Specialist Suppliers	Specialist Production Divisions of Global firms, e.g. Tyres and Windows
Small component manufacturers	Dominant industries in their fields located in developed countries

Adapted from: Nolan, et al (2007).

Table 10.3   Sub-System Suppliers by Product and Company

Companies	Product	Comment and notes
GE/Rolls-Royce/Pratt & Whitney	Engines	Pratt & Whitney is owned by United Technologies
Vought/BEA/Fuji/Mitsubishi Kawasaki/Finnemeccania	Main aircraft structures	Vought is the major B747 supplier
Honeywell/Goodrich/Rockwell Collins/Smith Industries	Avionics	All conjoint suppliers for the A380 and the B787
Labinal	Wiring	Snecma subsidiary 80 per cent world key supplier
Meggit	Smoke and Fire Detectors	Market Leaders
BEA/Recaro	Seating	Market Leaders
Messier Bugati/Messier Dowty	Landing Gear Systems	Leaders with Goodrich

Adapted from: Nolan, Zhang and Liu op. cit.

It was noted above that the supply-chain system extends to specialist production divisions of global corporations whose operations cross market boundaries both nationally and internationally. For example, the supply of aircraft tyres may be obtained from Michelin, Goodyear or Bridgestone. In turn aircraft windows can only be obtained from the global glass maker, St Gobain. At a more basic supply level aluminium components can be obtained from Alcoa who are contracted to supply about one million lock bolts for the A380 assembly.

The Processes from Initial System Integration to Final Assembly

It is also important to recognize the fact that central to the development of China's new enterprises is the notion of the lean enterprise. This moves the central focus of corporate attention, assert Dimancescu, *et al.* (1997), away from task-based planning in which the final solution that shapes a project is the sum of all individual tasks involved. In its place we find the concept of process which involves three key objectives, the development of new business, the need to recognize and respond to customer needs, and the introduction of new products that reflect the second objective, namely customer satisfaction.

All of these factors are both present and active in what we now identify as the cascade effect. As the previous discussion has illustrated the decision taken by the world's premier aircraft manufacturers, after the initial process of industry-wide mergers, to adopt a supply-chain model has led to a series of consequential mergers and acquisitions in the sub-assembly production tier across the entire aerospace component and services sub-sectors of the international industry. What is essentially a globally integrative process has created a pattern of leaders and followers, with the United States and the European Union on the leading edge. Given China's avowed intention to adopt a catch-up strategy over the next quarter of a century, the time has arrived to evaluate progress thus far.

External Views on China's Plans for Domestic and International Competitive Large Jet Production

The institutional history of China's ventures into aircraft production has been the subject of comments and discussion in the previous chapter. Responses to the current plan to move progressively into the big jet market both domestically and internationally have produced comments ranging from the positive through the sceptical to the negative. There can be no doubt that the sheer size of China's domestic market is able to give any growth plans a positive spin in the minds of both potential suppliers and customers. On the other hand a trenchant critic (Aboulafia, 2006) has suggested that the contracting-in by global producers is equal to approximately one-fifth of 1 per cent of the current total world jetliners value chain.

In turn, it has been suggested that the industry in China currently sits at a strategic nexus with a need to make a significant choice of direction. It is required to decide whether to look exclusively at the production of a domestic jet, using the Japanese system of component first models or, as an alternative, use a more cautious branding policy, that will create some degree of national pride. The strategic purpose of this choice of direction is to avoid the danger of disturbing the current status quo, in what is surely one of the world's most politically sensitive industries.

At this stage of discussion it is also important to introduce what can best be described as an innate state of confusion in the domestic processes for aircraft purchase in China. Despite the fact that the bureaucracy retains nominal central authority through CASG over fleet acquisitions (a practice shared with the military) by the key state-owned airlines, the principal carriers, as we have seen in earlier discussions, have repeatedly refused to buy either purely domestic products, or joint-venture outputs, notably the MD90.

It is also notable that the when Boeing acquired McDonnell Douglas, it stopped the MD90 programme, which if it had been supported in China, would have allowed the domestic industry a degree of positive shift up the aviation value chain. Airbus was to share this experience with their AE-100 joint-venture issue, which commenced in the early 1990s. In this case CAAC simply refused to assist the project on the grounds, according to some executives, that AVIC was incapable of building the aircraft. The end result saw the AE-100 fail for lack of orders, which then led Air China to buy the alternative A318.

The reasons for rejection have been subject to a range of possible explanations, of which the following would appear to be the most logical. It must be borne in mind that given the endemic liquidity problems that constantly confront airline operators, the existence of credit, leasing and buy-back services are considered to be an essential requirement for fleet maintenance. Their existence may be endorsed institutionally, by both manufacturers and host governments.

One must bear in mind that during the period covering the events described above, China's emergent domestic credit market could not cope with the need for massive, credit lines and easy payment plans. As a result Chinese banks which faced mountains of bad debt as the SRO closed down always required payments up front. By contrast the international aircraft leasing consortia were able to access, through various tax loopholes, the means whereby various forms of price depreciation could operate across borders. From a Chinese airlines perspective, this simply made the local model more expensive, when compared with their international rivals.

Contemporary Developments in China's Aerospace Manufacturing Industry – Market Protection versus Excessive Growth

There have been a series of important changes put in place by central government in China in more recent times. For example in January 2008, CAAC reported a 16 per cent increase (185 million passengers) in traffic during 2007. The agency also projected a further 14 per cent (210 million passengers) increase during 2008. The then head of CAAC, Li Jiaxiang, then announced that government intended to curb industry growth in the interests of air safety. According to Li the operational structure was imbalanced with rising safety risks and low economic returns.

The new measures required that those airlines reporting a serious shortage of pilots were not to be allowed to import new aircraft or open new routes. In addition a ban would be placed on applications to launch new airlines until 2010. As a further restraint future applications would see key factors such as investors, aircraft ownership and pilot qualifications brought under much greater official scrutiny. Existing domestic airlines were also to be encouraged to open up new international routes with a view to expanding their overseas market shares. The latter requirement is interesting, given the fact that the CAAC chief was widely known to be supportive of the idea that foreign airlines entering the domestic market, under China's growing number of bilateral agreements, should be prevented from gaining greater access to Chinese airspace.

At this juncture it is important to remember from discussion in earlier chapters that any plans or strategies for the continued expansion of civil aviation in China has to contend with the fact that the PLAAF continues to exercise significant control over available airspace. This means that the growing demand for aircraft as a function of an expanding passenger market is constantly being offset by serious limitations on the freedom to fly certain routes. This is an issue that will be addressed in more detail in the succeeding chapter.

Ownership Consolidation

In 2006 the X'ian Aircraft Corporation completed a deal whereby the production facilities for the building of the ARJ21 were to be purchased from AVIC I. The basis of the purchase involved an exchange of publicly trades stocks. This assured that production would be located in what is probably China's most technologically advanced aerospace manufacturing site. The fact that the locus of the deal was the international stock market, may also materially improve management transparency and accountability.

The Emergence of a Credit and Leasing Infrastructure for Aircraft

According to the Commercial Aircraft Corporation of China (COMAC) the order book for the ARJ21 stands at 206 on 6 November 2008. On the same day GE Commercial Aviation Services (GECAS) placed a firm order for five aircraft, with an option for a further 20. The event is a symbolic one for two reasons: GECAS's parent company GE, will supply the CF34 engine that will power the new 60–90-seat jet and the GECAS order, in turn, is the first from a global firm that is also very active in the aircraft leasing markets.

The emergence of an operational aircraft leasing infrastructure in China has been signalled by the activities of the Industrial and Commercial Bank of China (ICBC), the largest member of the country's major banking group. They are already working with the three major airlines and have completed contractual arrangements with China Eastern as well as with Shenzhen Airlines. The bank's financial leasing arm has assets with a value of RMB5 billion and the specialist firm set up in 2007 has a registered capital value of RMB2 billion. ICBC is joined in the market by the Bank of China (BOC), who has completed the takeover of a major Asian leasing company, the Singapore Asian Leasing Enterprise (SALE), which already has a fleet of over 60 aircraft available for rent.

What is remarkable about the opening up of leasing programmes by the major Chinese banks is the fact that they were technically bankrupt in the early years of the current decade and have only recently been able to return to relative liquidity. The primary cause of their problems can be found in the large mountains of bad debt that were constantly being uncovered with the opening up of the books that followed the government's decision to reform the SREs.

The potential for the Chinese banks to grow in the leasing market must also take into consideration the fact that the bulk of domestic bank activities involve straight cash transactions. These again have further serious limitations in cross-border business since the Chinese RMB is not free to float internationally. It has in fact been pegged against the US$, though from market experience since 2004 it is clear that the RMB has been tending to move upward toward its true market value. As a final comment the recent entry into the domestic market of the Hong Kong–Shanghai Banking Corporation, CitiBank, Standard and Chartered and the Bank of East Asia, may assist the existing indigenous institutions to move more quickly up their respective learning curves as they seek to expand their services in response to increasing market competition.

It appears that the leasing industry has been implicitly present in China for 20 years but is only now beginning to take off. As an important indicator of change, the government revised the rules relating to the leasing industry in 2007. These now require that firms wishing to enter the market have a minimum capital holding of RMB100 million. They must also be able to formally list major shareholders from recognizably qualified financial players as the source of their equity base

All of these developments signal a series of relatively progressive moves toward a more coherent management infrastructure for China's aerospace industry.

Unfortunately political rhetoric and the public endorsement of relatively short run-time tables for targeted outcomes would seem to be more indicative of national pride than serious progress. This is particularly so when measured against the harsh realities of strategic integration as practised in the hard competitive world of global aerospace.

Towards Merger and Consolidation: The Emergence of the China Aviation Industry Corporation

The year 2008 has seen a very significant return to organizational consolidation in China, commencing with the decision to create no less than five new super ministries within the central government. As earlier commentary has indicated, the CAAC has been incorporated into a new Ministry of Transport, and re-organized as a Civil Aviation Bureau. Now after several delays during 2008 the decision to merge AVIC I and AVIC II back into a single entity has been finally promulgated.

Critics, both international and local, would suggest that the decision has come not a moment too soon, given the fact that the previous decision to create AVIC I and AVIC II, produced a range of industrial plants, 80 per cent of which were principally engaged in non-aviation production as a means of creating revenue. Further comparison with the highly regarded shipbuilding industry, led one anonymous commentator to describe both the AVICs as a ministry masquerading as a corporation, and headed by politically connected bureaucrats with no business management experience.

The newly merged AVICs will retain the title of China Aviation Industry Corporation (AVIC) and the headquarters administration will comprise some 14 departments. The initial game plan calls for the introduction of a parent subsidiary relationship between the corporation and the six companies that constitute the total organization. It is further anticipated that the subsidiary firms will be spun off as independents at the point where their market performance and productivity makes such a move a logical one (see Table 10.4).

The new corporation will be market listed after the subsidiary amalgamations have been completed. From a strategic perspective current management has adopted a five-point programme that will be carried out in the following sequence. Market orientated reforms, professional integration, capital development, industrial development and international market development. After the formal launch of the new AVIC, it is intended to list each of the subsidiaries in turn on the stock exchange. The human resources plan also calls for recruitment up to the status of vice president in the various branch companies to be open to candidates from both China and overseas. The mission statement for the new venture has also targeted sales to the value of RMB1 trillion and a placing in the global *Fortune 500* by the year 2017. This projection in keeping with the growing decline in market demand will clearly need further adjustment in the future.

Table 10.4   The Organizational Structure of the New AVIC Corporation

New Company	Roles and Functions	Asset Bases
Commercial Aircraft Corp of China (COMAC)	Re-branding of CACC, with additional across-industry services functions	Shanghai
Transport Aircraft Corp.	Independent supplier of large international jets will compete against Airbus and Boeing	All non-defence assets and production centres in Xi'an, Chengdu and Shenyang.
Defence Division	Management of all military-related assets and production centres	All military-related assets in Chengdu, Shenyang, Xi'an and Hongdu
AVIcopter Corp.	Management of helicopter production	Production units in Harbin, Changhe, Jingdezhen
Aviation Engine Industry Corp.	Coordinates engine production and research	Liming, Xi'an, Chengdu, Zhuzhou China Gas Turbine – Jiangyou and Sichuan.
General Aviation Company	Management of medium-sized aircraft production	Production units in Guizhou and Shijiazhuang
Aviation Systems Company	Management of research and prototype units	Locations in Shanghai, Xi'an, Nanjing and numerous regional sites

Adapted from: China Economic Review.com.cn.

Government officials are at considerable pains to advise the international industry that the current consolidation programme is in fact the introductory phase of the new development. It also appears in the wake of some statements made at the International Aviation and Aerospace Forum in Zhuhai, during the first week of November 2008, that AVIC has plans to acquire a foreign-based general aircraft manufacturer, and act clearly intended to strengthen the existing demand for high levels of professional skill and experience in modern aviation technologies.

How far the plan to rationalize the aerospace industry implicit in current events will bring about positive results remains uncertain. On the other hand the relative haste and the sheer dimensions of the proposed changes indicate that the window of opportunity that will lead on to international success in aerospace manufacturing may not be open to China for very much longer. Such pessimism finds its source in the view of government expressed in the *People's Daily* that the new corporation might well close if China is not ready to roll out its big jet prototype (150 seats) on schedule and by 2020.

The newspaper also noted that in the matter of priorities, the need to first develop the requisite high level management skills might have to take precedence over the acquisition of advanced technology. The implications of this human resource imperative will be one of the topics discussed in some depth in the final chapter. The time has now come however to turn attention to another important dimension of China's progress in civil aviation. In the next chapter a brief review will be made of China's growing role in the emergent geopolitics of international aviation, as well as its interactive relationships with the United States and the European Union. The discussion of these themes will be balanced against the important geopolitical developments that are shaping China's relationship with the ASEAN group of Southeast Asian countries especially in the important area of China's possible role in what is scheduled to emerge as an FTA free aviation market incorporating a membership of those states which constitute the important ASEAN group of countries.

Chapter 11

ASEAN, Open Skies, and the Search for New Market Opportunities

The emergence of China as an important new member of the international aviation community has been somewhat fortuitous, given the fact that the industry has been undergoing many substantive changes economically, technically and geopolitically, as it strives to catch up with the Western countries. With this in mind, the time has come to address in a somewhat speculative fashion a number of issues which are still really now in the process of evolutionary development. Some of the events surrounding the dramatic emergence during the current decade of China as an important new and growing power in international aviation have already been addressed in previous chapters and need no further rehearsal here.

There are however very important implications still to be considered for both China and the evolving global aviation industry. This is because the core dynamics that are shaping international economic progress are still ultimately shaped by the international growth of business and trade relationships. It is these agendas that continue to influence the various bilateral agreements that the PRC has already signed with numerous countries across the globe.

In the strategic domain the ongoing development of open skies agreements with the United States and the European Union are currently the most significant of these numerous initiatives given the fact, that these parties occupy key roles in the international aviation industry. They are also being currently recognized for their innovative leadership in the attempts being made to plan the development of a more liberalized and open world aviation market. With regard to the international development of ASAs, it is clear that China is really no stranger to the world of bilateral arrangements. The CAAC is on record, as earlier comments have indicated, as reporting that by the end of 2006 the PRC government had signed off on some 106 ASAs with a group of countries that included Afghanistan, Algeria and Burma amongst the various signatory partners.

In addition the PRC is actively involved with the ASEAN countries of Southeast Asia, in what has been a significantly long-term search for a bilateral free trade agreement. The membership of what is already an existing free trade agreement (FTA) incorporates a number of strategically important states which range in their roles and scope from viable and rapidly developing modern economies to smaller political entities that are currently severely limited in their contribution to the aviation developmental scope.

This relative imbalance as discussion will reveal has particular relevance with regard to the ASEAN plan for a regional aviation arrangement somewhat akin to a free-market model. Further support for this assumption emerges from the fact that the parties appear to be visualizing a final outcome that will operate on the same basis as the European open skies system. These matters will become the primary focus of further discussion below. The consideration of these issues will then move on in turn to a somewhat larger context involving some further key external relationships currently under ongoing negotiation by the current PRC administration.

China's Primary Motivation for Change Revisited: The Need for Compliance with WTO Legal and Regulative Conditions

Progressive discussions with regard to the emergence of China as an important force in international civil aviation must first take as an essential item on its agenda an important geopolitical factor. Ever since the country's formal entry in 2001, as we have already discussed previously, China's government has been progressively seeking to satisfy some externally imposed and measurable forms of compliance with the legal requirements, regulations and rules that are a condition of full membership of the World Trade Organization (WTO). The event itself has had an important consequence for international business strategy. This is because China's election as a full member has resulted in a significant expansion of interest in bilateral aviation relationships by many of the Western developed countries who are now buoyed up by the possibilities for potential entry into China's domestic passenger and cargo markets.

Such interests grew at an accelerating rate as China's leadership followed through the decade the required schedule of reforms necessary for formal access as, for example, the liberalization of the limitations relating to the investment of foreign capital. As a direct result of what are now perceived to be consistently growing opportunities, civil aviation is but one of a wide range of industries which have moved into China. All of them now tend to be grouped within their various functional sets and subsets according to their perceived strategic importance. In the case of civil aviation international commercial interest also tends to be found within the area of multifunctional sectors, including manufacturing and MRO, as well as airline and requisite airport development.

The principal geopolitical driver underpinning these activities from a Chinese perspective is really one of the possible domestic gains to be made from potential Western involvement in what is rapidly becoming one of the world's largest economies. It involves at the bottom line and in practical terms an assessment of the relative value of various bilateral agreements with regard to their potential contribution to the CCP's own specific economic growth plans. These in turn include aerospace as well as aircraft manufacturing within future growth targets. The following example demonstrates the correlation between an ongoing macro-development programme and some further and specific developmental aspects relating to civil aviation.

The United States Strategic Economic Dialogue with the PRC

The United States has been conducting for a number of years a strategic economic dialogue (SED) with China at executive level which has allowed the parties to keep a watching brief on overall developments particularly with regard to aviation agreements. At the fourth meeting which concluded on 19 June 2008 the two governments signed a joint declaration to establish a Transportation Forum which is intended to assist China in the develop of its multi-modal strategies. The core purpose on the American side was to permit US firms who wished to help design, construct and equip China's transportation system in all its modes to enter China in order to attain these objectives. It also contained a condition that the final outcome would be to guarantee a future free flow of trade between the United States and the PRC. Quite clearly such an initiative has very important implications for civil aviation. It is with this possibility in mind that discussion can now begin to focus on the range, scope and current status of China's increasing number of aviation bilateral agreements.

The Distinctions between Traditional Bilateral and Open Skies Aviation Agreements

It will be timely at this juncture to establish the working distinction between the traditional forms of bilateral agreements (ASAs) and the emergence of open skies agreements as exemplified in the European single-market legislation which came into force in 1997 (see Figure 11.1). The benchmark agreement dates from 1946, when the United States and the United Kingdom set an administrative arrangement in motion which has led to nearly 4,000 agreements being lodged with the ICAO by 2005.

What later became the normative convention, as we have previously seen, allowed for city-pair arrangements to become subject to a set of restricted flight frequencies between two sovereign states. In more recent times what can best be described as a consistent pressure for more liberal market-orientated arrangements and increased competition, appears to be supported by the growing awareness that civil aviation is now a major contributor to future international economic growth. It has also emerged from the increasing trend toward the privatization of ownership of airlines and airports

It is worth noting here that while reform perceived as a formal relaxation of operational controls over the number of airlines permitted to fly specific cross-border routes has received strong support from some of the major players, the operational reality, suggests Rigas Doganis (2006), still reveals the continued growth of conventional ASAs, limited to the traditional form of a dual relationship. As a result they tend to monopolize the attention of the international regulative regime despite the manifest increase in moves by bodies such as IATA to promote greater liberalization.

Type of Agreement	Services Capacity	Service Frequency	Fares	Extended Traffic Rights
Traditional	Restrictions on operator numbers	Limits on number of markets serviced	Price restrictions	Restrictions on additional countries to be serviced
Open Skies	No limits on number of operators or number of markets	Zero restrictions	Zero restrictions	Open rights to include additional countries

Figure 11.1   Key Differences between Traditional Bilateral Agreements and Open Skies Agreements

Adapted from: US GAO-04-835, *Report on Transatlantic Aviation*, July 2004, p.11.

It should also be remembered that such agreements often have a much larger context, as already observed above, when they are located within the comprehensive trade agreements that exist either bilaterally between national governments, or in larger combinations involving multi-country and regional arrangements such as the ASEAN FTA. This latter format is clearly demonstrated in the case of China's relationships with the two major powers, the European Union and the United States. The EU as China's designated leading trade partner has developed a systematic relationship with Beijing within which a developing open skies agreement is really embedded.

The same series of developments have occurred within the China–US relationships. It must also be borne in mind that there is a second dimension to these geopolitical arrangements in that the EU and the United States are also engaged in intense negotiations leading to what the European partner has designated as progress towards a Common Aviation Area. This interaction forms part of a much larger game plan in which China is expected in the future to play an inevitable role. The larger context of these developments now requires some formal explanation with regard to the long-term objectives of the EU in its formulation of an integrated aviation policy that would cover all its member states.

The European Union's Single Aviation Market: Its Origins and Subsequent Development

The final stages of the development of a single aviation market in Europe saw final legal ratification take place in 1997. An important consequence from the point of view of the member states was a primary change in the status of national airlines to that of Community carriers. The consequent reaction from some member states was largely negative on fundamental grounds that questioned the competence of

Commission to act as the virtual agent for all of the national airline systems within the Union.

Prior to the passing of the Single Market Act, a number of traditional ASAs were signed between the United States and some seven leading members of what was then the European Community including Germany and the United Kingdom. As a consequence, the European Commission, as noted by Williams (2006), brought an action against the signatory states before the European Court of Justice (ECJ) in December 1998 on the grounds that such agreements infringed the internal competence of the Community as well as the terms of the EC Treaty.

After due consideration the Court ruled that while the status of bilateral agreements were outside its immediate jurisdiction, the nationality clauses in the agreements under review were contrary to the EC's rules on the right of establishment and as a consequence their existence discriminated against the carriers of other member states in each of the states which had signed the agreements with the United States. As a consequence the ECJ ruled that all existing bilateral agreements between member states and China were not sustainable in their current form and, therefore, they should be subject to significant amendments.

From a strategic point of view, the agreement allowed the European Commission in 2005, to consider and plan what is popularly called a roadmap for a future EU international open skies policy. The result led on to the formal emergence of a strategy based on three main developmental programmes.

---

1. The redrafting of ASAs as Horizontal Agreements on an EU external country basis.
2. The development of a Common Aviation Area comprising the EU in partnership with states located along its southern and eastern borders.
3. Subsequent international partnerships with the United States, Canada, China, Australia and New Zealand.

Figure 11.2   The European Three-pillar Model of Open Skies Agreements

Adapted from: European Union Commission Proposal (2007) 79.

The introduction of what are in effect horizontal agreements required that all ASAs between member states of the European Union and a given third country should be brought into formal compliance with EU law. In June 2003, the European Commission under a mandate from the EU Council began to renegotiate the existing ASAs, while the national governments of the various third-party signatories carried out the same task under agreement.

The advantage that stemmed from the adoption of the horizontal approach lies in the fact that the modification of one agreement can have a template effect on up to 27 other ASAs at the same time. By September 2007, this methodology had been applied successfully to a wide range of countries, while the same period saw more than 500 agreements brought into conformance with EU law and covering nearly a hundred partners. In the Chinese case some 22 ASAs would have required revision within that time period. These agreements covered passenger flights and cargo and had emerged from an important conjoint project with the EU that had commenced in 1999 and covering flight safety standards, production management, customer services and ATC.

The Search for an Open EU–China Aviation Agreement

Developmental linkages between the EU and China with regard to the potential emergence of material assistance in developing China's civil aviation industry have formed a normative part of trade development between Europe and China since 1990 and some important examples have been discussed in earlier chapters. In more recent times an Aviation Summit took place in Beijing in 2005, aimed at the discussion of possible further opportunities for collaboration. This seemed to offer a window of opportunity for the exploration of future aviation agreements. As to the strategic intentions of the European Commission, these are perhaps best exemplified in the opening speech of Jacques Barrot (Vice President of the EC) to the assembled delegates.

The future strategic directions proposed by the EU were to be found in the concluding stage of his speech when he said an EU–China aviation agreement would not be focussed exclusively on the terms and conditions of a free-market entry arrangement. In fact it would consider a broad range of issues of mutual interest including safety, security, environmental matters and the application of competition law. Further, it would also take account of the specific characteristics of the EU and Chinese markets respectively and would be guided by the joint commitment to facilitate operations for both airline systems for the benefits of the public at large. It is clear from the balance of the address, that technological and industrial cooperation would loom very large in the course of any further negotiations.

These views found official endorsement in the joint declaration of the parties at the conclusion of the summit. Further action that was listed for future agendas involved a range of economic, social and technical matters with specific attention drawn to security, air traffic management, infrastructural plans, investment opportunities and a wide range of further priorities. As the evidence demonstrates, the further progress of China–EU negotiations on civil aviation remains embedded in the larger context of geopolitical as well as trade discussions. These in turn range across layers of multifunctional purposes and intentions, which feed back into a multiplicity of consultations and exchanges, and will continue to do so over time.

The Current Status of the China–United States Liberalization Agreement

We can date the current developments in the China–US process of joint collaboration back to the establishment of the currently operational US–China Aviation Cooperation Programme (ACP). In 2004 a partnership arrangement was launched between the United States Trade and Development Agency (USTDA), the FAA and the CAAC. The programme identified very strong demands for US aviation products that emerged from the developmental funding that actually set up the ACP. As a working example, the proposed new regional jet the ARJ21, when it reaches the prototype stage, will be outfitted with US-made avionics and control systems.

The programme was expanded in 2007, with the decision to introduce human resource development through training systems that will include executive management education as well as courses that cover airworthiness maintainability analysis and certification training. There are also plans to assist in the development of an air traffic flow management system that will allow for a growth in regional services as well as in a general aviation market, in which a growing demand for private ownership will then be able to expand and develop. The USTDA has allocated close to $1.69 million as funding for this programme, which will be matched in the sum of $2.3 million by the various commercial member companies and organizations associated with the project.

The Initial US–China Aviation Liberalization Agreement

Beginning in 2006, negotiations began between the US and China with regard to proposed modifications in their existing ASA that would allow air services between the two countries to undergo a considerable expansion programme. The final terms of the agreement called for a phased process of implementation to take place in the period 2008–12. Under due process, the activities set out in Figure 11.3 would commence within the specified time period.

In the event each of the six major carriers – Delta, American, Continental, Northwest, United and US Airways – were awarded a route, with the services expected to begin on a staggered schedule through 2009 for five of the carriers. The exception, Delta, which was the only large carrier left without a route to China, was permitted to commence a Boeing 777 service from Atlanta to Shanghai on 30 March 2008.

The relative speed with which the new agreement will be fully functional is now open to question given the current crisis that has confronted the global economy in the second half of 2008 and on into 2009. China Eastern has grounded 20 aircraft as its persistent cost problems are made worse by the relative decline in demand for air services that is now hitting Asia. This is further reflected by the fact that while Chinese airlines carried some 141.4 million passengers up and through September 2008, the year on year increase over 2007, which was expected to reach 14 per cent, was in fact 1.7 per cent. From a global perspective, the speed

- Daily passenger flights to the gateway hubs of Beijing, Shanghai and Guangzhou, are to increase by two, thereby doubling US carrier entry.
- All limitations are to be removed on US cargo flights to any point in China. In addition an unlimited number of US carriers will be allowed to come into the domestic market after 2011.
- There will be an increase in the number of US carriers currently allowed to service the Chinese market from three to six by 2011.
- Opportunities for US carriers to code share on each other's Chinese schedules will be expanded.
- There is a formal commitment for both China and the United States to launch open skies negotiations in 2010.

Figure 11.3   The   Proposed   Liberalization   Agreement   Implementation   Process

Adapted from: United States Department of State, 23 May 2008, 2007/414.

of decline is reflected in the IATA projections for the second half of 2008. This has seen a possible profit increase in April of $4.56 billion turn into a projected $6.1 billion loss in November.

With uncertainties deepening, further speculation has little value until the degree, extent and the expected timeframe of the current global financial crisis is statistically made more certain. Attention as a consequence will now be turned to another dimension of China's international aviation strategy, namely its growing relationship in matters relating to aviation with the ASEAN states.

The ASEAN–China Free Trade Area Progress and Prospects

The Association of Southeast Asian Nations (ASEAN) was established on 8 August 1967 by Indonesia, Malaysia, the Philippines, Singapore and Thailand. It emerged under the influence of changing diplomatic and geopolitical priorities from the region's historical past when there were earlier joint defence arrangements previously in operation and duly managed under the Southeast Asia Treaty Organization (SEATO). It was then joined by Brunei in 1884, Vietnam in 1995, Laos and Myanmar (Burma) in 1997, and Cambodia in 1999. What might be termed the second wave of membership is reflective of the major shifts that occurred in the ideological and geopolitical directions taken by Vietnam, Laos and Cambodia in the 1990s.

In November 2001, China's aviation industry links with the ASEAN group, which were already set to some extent over time by geographical proximity, culture and trade, became formalized with the joint agreement to establish an ASEAN–China Free Trade Agreement by 2011. The programmes called for six major agendas to be covered in sequence, with implementation dependent on final decisions taken during the set time period (Figure 11.4).

The progress of the FTA included a decision to advance discussion, in parallel, toward an ASA between China and ASEAN. This in turn emerged from a memorandum of understanding (MoU) that was signed between the ASEAN governments and the PRC on Transport Cooperation in 2004. Before examining the terms and condition of this projected ASA, it is necessary to consider in some detail the important decision taken by ASEAN in the same year. This called for the ten ASEAN countries to adopt after a very long period of consideration a road map for the integration of air travel. The decision to do so fits within the longer-term plan of the ASEAN countries to fully liberalize its air services sector and create a single aviation market by 2015.

On 11 November 2008, formal agreements were signed in the Philippines capital to remove all restrictions on air and freight services and to allow regional airlines access to any capital city of a member country by 2010, on the basis of an extension of fifth freedom rights. In the interim, freight service liberalization was scheduled to commence early in 2009, when passenger services will obtain third- or fourth-freedom rights as a stepwise progressive measure. The final step leading to full liberalization will require the design of multi-lateral agreements which will be required in turn to follow eight implementation protocols.

There is however some scepticism abroad in the region that the formal launch of a total open skies system by 2015 will in the event simply not happen. Critics suggest that while the leading-edge economies will be supportive the balance of members will hide behind domestic protection and the tendency for various initiatives on free trade arrangements to become subject to high levels of impotence in the matter of their formal application within certain states. This possibility is further compounded by the constitutional inability of the ASEAN Council under its current mandate to invoke disciplinary procedures including, as in the EU case, the ability to demand compliance by a member state.

- Trade and Investment Facilitation Measures
- Provision of Technical Assistance and Capacity Building for Vietnam, Laos and Cambodia
- Promotion Measures consistent with WTO rules to be given to non-WTO member states of ASEAN
- FTA to be in place by 2011, with special and differential treatment given to new member states.
- Institutional agencies to be developed in order to manage the cooperation process.

Figure 11.4   ASEAN–China FTA Major Cooperation Development Agenda Requirements

Adapted from: Chirathivat (2002), pp. 677–8.

A problem also arises because some countries are still using protectionism as a protective tool. A noted example involves Indonesia's refusal to allow Singapore-based LCCs such as Tiger Airlines to fly into its four main cities, including Jakarta, as a form of protection for its national carrier Garuda. From a macro-economic perspective it must also be borne in mind that there are very large disparities in the general level of social and economic development between member states which has negative consequences for their air travel capacities. The question as to how these states – for example, Myanmar, Laos and Cambodia – will fare when facing competition from other regional carriers also serves to put a systematic timetable for implementation of the open skies strategy in doubt. It is against this background that the ASEAN–China Cooperation agreement can now be evaluated.

The ASEAN–China Aviation Cooperation Project

The plan for mutual cooperation is brought sharply into focus in the introduction to the proposal, which identifies its basic purpose. The primary aim is to allow the project to act as a supporting arrangement for the larger FTA. The further aim is to strengthen industrial cooperation in two major fields.

Air Services Arrangements

The proposal calls for the expansion of air service arrangements and connectivity either on a bilateral, regional or sub-regional basis and with the purpose of facilitating air traffic in both the passenger and cargo sectors with a view to increasing both trade and economic growth for the signatory partners. Negotiations were to commence with a view to a successful implementation by 2010, with implementation to run in parallel with the larger FTA.

With regard to the substantive elements of the ASA, it would include the requirements set out in Figure 11.5. At the same time provisions for the gradual liberalization of cargo as well as passenger services would be included but would not be limited to such subsequent arrangements.

Some Potential Policy Problems Facing the ASEAN–China ASA

The problems with full implementation of the agreement facing the ASEAN single aviation market proposal are also to be found in the ASEAN–China ASA. For example relative smallness of population does not deter member states such as Singapore or Brunei, each with high per capita incomes from overcoming the limitation of population size. This problem is clearly not an issue either with those countries such as Indonesia, the Philippines, Vietnam and Malaysia which are largely middle-income states. But for the balance of the ASEAN membership, the domestic aviation market is largely underdeveloped, with low traffic densities, service frequencies and small relatively high cost aircraft.

The Operational Rules to be Activated by the Terms of Agreement

Removal of restrictions as to the number of points in a route schedule.
No limitations on third and fourth freedom traffic rights between ASEAN states and China.
No limitations on fifth freedom traffic rights between ASEAN and China.
No limitations on frequency and capacity as well as type of aircraft.
Charter operations to be an element in services.
Multiple airline designations to be allowed.

The Specification of Cooperation in Other Aviation Fields

Airline Cooperation

Should include utilization of resources and business management services, including interlining, block-space arrangements and code sharing.

Airport Construction

To include infrastructural activities, design, construction, investment and financing.

Aviation Safety and Flight Standards

The parties should include information sharing, and mutual assistance in the use of investigation facilities and equipment. Cooperation should also be established with regard to recognition and certification of agencies including MRO and the flight operational standards.

Information Exchanges

This should cover all aspects of information on air transport infrastructure as well as industry development with a view to further facilitating the efficiency of ASA-designated air transport services.

The ASA Working Mechanism

Implementation should be driven by mechanisms at the working group level with negotiations and formulation as the first priority. Upon conclusion of all ASA requirements, the group shall continue work in other aviation fields. Technical assistance services for the group shall be rendered by the ASEAN Secretariat.

Figure 11.5   The Substantive Terms of the ASEAN–China FTA

Adapted from: ASEAN China Air Cooperation Framework aseansec.org.

A further imbalance can be found in a comparison of the various air fleets of the ASEAN group of member states. At one extreme Singapore Air ranks at number 20 in the world in terms of size and the scope of its operational services, while Malaysia and Thailand can also claim significant fleet size and network capabilities. By contrast Laos and Cambodia for example, tend to have seriously underdeveloped aviation policies, limited fleet size and subsequent route growth potential, marketing problems, little contact with alliances, or ASAs, and a major shortage of skilled personnel.

There is no gainsaying the fact that the positive economic potential to be obtained from the development of a viable open skies policy in ASEAN is quite considerable. It is also evident that the process of setting timeframes and due dates may end up being counter-productive. What appears to be called for as an alternative is a planned sequence of stages in which a clearly defined learning curve is to be followed at the operational level by the individual states. It is evident, given the ambiguities to be found in member state attitudes toward a single aviation market, that the potential for projects to meet their target dates is extremely low for all of the reasons cited above. There can be no doubt that the PRC government is aware of this, for further reasons that are really outside this chapter's brief.

Some Possible and Future Market Benefits for China

On the other hand and from that same Chinese perspective that is actively linked to China's identity as a recognized international player, the ASEAN cooperation agreement over time, could well deliver supplementary benefits in term of customers for such projects as the ARJ21. Given the fact that the new big jet project has clear potential for sale in developing aviation markets, China would have some comparative advantages, not least as a key supplier enjoying both geographical proximity to, and political membership within, the ASEAN aviation environment.

This would be further reinforced both by the growing momentum of final aircraft assembly being located both in China and by the short supply-chain potential offered by key ASEAN states such as Singapore. How far the PRC is willing to give its current negotiations a new and further geopolitical spin with these possibilities in mind, is no doubt on a number of agency agendas in Beijing.

It is now time to extend the current perspective on China's growing international experience in civil aviation to encompass a further and significant growing geopolitical debate. This is being largely shaped by what is being perceived in the world of international politics as a movement away from the unilateralist model of inter-state relationships based on the United States as the world's sole super power that has been associated particularly with the period in office of the second Bush Administration.

One side effect has been an emerging debate on multi-polarity running parallel to the countervailing possibilities of a return to a multi-lateral political environment. This has increasingly been taken up by those leading-edge developing economies whose sheer size and scale is now being equated with geopolitical as well as economic potential.

The Emergence of the BRIC Group of Countries

The language of political scientists and the media at large has recently included the term BRIC, which translates into Brazil, Russia, India and China. All four of these nation states are now identified, given their size and natural endowments, as leading-edge economies. In the context of international aviation Brazil, Russia and India share common links with China as the following examples will confirm.

We begin with a short case review of the decision of Embraer the leading Brazilian aircraft manufacturer to move to its first production location outside its home base in Sao Paulo. As a consequence a joint venture was developed, the results of which will be the subject of discussion below. Attention will then be given to the growing relationship between China and India in civil aviation matters, as it is reflected in the growth of their ASAs. Finally China's complex relationship with Russia will be considered, particularly since the beginning of the current decade.

Case Review: Harbin–Embraer Aircraft Industry Company Ltd (HEAI)

An agreement was signed in December 2002, which led to the creation of a joint venture and HEAI emerged as a consequence as the operational outcome. The new venture was planned to produce the ERJ-145, 30–50-seat regional jet. The first ERJ-145 rolled off the assembly line in 2004 with a completed order for six by China Southern; the final aircraft was delivered in February 2005.

The following year China's HNA Group placed an order on behalf of its new cargo venture, Grand Wall Airlines, which began operations in 2007 from its base in Tianjin. The contract called for the production and delivery of 50 ERJ-145s and a further 50 of the 106-seat Embraer 190s. Of these some six of the 190s had been delivered by November 2008, while another ten ERJ-145s has also entered service, one of which marked the 1,000th delivery, counting sales since it went into production of that specific model to a client airline.

The Growing China–India Market for Air Services

The year 2005 was an important time for ASAs between China and India. Under an MoU a dual agreement was introduced in which multiple carriers were permitted entry into their respective markets. The agreement called for each airline to schedule a sequential and weekly flight frequency commencing with 14 in the summer of 2008, rising to 28 in the winter of the same year and then reaching a defined peak of 42 in the summer of 2006. In addition no limitation was imposed on either aircraft type or designated seating. An equivalent arrangement in the matter of aerospace access was also introduced ranging from flight lanes at altitudes of 5,600 m through 11,200 m to a maximum of 16,800 m.

The ASA relationship became somewhat fraught over time with both parties refusing at one stage to finally confirm the formal arrangements. This resulted in delays for airlines wishing to take advantage of the ASA. It is also clear that by 2008 route utilization was severely skewed, with only Air India flying four times a week to its Chinese destination. By comparison, Air China, China Southern and China Eastern completed some 18 flights to India, in the same time period and with an average 90 per cent seat occupancy.

China and Russia: Ambiguity and Complexity in an Aviation Relationship

Any attempts to investigate the degrees of cooperation between the respective aerospace industries of these two countries are rendered extremely difficult at the current time. The reason why, suggests one European commentator (Kogan, 2004) lies in the fact that while Chinese officials do not like to reveal production details, their Russian opposite numbers simply refuse to confirm or deny the existence of relevant information. The problem is further compounded by the fact that there is a common tendency for the primary focus of aerospace cooperation to be usually presented in the media as relating only to military–technical cooperation. This is clearly the consequence of a long and previous history of reliance on Russia for PLAAF aircraft requirements, a relationship which has become subject to notable controversy over recent times with regard to Chinese access in to detailed data, dating from the SU-27SK Fighter Technology Transfer Agreement of 1995.

The consequent production in China of the new J-11B fighters for the PLAAF has been plagued with major managerial problems including a serious controversy over intellectual property rights. From a strategic perspective it would appear that both parties are in the process of a tactical withdrawal, with the available output from the agreement simply being absorbed by the PLAAF as much needed replacements for its ageing fighter squadrons.

In other matters relating to civil aviation a further pressure to disengage from production arrangements with Russia, comes from the fact that Boeing, Airbus and other major parties in the globally integrated aerospace industry are also becoming increasingly available for cooperative ventures, as the potential future demand for aircraft in China's domestic market becomes larger over time.

It is also a matter of record that the Chinese have proven to be apt pupils of Russia in the past, especially with regard to space technology. As the events of 2007 have clearly demonstrated, China is now a power to reckon with in that field, which raises again the growing importance of technological transfer rather than the delivery of finished technological products in cross-border trade as the key agenda item for future cooperative agreements.

The current dilemma from the Russian point of view is reflected in the fact that in September 2007, a private aircraft joint venture was agreed between the Moscow Aviation Institute and Dingxin Technology Company located in China's northwest Jilin province. The business venture has a total investment of RMB800 million ($106 million).and the distribution of equity was to be 60/40 in favour of the Chinese firm. The business plan calls for the production of some 500 two- and four-seat light aircraft and seaplanes each year, all intended for private purchase. There was also the expectation when the question of market risk was raised that total revenue from the project would have been at least equal to total investment.

The real problem lies in the fact that under the existing regulations covering the use of domestic airspace, aircraft used for executive business travel or pleasure are severely restricted in terms of airport locations and scheduled flight planning as well as access to designated route planning. In other words the plan was to produce an aircraft type whose potential is restricted before it enters the market by existing regulations, which thus confined such aircraft to a very limited operational span. From a safety perspective, devoted and current owners of such aircraft are reported to be prone to attempts to enter airspace by going under the radar, the results of which are very hard to uncover in terms of accident rates and other data.

The confusion that has resulted from this venture raises a strong sense of *déjà vu* reinforced by a recent event involving a high level meeting in Moscow. On 29 October 2008, Wen Jiabao and Vladimir Putin met in Moscow for their 13th Prime Ministers Meeting. In their joint communiqué they pledged support for the enhancement of further collaboration and cooperation including further commitments involving the mutual development of the civil aviation industry. How far these commitments will materialize, given the current unstable state of the China–Russia relationship in aviation matters is open to much conjecture.

Discussion has ranged broadly throughout this chapter with regard to the continuing development of China as an acknowledged major player in the world of international aerospace. It has also tried to identify some of the geopolitical as well as economic factors that are shaping not only the operational future of the industry, but its growing role as an instrument for the advancement of national as well as international aspirations. The final chapter will now attempt a speculative consideration as to the issues and problems that will require specific agenda attention, as China continues to seek the operational means to continue both significant operational growth and the reinforcement of its identity as a major power in the international aerospace industry.

Chapter 12
Some Major Issues Shaping the Future for China's Civil Aviation Industry

The various themes addressed in all of the previous chapters have attempted to both identify and demonstrate the range and complexity of the issues that have confronted the civil aviation industry in China in the era of political, economic and social liberalization that commenced in 1978. The balance of discussion in this final chapter will attempt to identify at least some of the substantive issues and problems that still tend to stand in the way of operational efficiency and planned development. It will also seek to evaluate some of the political implications that will follow the proposed change in leadership from the fourth to the fifth generation that is scheduled to be underway by 2012–13.

The chapter will begin with a sequential review of some major strategy problems, such as the inherent difficulties China's civil aviation industry faces given the fact that civilian services must co-exist in an overall system where military priorities have until now tended to shape the effective control of airspace. Discussion will then be expanded to consider the further problems that arise as the CAAC tries to fit a growing national demand for airline services into a current route network that constrains a large proportion of airline operations geographically to a limited area of domestic airspace, bounded by the Beijing, Shanghai and Guangzhou Mega-hubs.

The wider consequences, as well as the limitations of this current situation, will be reviewed from a number of perspectives, including a consideration of the many problems facing the smaller regional facilities, especially those airports which are to be found in the more remote districts of central, southwest and northwest China. Due consideration will then be given to the efforts that China has made with regard to compliance with ICAO regulations, especially in air safety matters.

A further consideration of the government's avowed intention to introduce a modern national ATM system by 2010, which is symbolically the final year of the 11th FYP, will follow logically in the sequence. The subsequent theme will critically examine some of the macro-problems facing China's economy as a consequence of the deepening and global economic crisis that confronts all international industries and especially commercial aviation at the current time. From a regional perspective the impact on the Asia–Pacific region has been most severe, and discussion will focus on the attempts China is currently making to come to terms with the increasingly fragile state of what has been an exponentially expanding economy.

The penultimate theme will address one of the substantive issues facing civil aviation development in China: it will examine the problematics that are inevitably going to arise as China considers ultimately going it alone as a direct competitor, both domestic and international, with the major players in the very important sector of aircraft manufacturing. The book opened with a basic review of the evolutionary reform process that has passed through four generations of government; it will return to this issue at the close, with some short and speculative comments on the possible changes in aviation policy and strategy that the fifth generation of CPC leadership might adopt after it comes into office post-2012.

Balancing Economic Development and the Protection of the National Interest

The protection of the sovereignty of national airspace in most countries conventionally strikes a balance between the degree of freedom enjoyed by all types of civil aviation, and the need to be prepared to take military control of any incursive activities by foreign aircraft, that might ultimately require the deployment of the national air force. These in turn may range from training flights for the simulation of combat air patrols (CAP) to real emergencies where there has been an illegal intrusion of some magnitude. This consistent balance between civilian and military activities tends in turn to influence such matters as the specification of flight plans, so that all parties in a normative situation can literally miss each other in time and space.

By contrast the conditions that govern airspace sovereignty in the PRC, as found in the Civil Aviation Act 1995, presents the terms of a very clear mandate under Article 4. This states that the use of airspace and the demarcation of a control area, control zone, restricted area, dangerous area and prohibited area shall be determined by the Ministry of Transportation and Communications (MORC) in coordination with the Ministry of National Defence.

The political reason for the control of national airspace can be found within the government's stated intention to uphold national security and unity and to ensure the continuing interests of national development. This involves the constant defence against violation of China's territorial sea and airspace as well as its multiple borders, a process that in the latter category and in the historical sense dates back over several thousand years. It is also strongly motivated by the post-1949 tensions and geopolitical conflict that have existed, notably over the political status of Taiwan which China has claimed on the grounds of geographical proximity, as well as previous colonization, to be a part of the mainland.

With regard to the operational context of airspace control, the PLAAF has seven military command areas located across China within which fighter aircraft, ground-to-air missile bases, anti-aircraft and radar facilities all have immediate and constant operational status. Whenever activation is deemed necessary the result often creates serious delays at prime times for many national airline services, since the air force has the further power to give priority to airspace use according to its own operational requirements. Confusion over the motivation for doing so is further advanced by the fact that on the positive side of commercial liberalization, the Central Military Commission (CMC), the controlling body of all arms of the PLA, is required to follow a developmental strategy for aviation under the 11th FYP which involves the opening of low altitude airspace to facilitate a growing market for business and private flying. This follows on the decision taken in 2000 to grant control over 29 routes to commercial aviation management.

An Example of Military Intervention

A working example of the major problems that can be caused by the current system emerges from a report in the *China Daily* dated 15 January 2008. The CAAC in compliance with ICAO requirements had recently implemented changes in the Reduced Vertical Separation Minimum (RSVM) for commercial aircraft. The developments that led to the formal introduction of this new system on 22 November 2007 will be described in more detail in later discussion. For the moment however the operational consequence of this decision was to formally increase the number of civil aviation flight lanes between altitudes of 8,400 m to 12,500 m from seven to13 in number.

The new route lanes were scheduled to come into operational force on 22 November 2007. In the event, the CAAC advised on Tuesday 27 November 2007, that airspace controls were to be introduced, effectively locking down the new lane schedule. Requests for information as to why this had happened produced a one-line message that the new system would be reactivated on the following Sunday. Apart from the fact that the decision was instigated at the request of the PLAAF no further explanations were forthcoming.

The consequential effect on traffic notably in and out of Shanghai was severe with some 150 flights delayed and about 15,000 passengers affected on the first two days alone. This event appears to be reflective of the commonly held view by passengers that the military has a sustained belief that civil aviation services are subject to a concessionary place in the priority allocations of airspace usage. The author having experienced in 2007 a 120-minute take-off delay in the China Southern service from Chengdu to Guangzhou, can vouch for the fact that rising frustration and anger amongst passengers especially business executives is exacerbated by the total official silence as to the cause of the delay that accompanies any pre-take-off waiting period.

Traffic delays in what appears to be a frequently skewed control system are now a constant factor in travel planning, especially in those key airports which are the busiest locations in the Chinese air traffic system. From an overall developmental perspective, growing congestion at airports is partially a product of the failure of airport development to keep pace with what has become until very recently an exponential growth in domestic passenger demand.

But there is an even larger demand for remedial action for example in the matter of the need for an effectively automated air traffic management (ATM) system. The current methods of manual control, for example, requires that large and medium-sized aircraft maintain an in-flight distance of at least 150 km at all times. Effective reductions in this distance along the developmental pathway taken by the leading members of the international aviation community cite reductions up to 55 km as the likely outcome of a system which has achieved full automation.

The growing problems created by the rising demand for services are fully recognized by the Air Traffic Management Bureau of the CAAC. As later comment will indicate an ATM operational coordination mechanism had been established, but the systematic integration of operational processes and the introduction of modern traffic flow technology have still to be set up. It is somewhat ironic that while China lacks a modern ATM system, the high technology aspects of airspace management are now the subject of very active research agendas for a number of leading scientific institutions in China. An important example can be found below with regard to studies of airspace management, being currently undertaken at Tsinghua University in Beijing.

A Working Example of High Quality Chinese Research into ATM Systems

International studies of air traffic flow management (ATFM), have attempted to discover the optimal allocation of a given set of airspace resources that would yield the optimum usage of that airspace over time. Current research at one of China's leading universities in Beijing has raised some second-order questions with regard to the building of an efficient air traffic network, which could then be automatically adjusted in real time as a flight proceeds. The result is the continuing development of an integer programme model known as the dynamic air route open closed problem (DROP).

The purpose of DROP is to advance current thinking further to include cost-based objectives which considers such new variables such as the shortest occupancy time on various routes. The implications for a better use of airspace through conjoint use of ATFM and DROP may, according to the research team, facilitate the further development of airspace management as a much more dynamic process. This raises an immediate question as to the correlation between such high level research outputs and the further possibilities for the sequential empirical testing of the results.

China's Need for a National Integration Policy in Air Transport

It is clear that the effective military control of some 80 per cent of the total national airspace is a major contributor in the economic sense to the current developmental problems facing Chinese civil aviation. From the perspective of the national growth of the aviation market, operational limitations are also being increasingly linked to the growing congestion at the few major airports that can handle high levels of service frequency. These are to be found in the triangular relationship between the three major urban nodes that were examined in Chapter 8, and their dominance of the passenger market is reflected in the Table 12.1. The data is also reflective of the economic interaction going on within the triangle on an inter-city basis. Its degree of growing intensity is reflected in the fact that while the nodal triad only contains 9 per cent of China's total population, the actual volume of air passenger movement has reached over 50 per cent of the national total. The distribution between hubs is found in Table 12.1.

Some Further Urban–Regional Imbalances in the Domestic Airport Sector

The statistical evidence that over 50 per cent of airline traffic in China is operating within the tri-nodal system described above has a number of developmental consequences which will now be considered in more depth. As a matter of clarification it is clear that the domestic airport system of China is somewhat hierarchical with the class 4D and 4E airports, which are low-capacity facilities serving smaller regional centres, at the base.

Further up the organizational pyramid are larger city locations, regional hubs and finally at the top we find the three international hubs that form the tri-nodal network. According to definitional practice, hub airports in China may be located either in a large city, according to Zhang (1997), or strategically located so that it has a large volume of connecting traffic, or alternatively a combination of the two. By comparison and according to a recent study, the current handling capacity of all China's regional airports is now at some 26 per cent of the total design

Table 12.1   The Shares of the Tri-Nodal Locations in Passenger Traffic (2005)

Node	Population Share %	GDP Volume (000)	National Share GDP	Pax Volume	Pax National Share
Beijing Tiajin Hubei Province	2.3	206.0	10.5	437.0	15.4
Yangtze River Delta	1.1	326.1	16.6	589.0	20.7
Pearl River Delta	0.6	181.2	9.2	405.0	14.2
Sum of all Nodes	4	713.2	36.3	1,431.0	50.3

Note: There are 14 cities in the Yangtze Delta linked with Shanghai and some eight linked with Guangzhou in the Pearl River Delta.

Adapted from: Wang and Fang-Jung (2007).

capacity. A recent national audit of some 38 operational sites discovered 37 were suffering financial losses and some who were moving toward financial insolvency, had suspended services and reported asset wastage.

In the matter of operational schedules, notes Fulbrook (2004), the CAAC is aware that only 4.5 per cent of regional routes have more than one flight per day. To compound matters, according to Chen (2006), 86.5 per cent of regional city-pairs have an average per trip traffic of less than 80 passengers. A further 81.7 per cent city-pairs cannot guarantee a daily return trip, 10.9 per cent city-pairs can guarantee one to two return trips daily, while those routes that provide more than two round trips per day, amount to 7.4 per cent. Further limitations are imposed by regulations that place official constrains on important matters such as the types of aircraft that may be allowed to operate as well as regulative restrictions on cross-regional operations.

An inevitable consequence of these limitations has seen the tendency already noted above for the regional airport sector to experience a degree of relative stagnation. This has been partially shaped by the effective transfer of responsibility for funding developments to local government and private interests. The range of issues discussed above immediately brings up questions relating to operational efficiency and subsequent productivity and these now return to centre stage.

A recent study which investigated the pattern of productivity changes in a sample of 25 regional airports for the period 1995–2004 revealed, as discovered by Fung, *et al.* (2008) an annual average productivity growth above 3 per cent. The results indicated that the major source of productivity growth did not emerge from improvements in efficiency but, rather, from technical progress. The disparity effects came from the polarization of efficiency. The authors suggested that reform policies needed to make changes in direction with regard to the more dependent and physically remote locations. However, given the fact that the accumulation of necessary funding for further institutional development is in the hands of local administrations, the question of capital availability immediately comes to the fore.

According to a recent report on China's airports by CAPA (2008) western regional airports are the subject of a new wave of investor interest. The Asian Development Bank (ADB), for example, has a US$50 million equity investment in support of the private Chinese company, HNA Airport Holding Group. In making this market entry the ADB joins a number of companies already busy in China including ARC Capital Holdings Ltd, as well as Pacific Alliance Asia Opportunity Fund Ltd. In addition there is evidence that Changi Airports International will be placing significant investment funding into a number of airports commencing with the Nanjing Lukou International.

In turn the growth of private sector interest in the general state of regional aviation has most recently (April 2008) become the focus of quite serious government intervention. It was in that month that the CAAC announced State Council approval had been obtained for a conjoint financial intervention with the Ministry of Finance. The regional industry now has access to subsidies covering medium to small airports, in addition the state has also provided further subsidies for regional aviation as well as announcing its willingness to subsidize interest payments where a specific operator has raised loans for capital construction. These new arrangements incidentally supersede a previous policy on the subsidization of operator losses.

The policy intention is to target airports with annual traffic of less than five million passengers. In turn regional subsidies will be available both for airports within a given province as well as for operations between provinces, where the flight distance is less than 600 km, and load factors are below 80 per cent. Finally the geographical distribution of the new policy is planned to cover central, west and northwest China.

It is notable that no mention is made here with regard to either expected yield for carriers from these changes, or the fact that both the rail and road modes of transportation offer increasingly viable alternatives to air transport in some locations. This strategy change does however have clear links to the larger and popular perception of a future national airline industry whose fleet requirements and replacement cycles will be met by indigenous suppliers.

It is also clear that part of the current regional problem with load factors has arisen from the propensity noted in earlier discussions for domestic airlines to purchase their fleet requirements from the international market. This has led critics to suggest that a significant proportion of the regional market is lost because the actual aircraft in service are operationally split for choice between 737/A320 twin-aisle carriers on the one hand and small regional aircraft designed to carry 50 persons on the other. The consequence has been described as a market that in the final analysis sees passengers complain about high fares and airport services and airlines in turn express concern over low yields that barely cover their operational costs.

While there is a growing interest in low-cost carriers now well established in China, their ability to operate is clearly dependent on a change in operational rules that permit both a competitive supply and demand paradigm to dominate the market and at the same time, allow direct competition on domestic routes with established carriers. If it was implemented of course it would be essentially a reprise of the past American and European experience. Whether it would work in China, requires a significant number of entrepreneurial investors to be both forthcoming and very active.

Its further potential is also dependent upon what sort of market conditions the government will be facing, when it raises the moratorium on new market entrants that is due to end in 2010. Given the current state of the passenger market in late 2008, the expectation is that China, in keeping with the rest of the world, will face a considerable degree of uncertainty.

China's Changing Approach to the Need for New Air Safety Standards

Throughout the 1980s and into the 1990s China did not enjoy a good reputation for air safety. Airline fleets comprised obsolescent Russian models as well as local products. In turn pilot error was a constant problem, while MRO standards varied widely and the general level of official oversight was not good. These problems were seriously compounded, especially for airlines operating outside national airspace, by the fact that Chinese pilots often lacked an effective level of English, the key language required by international ATM standards.

During the decennial period to 2005 according to Wang and Fang-Jun (2007) it is officially recorded that there were 32 fatal accidents, of which nine involved aircraft in the commercial sector. The aggregate number of fatalities for the period was 482, with the growing general aviation sector accounting for 23 accidents and 41 losses of life. There appears as a consequence to be growing recognition amongst Chinese officials that while a general improvement in air safety has been taking place, continuing market expansion now demands that persistent efforts be made to lower accident rates. This has led in turn to recognition of the fact that the long tradition of attempting to regulate through administrative directives, needs to give way to more concrete and tangible action, involving aviation education and training.

Proposals for further development include human resources development programmes with an estimate that China will need a safety administration labour force in excess of 10,000 members. In addition a special fund will be created with the intention of developing safety data collection and analysis as well as expanding the range and utilization of safety technologies. The CAAC will also aim at the continuous development of a strong international relationship with bodies such as ICAO as well as various national CAA departments.

The fact remains however that the ability to put in train increasing efficiencies in air safety control are still being hampered by lack of an integrated national infrastructure, scarcity of airspace, legal and regulatory confusion and the need to give safety management key priority. The requirement for action is further limited by the fact that there is a shortage of key and trained personnel in all operational areas covered by air safety requirements. With regard to the organizational modernization of civil aviation in China a major question now arises: What reformist initiatives will there be needed in the short to medium term, to ensure that any future expansion in the size, range, roles and scope of commercial services, will see the quality of air safety provisions improve in tandem and at the required rate of growth? We can now turn to an assessment of efforts now being made in China to redefine the infrastructural needs that should shape the reform process.

National Plans to Develop a Modernized Air Traffic Management System

What might be called a first step in matching the supply of quality ATM services with what has been identified as a growing level of demand was taken in November 2007 when China implemented its plan to introduce a new reduced vertical separation minimum (RVSM) into domestic airspace. The event was a subject of some comment already noted above because within hours of the prescribed implementation of the changes, the system was deliberately closed down for several days without a formal explanation from the ATMB, though a strong rumour was circulated that the PLAAF had unilaterally instigated the closure. The effects already described led to serious delays and flight cancellations before operations recommenced.

Offsetting the negativity of the incident on the positive side, the decision to implement the new RVSM marked an important step forward for China, both in domestic and international terms, since it formed a part of a much larger developmental project carried out with the ICAO. The Beijing event was the product of considerable research and testing in liaison with an international working party of member states and involved the following programme of changes proposed by CAAC, to both improve airspace capacity and operational efficiency. The initiative proposed to implement a 500-metre vertical separation between the flight levels of 8,400 m to 8,900 m, together with a 300-metre vertical separation in other altitude blocks below 12,500 m. The new RVSM was also designed in a way that would allow statistical congruence between China which employed the metric system and neighbouring countries which did not.

To accommodate the problem, the operational difference between metric and imperial values would not be allowed to exceed 30 m for RSVM flight levels. Formal implementation was intended to begin on 21 November 2007 with their operational parameters designed to cover Beijing, Guangzhou, Kunming, Lanzhou, Shanghai, Shenyang, Urumqi and Wuhan Flight Information Regions (FIRs). In addition the airspace over Sanya FIR (sector 01), with the further oceanic airspace around this offshore island, brought into the range of implementation the South China Sea.

The implementation of the RSVM is really a first step, since clearly a reduced horizontal separation minimum (RHSM) will become a logical extension, especially when incoming banks at the various airports are reaching their busiest time periods in the operational cycle. This raises again the question of national strategic priorities for ATM improvement, which were recently made public by the CAAC at a major conference in Montreal in September 2008, the details of which will now be described below.

China's Game Plan for a Modern and Efficient ATM System

One of the core questions that face Chinese government planners continues to involve the apparent imbalance between the current and potential future demands that will need to be addressed by the national ATM system. Three important shortcomings are identified as central problems that have to be overcome. First, they involve the current limitations imposed by managerial and access policy limitations. Secondly, the national ATM technological infrastructure is simply inadequate in the face of sustained and increasing growth in the demand for operational services. This applies especially in the west and north where civil aviation is required to play a major role as a developmental agency. Finally, the need to introduce managerial systems and technology that fit rising traffic flows is yet to be formalized into a real time strategy. The ground plan for change involves a comprehensive review and overhaul of a series of sub-systems as shown in Figure 12.1.

What is apparently being sought is a strategy that will build an ATM system that attaches equal importance both to the use of traditional infrastructure as well as the introduction of new technologies. The term traditional infrastructure is intended to denote the need for a progressive evolution of the modernization of all ATM services rather than an attempt to address the massive need for technological progress in the very short run. The official position with regard to the transitional development programme can be seen in Table 12.2.

The proposed programme plans in the short term to cover airspace, infrastructural and research and development measures. The intention is to sequentially combine and enlarge current ATM control areas, put further action in train to reform airspace management and to remove the utilization mechanisms that currently cause serious

---

The reforms will cover, in both function and extent, the following range of professional activities:

> Airspace System
> Flight Planning System
> Air Traffic Flow System
> Air Traffic Services System
> Aviation Information System
> Meteorological System
> ATM Automation System
> Dynamic System for Airports and Runways
> Information and Exchange Network

Figure 12.1　The Plan to Integrate ATM Sub-Systems in China

Source: Avbuyer.com.cn 8 October 2008.

congestion. These initiatives will be supported by the introduction of major ACCs, better radar, increased automation and ATFMS, and the creation of an integrated information management programme for ATM.

In the anticipated short term the research and development programme will include ADS-B route trials, work on ATM trial and deployment exercises, GNSS integrity monitoring as well as RNP/RNAV trials and implementation. A further research and development programme will attempt to assess a range of equipment and technologies, where implementation is not constrained by intellectual property rights. In the matter of the last category, it is interesting to speculate whether the major controversies that have often surrounded the question of international intellectual property rights in China are being seen as a possible hindrance to the last item proposed for the ATM reform agenda. This calls for consistent attendance to the larger questions of harmonization and coordination within the larger international context of the ICAO's support for an evolving and future global ATM system, within its longer term FANS context

The CAAC agenda also requires the strengthening of communications with countries, regions and other organizations. Quite clearly the answer to the speculative question raised above depends on the meaning the CAAC is giving to what the late neo-liberal economist Friedrich von Hayek would call the weasel word, independence. From a managerial perspective, a practical indication of the reformist intentions is the decision to ease current control requirements over domestic air route operations. The existing rule requires that a carrier apply for transit rights over a given route, which must then be approved by the requisite Air Transport Bureau (ATB). In 2010 it is intended that this process be replaced by a new rule, discussed in an earlier chapter, that will permit airlines to simply advise of their intentions to fly a given route.

Table 12.2   GCAAC's Air Traffic Management Bureau Transitional Reform Programme

Current Facilities 2008	Proposed Facilities 2010 following
Ground-based Navigation	Satellite-based Navigation
Sensor-based Navigation	Performance-based Navigation
Voice Communication	DL/Voice Communication
Ground Radar Systems	Integrated ADS-B/MDS Radar Systems
Separate ATM Automation Systems	Networked ATM Automation Systems
Flight Plan Management	Air Traffic Flow Management
Internal Information Exchange	Integrated Exchange for all Services

Adapted from: Lu Xiaoping CAAC-ATMB Presentation CANSO Conference, Montreal, 14–20 September 2008.

The prevailing tone of discussion thus far has been fraught to some degree with uncertainty. What has been presented has really been a series of snapshots of a wide range of issues whose sheer size and complexity remain daunting with regard to the search for coherence and direction in both policy and management in civil aviation. This has been further exacerbated by the major global crisis that has struck first financial markets and then individual nation states, with a deepening effect in the last financial quarter of 2008. This has continued into 2009 as individual states including China publicly acknowledge that they are in an economic recession.

International civil aviation has been no exception to this general trend in terms of the consequences for all industries as the banks begin to fall apart, led by some household names in the United States and Europe. In the international aviation sector, there have been reported downturns in customer demand and a general problem with rising costs which have struck low-cost as well as legacy carriers in turn. China has not been exempt from what has become a very serious crisis for the industry, as further discussion below will indicate.

The New Financial Reality: Civil Aviation and the Global Credit Crisis

The events that have shaken the global financial world to the core, especially in late 2008 and into 2009, have had an immediate effect on major industries including civil aviation. As a consequence the assumptions of the continuing and long-term increasing growth of China's airline industry, which have been reflected in both analysis and comment since the first chapter, must now be considered against the conflicting pressures of current economic events.

It is clear that international civil aviation is in the process of trying to absorb the knock-on effects of a growing global credit squeeze which has destabilized virtually every aspect of the industry, from falling airline stocks, through to an increasing, rapid and widespread decline in passenger demand. According to the CEO of IATA, the relative high speed of the slowdown has effectively reduced the ability of carriers to respond. Even positive developments such as the fall in oil prices is offset by the hard fact that the current price is still 30 per cent higher year on year than it was in 2007. Current negative expectations according to IATA are supported by the estimate that the aggregate loss by passenger traffic for 2008 will be US$5.2 billion and rising within the Asia–Pacific region which is at the leading edge of the overall trend.

The effects of an international fall in global trade activities are reflected in turn, by the fact that air freight has been in significant decline since August 2008. Again the Asia–Pacific region comes to the fore with a reported 6.8 per cent reduction in August after a 6.5 per cent fall in July. These results signal the growing slide into economic recession, given the fact that the Asia–Pacific region's freight market represents 45 per cent of the global air cargo markets.

Expectations within the Association of Asia–Pacific Airlines (AAPA) are for market conditions to get even worse. Weakening passenger demand particularly in the yield earnings gained from premium and first class services is being reported on a membership-wide basis, which is significant since there are 18 carriers in the group, including all of the key players in the region. In addition the AAPA has suggested that some airlines may not survive if the global crisis continues to deepen and its duration extends over significant time.

The pattern is repeated from the perspective of China's big three carriers, which are all currently deeply in the red. Declining domestic demand coupled to higher fuel prices have seen operating revenues fall while expenses increase. Of the three, China Eastern has seen its relative market decline over some time, and has also lived through a failed attempt to merge its ownership with Singapore International Airlines. These cumulative events has left it with a debt to equity ratio of the order of 98 per cent on the basis of a capital value of RMB7.55 billion against debt totalling RMB7.47 billion. It is now throwing the deck chairs overboard with plans to cut long-haul flights, reduce salaries across the board and postpone new aircraft deliveries. In addition it is going through the preparation stages of a possible merger with Shanghai Airlines.

A much more important sign of infrastructural cost problems is the fact that the parent companies of China Southern and China Eastern after actively canvassing in Beijing for a major capital injection from the government of the type that has already been granted to the state-owned banks, have both been promised cash injections in the order of RMB3 billion (US$437 million). In the China Eastern case, this has been followed by a further cash injection of RMB4 billion, which incidentally coincides with the airline's request to various stock exchanges to suspend trading in its shares. In turn Air China has approached its parent company for a cash injection to reduce its debt ratio. Both Shanghai Airlines and Grand China Airlines (HNA) are also now signalling that they too will seek some form of government support. They have very recently been joined by Grand China Express the flagship carrier of the HNA Group which now expects to receive a cash injection from the Tianjin municipal government in the order of RMB200 million.

The Group has also made an application for a capital subsidy from the Hainan provincial administration. To add to what can only be described as a symbolic example of total managerial confusion over business aims and objectives, there are reports that while the cancellation of some unprofitable routes is being considered, HNA has still got active plans to buy a 45 per cent stake in the Beijing Yanjing Hotel as well as a 95 per cent equity share in a leading real estate firm in the capital.

As an additional sign of the current economic uncertainties on 19 December 2008, the government cut the domestic price for aviation fuel for the sixth time. The fact that these prices are managed by government has meant that Chinese airlines have been unable to obtain the benefits of a falling international price for oil. This means that the purchase of fuel accounts for between 40 per cent and 50 per cent of airline operating costs. In addition the CAC have cut fuel surcharges on domestic routes by an unspecified margin.

There has developed a popular view that China has sufficient resources in terms of its various fiscal surpluses, to at least slow down the current collapse of the international credit system. This assumption is again increasingly under pressure from an aviation perspective as the following evidence will reveal. In a very recent 2009 conference reported by the ATW on 9 January 2009, the CAAC Vice Director General, Yang Guoqing, reported that China's airlines had made a net loss of RMB7.7 billion ($1.13 billion) in the period January to November 2008. The most negative effects were felt on international routes where by rough estimate the carriage of 192 million passengers in the measured period was 13 per cent lower than the total reported for 2007. In turn the fall in cargo volume was even larger at 14.3 per cent or 4 million tonnes.

The expectation of a steeper fall in 2009 was acknowledged, while at the same time, the hope was expressed that Beijing's intention to aim for an 8 per cent growth rate in GDP will effectively boost the CAAC's projection of a growth of 11 per cent in passenger traffic and 4 per cent in cargo volume. On the other hand it is proposed that capacity increase and market access by China's airlines be controlled by the return of leased aircraft, the sale of older fleet planes, a reduction in the delivery of foreign-made new aircraft and the sustaining of the current ruling that no new aircraft should be purchased until 2010. A further indicator of hard times comes from China Southern which offered in December 2008 four of its B777-200s from its fleet of 360 aircraft for sale in order to offset steeply rising costs. These events in sum give weight to a serious contradiction, since the scheduled expectations of growth are expected to be obtained by airlines who, at the same time, are expected to operate with a diminished capacity to respond if the market does turn up.

The Inevitable Impact of the Credit Crisis on the Economy of China

According to official data released in October 2008, China had experienced five consecutive quarters of decline it its GDP growth rate. This has delivered a current GDP increase of 9 per cent on the last quarter which is probably the healthiest growth rate in the world at the moment, but actually below the country's recent year on year improvements. What is really a source of concern for the government however is the fact that as an export dependent economy the contribution of that key sector to GDP was in September 2008 running at 1.2 per cent. This result signals a fall from the 2007 figure of 2.4 per cent.

From a Chinese viewpoint this decline is a matter of considerable concern because exports to Japan and the United States make up approximately 49 per cent of the export trade, which in turn has contributed 32 per cent of China's GDP growth in the period 2005–07. A further indicator that the downward trend in the national economy is not a short-run phenomenon may be found in the fact that share prices on China's stock exchanges have been falling consistently since 2 November 2007 until the same date in 2008. This reflected on average a daily loss by each individual investor in the order of RMB1,570 ($229.5) per day. Further estimates of corporate performance reveal that PetroChina, the leading oil producer and the largest equity holder in the market, had seen its share value virtually evaporate to the tune of RMB2.2 trillion over a period of 241 trading days.

Perhaps the most dramatic sign of the government's growing concern has been the recent announcement that the retirement age of members of the public service will be adjusted downward by five years so that men will be required to leave their jobs at 60 and women at 55. This decision has been ascribed to a rising level of unemployment amongst middle-class business and professional employees. It appears that the problem is also being compounded by the increasing difficulties being faced by university graduates in obtaining a first job appointment.

This view is supported by the subjective comments of some of the author's recent Chinese graduate students. It has also been estimated that some 1.5 million students are still seeking employment after graduating in 2008. Recent advice received regarding a specific MBA graduating class reveals that six months after the event in June 2008, only five members out of a total class of 60 have been able to obtain meaningful employment.

There can be no doubt that China will bear its own share of the problems being created by the current economic crisis. What is significant however is the experts ongoing debate over the proposed RMB4 trillion (US$586 billion) economic stimulus package announced early in November 2008. There is some concern being expressed with the possibility that the old mode of relying on government loans and subsidies, as a form of throwing money at the problem when markets turn down, might be taken up yet again by the PRC administration.

Critics suggest that this would be a counter-productive exercise and that China should not continue to rely on fixed-asset investment and exports to fire up economic growth. They would rather see a major change of economic direction that would allow for an expanding rate of domestic consumption to lead on and into a major contribution to long-term sustainable growth. The issue has relevance since the contribution of domestic consumption to GDP tends to be quite small, due to the fact that most people tend to be net savers rather than active consumers. This becomes increasingly apparent when domestic consumption is compared with the relative size of the now rapidly falling rates of export sales.

The stimulus package covers a range of social, environmental and technological interventions financed directly by government in the amount of 30 per cent with the balance of funds coming from local governments' banks and businesses. While there is no clear current indication as to the distribution, project by project, of the funding, there is a wide belief that transportation will be the primary infrastructural beneficiary. While airport construction appears to be mentioned in passing, the key battle for resources has already opened up however between railways and roads, with railways as a stand-alone ministry, rumoured to be gaining a probable one quarter (RMB1 trillion) of the designated package on offer.

This produces a degree of potential distortion in product outputs, given the fact that both rail and road construction already has significant government funding. The rail industry also has a political advantage in the sense, already discussed earlier, that it enjoys the status of a stand-alone ministry, while both aviation and road transport have been collectivized under one of the new super ministries.

Significant gaps also emerge from a closer look at government intentions. The proposals call for more spending on social services, farmers and the poor, as well as an increase in personal incomes, but there appears to be no thought being given to individual tax incentives, despite the fact some 6.5 per cent of state revenues comes from that source. The government tendency to return to state-funded infrastructure building also fails to find favour with research economists who point out the various dangers that such initiatives can produce. The lack of a clear market-driven set of objectives has in the past led to over-production with government monopolies also squeezing out private investors.

It is also notable that in China, government-funded infrastructure development is considered to be high risk with regard to the inevitable emergence of often large-scale official corruption. This is frequently due to the fact that many officials have the power to handle both the processes of land requisition and the contracts for the subsequent projects that are to be constructed on site. People also have in mind the fact that in the last construction boom that followed the 1997 Asian financial crisis, at least ten officials holding ministerial rank ended up in jail. With this experience already on record, special inspection teams appointed by the Central Commission for Disciplinary Inspection (CCDI) are already setting up surveillance systems in a number of provinces. It is also clear that there is an inherent condition of fragility in the economy of the PRC which has been aggravated by the global financial crisis. It relates directly to the need to build a more consumer-friendly economy, in which the enormous potential of significant level of domestic consumption can be added, as we have already noted, to the GDP.

How far the current fiscal intervention will succeed in China lies really outside the terms of the current discussion, except perhaps in one particular. The fact that by the active encouragement of the expansion of both railways and roads, both of which have already received massive investment, the potential grows for serious inter-modal competition between them and the civil aviation industry especially will increase over time. This has specific possibilities in the area of short-haul and shuttle services in major urban centres, where very efficient high-speed railway technology is being introduced.

As a working example, business travellers moving between the cities of Guangzhou and Shenzhen, a distance of approximately 150 km, can complete the journey either way in 47 minutes and at a current peak speed of 210 kph. Of equal importance is the fact that these services will deliver passengers to stations which are located either in or close to the central business districts.

It is now time to move back to a more specific and important question facing the aerospace industry, which relates to very recent events involving China's future in aircraft construction. Its intended focus is revealed in the title of the next theme for further discussion.

What are the Prospects for the Further Development of an Autonomous Aerospace Industry?

According to the *Shanghai Daily* of 3 November 2008, a bilateral trade mission comprising a large number of American aerospace firms had arrived in China in search of investment opportunities in the aerospace industry. The delegation's schedule included visits to the key cities of Shanghai, Beijing, Suzhou and Guangzhou and it also carried the official status of a bilateral exchange. The ostensible reason for the visit, according to a senior consultant attached to the delegation, can be found in the persistent belief of the delegates that the massive industrial slow-down being experienced in the United States, can be offset to some extent by corporate movement into what are perceived to be the burgeoning aviation markets in China and probably India and Russia.

The confidence of the delegation that joint ventures and supplier contracts might flow from the visit stands in marked contrast to the decision of US airlines to attempt what has been referred to in a formal request to the USDOT the introduction of a blanket waiver of all dormancy conditions. This would allow US airlines to either scale back services on limited entry international routes, or to withdraw from the scheduling of specific international services for a period of up to two years. The request which was granted on the basis of individual applications by airlines, reflects a very significant change in the US carriers strategies to progress the development of long-haul non-stop services. It also suggests a restrictive possibility that the scheduled development of the current ASA might also be subject to a progressive slow-down.

But as the Zhuhai Aviation Fair has already indicated the assumption that China's demand for a consistently large number of commercial aircraft including freighters will remain a growing market opportunity well into the future, still remains at the core of international supplier expectations. This view tends to be supported by the way in which existing contractors who have been located for some time in the Chinese market, have become embedded in a series of cooperation programmes which entail both a specialist and broad spectrum approach to the industry's marked shortage of skilled workers.

The result is revealed in a growing range of training opportunities which include executive development, then on through technical competencies and environmental studies with perspectives ranging from airline development through to manufacturing and into general aviation.

United States–China Aviation Cooperation Programme (ACP)

The programme was launched in 2004 with the intention to train Chinese aviation professionals in a broad spectrum of activities. Its membership has since grown from some eight original corporate members to 31 in 2008. It is also clear from official documentation that the American initiative has a geopolitical motive at base. The incentive to set up this programme was really a tactical response to the fact that the EU as a major international competitor had already set up a similar programme in China which promoted European aviation products, methods and standards, with some success.

The transparency of American intentions is further revealed in the fact that the ACP has also obtained the formal support of major agencies such as the US Commerce Department and the USTDA which is funding a number of important projects, as well as the FAA. The programme is also materially assisting the CAAC in its various research and development initiatives including the current ATM modernization project.

CAAC–Rolls-Royce Top 100 Programme

The programme began in 1990 with a strong emphasis on English language training as well as teaching methodology courses. It has since moved on into group specific senior management skills for high potential candidates and the establishment of an official CAAC–Rolls-Royce Training Centre. During the current decade the programme has introduced specialist training for Airline Presidents and CEOs. In 2006 a further agreement was signed extending the learning partnership Airline Presidents courses, an event that coincided with the tenth Anniversary of the Top 100 series.

Beijing–PanAm Aviation Academy

Established in 2003, this programme was the first business-orientated professional pilot academy to be granted CAAC authorization. Driven by an international team of professional instructors, it has since become recognized for its curriculum which has involved the adoption of an advanced US–Europe style of training syllabus as well as a range of consultancies within the aviation industry. The core programme has been designed to produce high quality graduates over less time and with a more cost-effective programme. The academy has also developed some 12 flight training agreements with Chinese airlines for the supply of trained pilots.

The most important aspect of these programmes is their ability to act as a modernizing agent in those key areas of labour market demand, where China has significant and continuing shortfalls in the quality and supply of skilled labour. The active assumption however on the Chinese side that this kind of programme, will lead to the organizational replication of indigenous firms able to fully take over such roles and functions, remains clouded in uncertainties. The following discussion will address some of these implicit problematics.

How Viable is China's Current Plan for an Autonomous Aerospace Industry?

The repeated assertion by CAAC and other indigenous providers in the aviation industry that China will by 2020 be designing, building and operating its own autonomous large-jet aircraft, raises some very important issues in regard to its current and future ability to move from component production and assembly into a fully integrated production system. The competencies currently enjoyed by indigenous firms has raised some serious and substantive doubts that will now be considered in more detail.

The development of an indigenous labour force with operational skills in production systems has clearly been a major component in the strategies of international companies entering China, suggests Warner (2008), with the opening up of market access to FDI. In the case of aviation they have been involved in a range of activities, either individually or in the form of joint ventures across a variety of projects. Much of the requisite work has involved a range of sub-contracts for components, with a strong emphasis on structural assemblies. It has also included at the core of some ventures, as noted by Kelly (2008), as a set of risk and revenue sharing arrangements.

The emphasis on structural assemblies already noted above marks the constraining limit faced by indigenous firms in China at the current time. To date the development of technological systems and integration packages remains firmly in the hands of the dominant US companies located in China, with no sign to date that their corporate plans will allow for China in the future to become a major international force, notably in the core practice of system integration. An interesting example of what is a continuing dichotomy can be found in the following comparison.

In 2007 Chinese aviation firms won US$700 million of component and structural contracts for North American and European airlines projects. In the same year recent research has noted (Sweeney, 2008) that Parker, a very large US aircraft control system builder, was the successful winner of a single contract to supply the new Bombardier series C model with a fly-by-wire system. The important difference lies in the fact that the market value of the Bombardier contract was US$3.5 billion. During the same period it is rumoured that US suppliers gained various contracts for work on the new ARJ21 series of regional jets which were considerably in excess of the nominal gains made by what can best be described as competitive indigenous firms.

The expansion by major international players within China's manufacturing sector has to a considerable extent masked its real shortcoming with regard to any clear and logical direction in the growth of its manufacturing capability. This is especially true at the next and crucial level of complex supply-chain design and the integration of aggregate production systems internally and inevitably across national borders.

This issue raises the ultimate question with regard to the development of an indigenous aerospace manufacturing industry. Given heavy dependence on externally created learning curves will China ever possess a stand-alone set of systems and an indigenous integration technology, given the inevitable propensity for the big Western players to shut China out of those areas of programmes that yield the best returns in value, revenue and profit? This question becomes increasingly important when it is noted that China's popular and comparative advantage as the world centre of low-cost production is beginning to be overtaken now by its emergent neighbours such as Vietnam.

The current stage of what appears to be a very convoluted approach to an overall manufacturing strategy is reflected in two recent government publications. The first proposes a guideline for the promotion of civil sectors of the national defence industry, while the second called for military aircraft manufacturers located in major provincial centres to accept and use commercial capital to develop military products with civilian applications. It was also indicated that this latter proposal was to proceed as a corollary to continued and heavy investment in the aeronautics and space industry.

Discussion thus far has attempted to illustrate the essential uncertainties that confront the Chinese aviation industry as it seeks to become a unified, efficient and broad spectrum industry. Further comment given the manifest issues that have already been considered must clearly await the events of 2009, which if market signals are to be believed will require considerable revision of current projections for continuing growth. With this thought in mind it is now time to return to the core issue of political leadership during these interesting times.

The Prospective Influence of Changing Ideological Leadership on China's Aviation Future

A primary theme throughout the book has considered the dominant role of the CCP as the ideological force shaping government and the policy directions taken by China since 1978. Two examples of the importance of this dynamic will be considered as the concluding themes for this chapter. The first will examine the major change that has recently occurred at the most senior level of management in the CAAC. The second will look at the implications of the major political changes that are expected to take place in Beijing, when the 11th FYP comes to an end and a new leadership takes office as the fifth generation in the 2012–13 period.

The Important Administrative Change Strategies introduced by Yuan Yuanyuan as Minister of the CAAC

The various strategies that have shaped and directed China's aviation industry, during the modernization of current operational forms and managerial style, began to emerge with the appointment of Yang Yuanyuan as Minister of the CAAC in 2002. The scale and scope of the activities introduced by this former international commercial pilot spanned the total reorganization of the airline and well as the service industries, and as a working example, the transfer of operational rights to some 89 airports.

From a managerial perspective, the effects on the CAAC were equally profound, with the structural change in the organization's primary role from being an active participant in the management of the industry to that of an industrial and market regulator. It is also interesting that the period during which he was in office was notable for the fact that the airline sector began to signal very positive growth in both revenues and profits.

Within the international sphere Yang's period as CEO occurred at a time of significant growth in the number of bilateral aviation agreements. As a result and given his deep professional interest in the airline industry, he gave great stress during his term of office, to the important need to vastly improve the economic performance of the domestic passenger carriers in order to meet the demands of international market competition. He was to leave office somewhat abruptly in late 2007 and the detailed reasons for his departure still await further clarification and final confirmation.

The Accession of Li Jiaxiang as Minister of the CAAC in 2007 and the Commitment by the CAAC to a Super-carrier Programme

At first glance Li Jiaxiang is a representative of the pre-reform age in Chinese aviation. A major-general in the PLAAF, he was until 2002, the deputy air force commissar in the Shenyang Military Region. Appointed chairman of Air China in 2002, he presided over the airline's return to profit with a resultant move from its position as the weakest to that of the strongest of the major state-carriers group.

His experiences at Air China have clearly shaped Li's primary interest in what he calls the development of a Chinese super-carrier that would effectively match competitors like Lufthansa, Emirates and Air France–KLM. This has evolved directly from his belief that China's international carriers are in danger of being marginalized in a competitive international market. He is also concerned with the fact that between 2000 and 2007, the cargo sector in the domestic market shrank from 44 per cent to 18 per cent, while the share of internal passenger traffic fell from 56 per cent to 44 per cent. The conjoint effects of these events have clearly been influential in shaping current CAAC policy.

It has become apparent that the strategy preferred by Li in terms of market growth, spins off from his liking of super-carriers, which means that he favours growth by a merger and acquisition policy in which the domestic carriers would be the target group. By contrast Yang would be have been much more inclined to develop a strong marketing approach that would lead to a more open market-orientated system, a view that has some considerable support from senior industry specialists.

The general consensus however suggests that while the opening up policy might slow down under Li, it would still continue an active life as a primary goal to be pursued by the CAAC. In the final analysis however the prescribed role and scope of the CAAC in shaping the future of civil aviation now seems to depend on the will of its new parent body, China's Super Ministry of Transportation.

Ever since the seminal changes introduced in Chinese power politics in 1978, the question of the ongoing leadership of the CCP has continued to be a matter of public concern. The final theme of the book will now selectively examine some of the profound issues that will surround the next accession to power by what the Chinese people are calling the fifth generation of CPC leadership.

Aviation's Potential Future under Fifth Generation Political Leadership

Many of the themes addressed throughout the book have been shaped by the continuing prevalence of a high degree of ideological evolution which reflects, in turn, the fact that market-driven reforms in China are ultimately subject, at least in principle, to total governmental control. From the official perspective of the CCP Politburo all changes since 1978 have reflected an ideological continuity which is now claimed to have really existed from the time of Mao Zedong to the current period in office of Hu Jintao and Wu Jiabao.

The political reality however does show a distinct shift over time away from the Great Leader model with its inevitable drift toward factional politics. The trend today is toward a more collective form of leadership. This view was endorsed by Hu Jintao at the 17th Party Congress of the CCP, when he actually called for a commitment to collective leadership with a formal division of authority and responsibility between individual cadres as a system able to replace the present arbitrary decision-making process, as exercised in the past either by an individual or a minority of people in the party.

The emergence of collective leadership has been signalled in China by the election of a number a key new members to the Standing Committee of the Politburo and to other important posts that signal both a generational shift and a new range of managerial potential. The leading-edge candidates at the moment for the Presidential and Prime Ministerial posts in 2012 are aged 54 and 52, and both hold PhDs, in Law and Economics respectively. Their formal careers which have been developing since 1978 include senior appointments and resultant managerial experience at the level of regional and provincial government.

Bearing in mind that reform thus far in the fourth generation has been driven by engineers and technocrats, the fifth generation will be able to call upon a strong entrepreneurial element in the State Council and Politburo, which includes the CEOs of three of China's largest flagship firms, Sinopec, First Auto Works and China Telecom. This group of some 18 persons also includes the heads both of joint-venture corporations and indigenous firms within the emergent private business sector. Their presence also tends to give further support to the notion of a structural shift in the generational age of the membership since they tend to be mostly in their 40s. When it is reviewed as a total group what appears to emerge is a strong balance of party elites, comprising the children of prominent figures in the CCP as well as a variety of administrative, commercial and industrial interests.

It would appear at first glance, that the distribution of industrial and commercial experience represented in the fifth generation could have an important influence on the urgent need to bring China's expectations for the future growth of the aviation industry into line with current economic and social uncertainties. With this in mind, it is clearly hoped by the collectivist lobby that a growing political pluralism can overcome the tensions and conflict inherent in the CCP and go on to reach a positive consensus on industrial policies that will give Chinese aviation both stability and operational strength in the future.

There can be no doubt that the fifth generation will come to office at a time when the future will contain manifest uncertainties, especially with regard to the need to bring the national economy back into economic, social and political balance. Quite clearly the initial policy and reform issues that require identification and placement on the growing agenda for further government action will be dominated, until and perhaps even beyond 2012, by the immediate need to attend to and ameliorate the various infrastructural problems created by the international recession.

As a consequence the current situation suggests a need for agendas addressing the short-run issues that need priority as the means for bringing China's economy back into medium to longer-term balance. From a strategic perspective this will require in turn that sight is not lost of the key roles that important industries like civil aviation will still need to play in China's industrial future. This recognition thus calls for consistent attention to be paid to the need to look forward and continue to plan for aviation's continued market growth. As to what will be the final shape of the industry after 2012 and the accession to power of the fifth generation of leadership, there can only be one certainty for those working on the planning agenda at the current time: that, quite irrespective of the material consequences of world recession and falling demand, the future administrative, managerial and operational directions taken by all sectors of China's aviation industry will inevitably aim to produce a final result famous for its uniquely Chinese characteristics.

Bibliography

Abbas, A. 1997. HKIA City as Airport: Other Histories other Politics. *Public Culture*, 9(3) 293–313.

Abegglen, J.C. 1994. Sea Change: Pacific Asia as the New World Industrial Center New York: The Free Press.

Aboulafia, R. 2006. *The High Cost of Building Jets*, Aerospace America, available at http//www.aiaa.org/aerospaceimages/articleimages/pdf/AA_Apr06_11pdf (accessed 2 February 2007).

Agenda21 1996. Sustainable Development of Industrial Transportation and Communications, Transportation White Paper, Ministry of Transport, Beijing.

Agnew, J. 2002. *Making Political Geography*. London: Edward Arnold.

Annual Review of China Civil Aviation, 2008, available at AvBuyer.com.cn (accessed on 25 August 2008).

Air Cargo World, 2007. Feature Focus: World Top 50 Cargo Airports, July, 20–22; Top 50 Cargo Airlines, 26–9.

Air TN-EU. Web.http//.www.airtn.eu 2007.

Air Transport World, Daily Newsletters 2003–08.

APCO International Inc. 2008. *Report on the 11th National People's Conference,* Beijing, 1–15 March.

Armstrong, D. and Terry, E. (eds) 2003. *Pearl River Developmental Zone; Tapping into the World's Fastest Growing Economy*, Hong Kong: SCMP Publishing.

Asia Development Bank 2007. Policy Reform in Road Transport, Final Report, Manilla.

Asland, A. 2007. Russia's Capitalist Revolution: Why Reform Succeeded and Democracy Failed, *Petersen Institute for International Economics Occasional WP Series 07*.

ATM Bureau 2008. (online) available at http//www.atmb.net.cn. (accessed on 17 June 2007).

Bagnai, A. and Ospina, C.A.M. 2007. Structural Changes and the Transition Process: A Macroconometric Model of China, *Luiss Laboratory of European Economics, Working Document No. 47*.

Barrot, J. 2005. *Opening Address,* on Behalf of the European Union Commission, China European Conference on Developments in Open Skies Agreements, Beijing, 30 June.

Baum, R. 1994. *Burying Mao: Chinese Politics in the Age of Deng Xiaoping*, Princeton: Princeton University Press.

Baumol, W.J., Panzar, J. and Willig, R. 1987. *Contestable Markets and the Theory of Industry Structure,* San Diego: Harcourt, Brace Janovitch.

Beall, B. 2005. *US–EU Open Skies International Aviation Agreement Case Study Working Paper.* George Washington University Working Paper Series, Washington DC, 3 May, 1–9.

Bisignani, G. 2008. *Editorial*, IATA Industry Times Edition, 10 October.

Bitzinger, R.A. 2004. Civil Military Integration and Chinese Military Modernization, Honolulu, *Asia Pacific Center for Security Studies*, 3(9), 1–9.

Bliss, C. and Haddock, R. 2008. *Integrating China into Your Global Supply Chain,* New York: Booz, Allen and Hamilton Inc.

Boatai, C. 1986. *Foreign Investment in China,* Beijing: Foreign Languages Press.

Bolton, J. and Sleigh, A. 2007. China the Infrastructure Imperative, Outlook, *Journal of High Performance Business*, Accenture Consultants Inc. 2, 1–8.

Bomal, C., Foramin, A. and Perez, A. 2007. *A New Leap Forward for China's Overseas Investment Development,* Bangkok, Thailand: The Asia Institute of Technology, School of Management,.

Bounova, G., Silvis, J., Li, Q., Huang, Y. and Li, J.L. 2006. Analysis and Optimization of Airline Networks: A Case Study of China, Santa Fe Institute of Theoretical Physics and Chinese Academy of Social Sciences CASS.

Brahm, L.J. 2002. *Zhu Rongji: The Transformation of Modern China*, Singapore: John Wiley and Sons.

Bromnelhorster, J. and Frankenstein, J. (eds) 1997. *Mixed Motives: Uncertain Outcomes Defence Conversion in China,* Boulder, Colorado: Lynne Reiver.

Burns, J.P. 1989. Chinese Civil Service Reform: The 13th Party Congress Proposals, *The China Quarterly*, 120, 739–70.

CAAC (now General Administration of Civil Aviation in China (GCAAC)) *Reports on the Development of China Air Transport System 2000–08*, accessible on China.govt.cn

CAAC Decree No 110 1986, On the Provision of Foreign Direct Investment in China's Civil Aviation Industry, Beijing, China.govt.cn

Caijing Annual Year Book 2008. Business Forecast Studies, *Aviation in 2008, Turbulence Ahead,* 44–8.

Cao, C. 2004. Challenges for Technological Development in China's Industry, *China Perspectives,* 54, 1–20.

CAPA (Centre for Asia Pacific Aviation) 2007. China Aviation Daily Newsletters, 2005–08, publications@centreforaviation.com.

CAPA, 2008. *Monthly Essential China,* Issue 68, February.

CAPA, 2008. China Airports Outlook, 2–12.

Carter, C. 2001. *Globalizing South China,* RGS-IBE Series, Oxford: Blackwells.

Chandra, S. 2000. *Strategy Lessons from the Spectacular Growth in China Civil Aviation: A Viewpoint,* Bangalore, India: National Aerospace Laboratories.

Changshun, W. 2007. China is Focused on Safety Improvements in Spite of Rapid Industry Growth, *The ICAO Journal*, 61(2), 7–10-33.

Chen, K. 2006. Joint Efforts to Promote and Expand China's Regional Aviation, Strategic Development and Planning Department, Hainan Airlines, Zhuhai International Aviation Fair, October.

Chen, X.P. 2004. On the Intricacies of the Chinese Guanxi, *Asia Pacific Journal of Human Resource Management*, 21(3), 305–24.

Chen, Y.F and Tjosveld, D. 2005. Cross Cultural Leadership, *Journal of International Management*, 11(4), 417–39.

Cheng, T.C.E. 2003. Supply Chain Performance in Transport Logistics by Service Providers, *International Journal of Logistics Research and Applications*, 6(3), 151–65.

Cheung, T.M.M. 2007. The Remaking of the Chinese Defence Industry with the Rise of the Dual Economy, Testimony before the US–China Economic and Security Review, Washington, DC.

Child, J 1997. Management in China, in Dickson, D. (ed.), *Exploring Management Across the World*, London: Penguin Books, 303–30.

Chirathivat, S. 2002. The ASEAN–China Free Trade Agreement: Background, Implications and Future Development, *Journal of Asian Economics,* 13(5) September, 671–86.

Chow, G.C. 2007. *China's Economic Transformation*, 2nd edn, Oxford: Blackwell.

Chung, H.J. 2003. The Political Economy of Industrial Restructuring in China: The Case of Civil Aviation, *The China Journal*, 50, 61–82.

Chung, H.W. 2003. Economic Reform and Path Dependence in China: A Comparative Study of Reform and Development in Nanjing and Suzhou, *Asian Perspective*, 27(2), 205–39.

Clegg, S., Wang, K. and Berrell, M. (eds) 2007. *Business Networks and Strategic Alliances in China*, Cheltenham: Edward Elgar.

Dawson, S. 1996. *Analysing Organizations,* 3rd edn, London: Macmillan Business.

Dimancescue, P., Hines, P. and Rich, N. 1997. *The Lean Enterprise: Designing and Managing Strategic Processes for Customer Winning Performance*, New York: Amacon.

Doganis, R. 2001. *The Airline Business in the Twenty-first Century*, London: Routledge.

Doganis, R. 2002. *Flying of Course: The Economics of International Airlines*, 3rd edn, London: Routledge.

Doganis, R. 2006. *The Airline Business,* 2nd edn, London: Routledge.

Dual, D.T. 2008. Regulation, Competition and Politics of Air Access Across the Pacific, *The Journal of Air Transport Management*, 14(5), 237–42.

Enright, M.J. and Scott, E.E. 2007. *The Greater Pearl River Delta: Invest in Hong Kong,* 5th edn, Hong Kong: Enright Scott and Associates.

European Commission, 2007. *Flying Together*, Directorate General for Energy and Transport.

Fan, S. and Chan-Kang, C. 2005. *Road Development, Economic Growth and Poverty Reduction*, International Food Policy Research Institute, Research Report No. 138, Washington DC.

Fan, T., Vigeant-Langlois, L. and Geisler, C. 2001. Evolution of Global Airline Strategic Alliances and Consolidation in the Twenty-first Century, *Journal of Air Transport Management*, 7(6), 349–60.

Ferguson, N. 2001. *The Cash Nexus: Money and Power in the Modern World, 1700–2000*, London: Penguin Books.

Ferguson, N. 2004. *Empire: How Britain Made the World*, London: Penguin Books.

Ferguson, N. 2006. *The War of the World*, London: Penguin Books.

Findlay, C. and Goldstein, A. 2004. Liberalization and Foreign Direct Investment in Asian Transport Systems: The Case of Aviation, *Asian Development Review*, 24(1), 37–65.

Fleming, D.K., Hayuth, Y. and Spatial, P. 1994. Characteristics of Transportation Hubs Capability and Intermediacy, *Journal of Transport Geography*, 2(3), 3–18.

Forsyth, P., King, J. and Rodolfo, C.L. 2006. Open Skies in ASEAN, *Journal of Air Transport Management*, 12(3), 143–52.

Francis, C.-B. 2000. *The Defence Sector as a Window into China's National System of Innovation*, Peace Studies Programme, Cornell University, Ithaca, New York, Occasional Paper, 25, 168–73.

Fulbrook, D. 2004. China's Regional Airlines Fail to Takeoff, *Asian Times*, 9 September, 1–2.

Fulin, C. 2008. *Starting Point: Thirty Years of Reform in China*, Beijing: Foreign Languages Press.

Fung, M.A., Zhang, A., Leung, L. and Law, J. 2005. The Air Cargo Industry in China: Implications of Globalization, *Transportation Journal*, 44, 44–62.

Fung, M.K.Y., Wan, K.K.H, Huy, Y.Y. and Law, J. 2008. Productivity Changes in Chinese Airports, 1995–2004, *Transportation Research Part E, Logistics and Transport Review*, 44(3), 521–42.

Gang, F. 2001. *Report on the Regional Use of Relative Indices in Marketization in China*, (online) http://www.govt.cn.

Garnaut, R. and Song, L. (eds) 2005. *The China Boom and its Discontents*, Canberra: ANU Asia Pacific Press.

Garran, R. 1998. *Tiger Tamed: The End of the Asian Miracle*, Adelaide: Allen and Unwin.

GCAAC Decree No. 10 2005. *Report on Changes Relating to the Provision of Foreign Direct Investment in China's Aviation Industry*, Beijing: China.govt.cn.

GCAAC. *Report on the Development of China's Air Traffic Management System: 2006–2007* China.govt.com

Gelb, C. and Chen, D. 2004. Going West a Progress Review, *China Business Review*, 10 May, 1–10.

Gelber, Harry G. 2007. *The Dragon and the Foreign Devils: China and the World, 1100 BC to the Present*, London: Bloomsbury.

Goldstein, A. 2005. *The Political Economy of Industrial Policy in China: The Case of Aircraft Manufacturing*, Proceedings of the CEAUK-ACESA International Conference, Chongqing University, 31 March.

Gong, T. 2002. Dangerous Collusion: Corruption as a Collective Result in China. *Communist and Post Communist Studies*, 35(1), 85–103.

Gray, J. 1990. *Rebellion and Revolutions: China from the 1800s to the 1980s*, Oxford: Oxford University Press

Gries, P.H. 2004. *China's New Nationalism, Pride, Politics and Diplomacy*, Berkeley: University of California Press.

Groves, T., Hong, Y., Macmillan, J. and Naughton, B. 1995. China's Evolving Managerial Labour Market, *The Journal of Political Economy*, 103(4) August, 873–92.

Guangyuan, Y. 1984. *China's Socialist Modernizations*, Beijing: Foreign Language Press.

Guoguang, L. and Wensen, L. 1987 (2nd edn 2000). *China in 2000*, Beijing: New World Press.

Gurtov, M. 1993. Swords into Ploughshares, *China Quarterly*, 134, June, 213–41.

Hanxian, L. 1985. *Economic Changes in Rural China*, China Studies Series, Beijing: New World Press.

Hassard, J., Morris, J., Sheehan, J. and Xioyo, Y. 2006. Downsizing the Danwei China State Enterprise Reform and the Surplus Labour Question, *International Journal of Human Resource Management*, 17(8), 1441–55.

He, J. and Yang, Y. 1999. *The Political Economy of Trade Liberalization in China*, ANU Asia Pacific School of Economics and Management, Working Paper Series, 1–24.

He, W. and Lyles, M.A. 2008. China's Outward Foreign Direct Investment, *Business Horizons*, 51(6), 485–91.

Holz, C.A. 2006. *China's Economic Growth 1978–2005. What We Know Today about China's Economic Growth Tomorrow?* Hong Kong: University of Science and Technology.

Hong, J., Liling, R. and Hansman, R.J. 2002. *Market and Infrastructure Analysis of Future Air Cargo Demand in China*, Washington DC: American Institute of Aeronautics and Aerospace.,

Houser, T. 2008, *Finding Agreement on Climate in a Crisis*, Petersen Institute for International Economics (Op-ed distributed through Project Syndicate, 23 December 2006).

Hughes, N. 2008. *A Promising Future for China's Aviation Industry*, Washington DC: National Defence Policy Association.,

Huang, D. 2000. Unrest in Airline Markets, *Beijing Morning News*, 19 April, 1–2.

IMF 1993. *China at the Threshold of the Market Economy*, Occasional Paper No 107, Washington DC.

ICAO, 2007. China Focused on Safety Improvements in Spite of Rapid Industry Growth, *ICAO Journal,* 62(2) March–April, 7–12.

ICAO, 2007. *Review of RVSM Flight Level Allocation System in China, Bangkok,* Agenda Item 2, 12–16 March, RVSM/TF/30-IP/02.

ICAO, 2007. *Review of the 30th Meeting of the ICAO RVSM Implementation Task Force*, Paris, TRASAS/I-IP/02, 12 April.

ICAO, 2007. *Working Paper RVSM Implementation Plan and Flight Harmonization in China*, Technical Commission A36-WP/176 TE/48, 14 September.

ICAO, 2007. *Implementation of the RVSM in Sovereign China Airspace*, Agenda Item 3, Report on the Relevant Outcomes from Other Pertinent Meetings, Edmonton, Canada, CPWG/4-IP/7, 1–21 September.

ICAO, 2007. *The Thirty-second Meeting of the ICAO RVSM Implementation Task Force*, Beijing, RVSM/TF/32-WP/9.

Jaggi, G., Randle M., Resen, D. and Takahashi Y. 1996. *China's Economic Reforms, Chronology and Statistics*, Washington DC: The Petersen Institute for International Economics, Working Paper 96-5, 1–31.

Janso, J. 1998. Post-merger Strategies of the Leading US Aerospace Companies, Stockholm Defence Research Establishment SDRE FAO-R-98-oo941-170-SE.

Jenkins, M. 2002. 30 Years and Counting: The Boeing Company m.jenkins@boeing.com

Jiang, H., Ren, L. and Hansman, J. 2003. *Market and Infrastructural Analysis for Future Air Cargo Demand in China*, AIAA 3rd Annual Technology and Operations Conference, ATIO, Denver, Colorado, 17–19 November.

Jin, F. Wang, F. and Liu, Yu. 2004. Geographic Patterns of Air Transport in China 1980–1998: Imprints of Economic Growth, Regional Inequality and Network Development, *The Professional Geographer*, 56(4) November, 471–87.

Kah, A.E. 1988. Surprises of Aviation Deregulation, *American Economic Review Papers and Proceedings*, 78(2) May, 316–22.

Karaev, Z. 2005. Border Disputes and Regional Integration in Central Asia, *Harvard Asia Review*, 9(4), 1–15.

Kasarda, J. 2000. *Aeropolis Airports Drive Urban Development in the Twenty-first Century*, New York: The Urban Institute.

Kasarda, J. 2004. Asia's Emerging Airport Cities, *Urban Land Asia*, December, 18–21.

Kasarda, J.D. and Green, J. 2004. *Air Cargo: Engine of Economic Development*, IACA: Air Cargo Forum, Bilbao, Spain, 15 September, p. 5.

Kelly, E. 2008. China not Ready to take the Next Step, *Asian Aviation*, 5(8), 32.

Kemerade, W. Van 1996. *China, Hong Kong, Taiwan Inc. – The Dynamics of a New Empire*, London: Little Brown and Company.

Kogan, E. 2004. Russia China Aerospace Industries from Cooperation to Disengagement, Association for Asian Research, .org

KPMG 2008. *Transport in China, Property and Infrastructure Report*, Hong Kong.

Kynge, J.K. 2006. *China Shakes the World the Rise of a Hungry Nation*, London: Nicolson.

Lam, N.M. and Graham, J.L. 2007. *China Now: Doing Business in the World's Most Dynamic Market*, New York: McGraw-Hill.

Lau, K.H. 2003. Supply Chain Performance in Transport Logistics: An Assessment by Service Providers, *International Journal of Logistics Research and Applications*, 6(3), 151–65.

Le Thuong, T. 1997. Reforming China's Airline Industry: From State Owned to Market Dynamics, *Transportation Journal*, 22 December.

Li, L. 2001. Deregulation of Air Fares, *Aviation Market News*, 3 March, 6.

Li, X. 1998. *Development, Conception and Implementation of China's Air Traffic Management System*, CANSO Civil Air Management Sources Organization, Proceedings of the Conference on the Economics of Airport and Air Navigation Services, Montreal, 14–20 September.

Liebenstein, H. 1966. Allocative Efficiency versus X-Efficiency, *American Economic Review*, 56, 392–415.

Liew, L.H. 2005. China's Engagement with NeoLiberalism, Path Dependency, Geography and Self Reinvention, *Journal of Development Studies*, 41(2) February, 331–52.

Lin, C. 2001. Corporatization and Corporate Governance in China's Economic Transition, *Economics of Planning*, 34, 5–35.

Lin, G.C.S. 2002. The Growth and Structural Change of Chinese Cities: A Contextual and Geographical Analysis, *Cities*, 19(5) October, 299–316.

Lin, J.Y., Cai, F. and Zhou, W. 2003. *The China Miracle: Development Strategies and Economic Reform*, revised edn, Hong Kong: Chinese University of Hong Kong Press.

Lin, Y.M. 2007. *Between Politics and Markets: Firms, Competition and Institutional Change in Post-Mao China*, Cambridge: Cambridge University Press.

Linbeck, A. 2006. An Essay on Economic Reform and Social Change in China, *World Bank Policy Research Paper No. 4057*, Geneva.

Liu, D. 2000. *Introduction to Civil Aviation in China*, Beijing: China Civil Aviation Press.

Liu, Q. 2006. The First Step toward Super Ministries, Chinatoday.com.cn.

Loveridge, R. and Mok, A. 1979. *Theories of Labour Market Segmentation*, The Hague: Martin Nijhoff.

Ma, G. and McCauley, R.N. 2008. Efficacy of China's capital Controls: Evidence from Price and Flow Data, *Pacific Economic Review*, 13(1), 104–23.

Ma, Hong (ed.) 1990. *Modern China's Economy and Management*, Beijing: Foreign Language Press.

McGregor, J. 2005. *One Billion Customers*, New York: Wall Street Journal Books, Free Press.

Me, E. R., Renzhang, Y. and Haoshing, B. 1985. *An Outline of China's Physical Geography*, China Knowledge Series, Beijing: Foreign Language Press.

Meyer, M.W. 2008. China's Second Economic Transition: Building National Markets, *Management and Organization Review*, 4(1) 3–13, Oxford: Blackwell.

MOFCOM 2005. *China Trade in Services: Supplementary Provisions to the Provision On Foreign Investment in the Civil Aviation Industry*, Order 139 of the CAAC-MOC-NDRC.

Morck, R., Yeung, B. and Zhao, M.Z. 2008. Perspectives on China's Outward Foreign Investment, *Journal of International Business Studies*, 39(3) April, 337–50.

Nathan, A.J. and Gilley, B. 2002. *China's New Rulers, the Secret Files*, London: Granta.

Naughton, B. 2007. *The Chinese Economy Transitions and Growth*, London: MIT Press.

Ngok, K. and Zhu, G. 2007. Marketing Globalization and Administration in China: A Zig Zag Road to a Promising Future, *International Review of Administrative Sciences*, 73(2), 217–33, London: Sage.

Ning, Y. 2007. *Yangtze Delta Region Urbanization Development and Megalopolis Restructuring*, Proceedings of the International Conference on Population Geographies, 10–13 July, Hong Kong: Chinese University of Hong Kong.

Nizhe, J. 2000. (online) *Introduction to the Implementation of the GWDS in China*, available at Beijing Chinagate.co.cn.

Nogalis, A. 2004. *Transport Sector Brief, East Asia and the Pacific Region*, Manilla: World Bank–Asia Development Bank..

Nolan, P.2001. *China and the Global Economy, National Champions, Industrial Policy and Big Business*, Basingstoke: Palgrave.

Nolan, P. 2003a. *China at the Crossroads*, Cambridge: Polity Press.

Nolan, P. 2003b. *Evaluation of the World Bank's Contribution to Chinese Enterprise Reform* Washington DC: World Bank Operations Evaluation Department..

Nolan, P. 2003c. *System Fragility, Industrial Policy and China's International relations with Special Reference to Strategic Industries*. Evidence before the US Congress: US–China Economic and Security Review Commission, Washington DC.

Nolan, P. 2004. *Transforming China, Globalization, Transition and Development*, London: Anthem.

Nolan, P. and Zhang, J. 2003. Globalization Challenges for Large Firms from Developing Countries: China's Oil and Aerospace Industries, *European Management Journal*, 21(3), 285–99.

Nolan, P., Zhang, J. and Chunhang, L. 2007. *The Global Business Revolution: System Integration in Global Aerospace, Beverage and Retail Industries*, London: Palgrave.

Nolan, P., Zhang, J. and Chunhang, J. 2008. The Global Business Revolution: The Cascade Effect and the Challenge for Firms from Developing Countries, *Cambridge Journal of Economics*, 32, 29–47.

OAG 2008. Press release, 21 May.

Oster, C.V. and Strong, J.S. 2007. *Managing the Skies: Public Policy Organization and the Financing of Air Traffic Control?* London: Ashgate Aviation.

Oum, T.H., Park, J. and Zhang, A. 2000. *Globalization and Strategic Alliances: The Case of the Airline Industry*, Oxford: Pergamon Press.

Oum, T.H. and Lee, Y.H. 2002. The Northeast Asian Air Transport Network: Is there the Possibility of Creating Open Skies in the Region? *Journal of Air Transport Management*, 8(5) September, 325–37.

Panitchpakdi, C. and Clifford, M.L. 2002. *China and the WTO: Changing China Changing World Trade*, Singapore: John Wiley and Sons Ltd.

Park, J., Zhang, A. and Zhang, Y. 2001. Analytical Models of International Alliances in the Airline Industry, *Transportation Research B (Methodological)*, 35, 865–86.

Park, J., Park, N. and Zhang, A. 2003. The Impact of Alliances on Firm Value, *Transportation Research E (Logistics)*, 39, 1–18.

Pearson, M.M. 1997. *China's New Business Elite: The Political Consequences of Economic Reform*, Berkeley: University of California Press.

Pearson, M.M. 2005. The Business of Governing Business in China: Institutions and Norms of the Emerging State, *World Politics*, 5(7) January, 296–322.

Porter, M.E. 1990. *The Competitive Advantage of Nations*, London: Macmillan.

Protopenko, J. 1997. Privatization: Lessons from Russia and China, *Enterprise and Management Development Working Paper EMD/24/E,* ILO Entrepreneurship and Management Development Branch, Geneva.

Pudong Government Commission.gov.cn.

Quah, D. 2002. Technology Dissemination and Economic Growth: Some Lessons for the New Economy, *LSE-CERR Discussion Paper 320/07*, The London School of Economics.

Quong, Liu. 2006. *The First Step Toward Super Ministries*, Chinatoday.com.cn.

Ralston, D.A., Holt, D.H., Temstra, R.H. and Cheng, Y.K. 2008. The Impact of National Culture and Economic Ideology on Managerial Work Values: A Study of the US, Russia, Japan and China, *Journal of International Business Studies*, 39(1), 8–26.

Ren, J. 2006. Strategies for the Economic Reform and development of Western China, *International Studies*, 43(3), 411–18.

Rimmer, P.J. and Comptois, C. 2002. China's Transport and Communications: Transforming National Champions into Global Players, *Asia Pacific Viewpoint*, 43(1) April, 93–114 (revised 2006).

Rui, G. and Peng, C. 2007. Dynamic Air Routes and the Open-Close Problem for Air Space Management, *Tsinghua Journal of Science and Technology*, 12(6), 647–51.

Russell, E. 2007. China Blocks Take-off of New Airlines, *Asia Times,* 30 August, 1.

Saich, A. 2001. *Government and Politics of China*, Basingstoke: Palgrave.

Savant, K. 2008. Chinese MNEs make Steady Progress, Fudan-VCC Fudan University and Vale Columbia Center, Columbia University, Press release, 22 October.

Senguttavan, P.S. 2006. Air Cargo: Engine for Growth and Development: A Case Study of the Asian Region, Metrans Transportation Center, School of Policy Planning and Development, University of Southern California, National Urban Freight Conference, February 1–3.

Service, R. 2002. *Russia: Experiment with a People*, London: Macmillan.

Shambaugh, D. 2005. *Power Shift; China and Asia's New Dynamics*, London: Macmillan.

Shen, Li, The Eight Key Tasks for Future Western China Development, Chinagate. co.cn.

Sheng, J.L.J., Li, B. and Miao, J. 2003. *Investment in China: Opportunities in Private Equity and Venture Capital*, Beijing: Tsinghua University Press.

Shenguan, G.S. and Fulin, C. 1996. *The Development of China's Non-governmentally and Privately Operated Economy*, Beijing: Foreign Language Press.

Shenkar, O. 2006. *The Chinese Century*, Philadelphia: Wharton School Publishing, University of Pennsylvania,.

Shun, Z. 2008. Reform of China's Defence Industry, in Pilsbury, M. (ed.) *Chinese Views of Future Warfare*, Washington DC: Institute for National Strategic Studies.

Sigurdson, J. 2004. *PRC Technological Capability, Latin America, Caribbean and Asia–Pacific*, Economics and Business Association Conference, Working Paper 25, Beijing, 3–4 December.

Sims, T. and Schnelt, J.J. 2000.The Great Western Development Strategy, *The Chinese Business Review*, November–December, 1–10.

Snow, E. 1956. *The Birth of Communist China*, London: Pelican Books

Sunian, L. and Qungan, W. 1986. *China's Social Economy an Outline History: 1949–1984*, Beijing: Review Publishing.

Su, Y., Xu, D. and Phan, P.H. 2008. Principal–Principal Conflict in the Governance of the Chinese Public Corporation, *Management and Organization Review*, 4 (1) 17-38, Oxford: Blackwell.

Sweeney, P. 2008. Flying without Succeeding: Assessing the Future of the Civil Aerospace Manufacturing Sector in the PRC, *The Journal of Policy Solutions*, 8, 1–17.

Tanger, R.H. 2008. *The Air Cargo Market between China and the United States: Demand, Developments and Competition, Kellogg School of Management*, Northwestern University, Booz Allen Hamilton, McLean, Virginia, China Air Cargo Summit, Guangzhou, PRC, 27 March.

Ting, A. 2008. *Can ASEAN fully Liberalize its Aviation Market by 2025?* (online 2 November) Available at http://www.com/my bernana/US/news_lite.php? id =369434.

Terry, E. (ed) 2007. *Pearl River Super Zone, Tapping into the World's Fastest Growing Economy*, Hong Kong: SCMP Book Publishing.

US Department of State, 2008. *US–China Dialogue Fact Sheet* (accessed 30 July).

US Government Accounting Office, *Transatlantic Aviation Effects of Easing Restrictions on US European Markets*, GAO-04-835.

Vasigh, B. Fleming, K. and Tacker, T. 2008. *Introduction to Air Transport Economics: From Theory to Applications*, Aldershot: Ashgate.

Vines, S. 1999. *The Years of Living Dangerously: Asia from Financial Crisis to the New Millenium*, London: Orion Books.

Wang, J.E. and Fang-Jun, J. 2007. China's Air Passenger Transport: An Analysis of Recent Trends, *Eurasian Geography and Economics*, 48(4), 469–80.

Wang, S. 2008, Changing Models of China's Policy Setting Agenda, *Modern China*, 34(1), 56–87.

Wang, Y. and Li, J. 2006. Business Planning Management for Sustainable Transportation, *World Transport Policy and Practice*, Special Issue on Transportation in China, 12(4), 29–34.

Warner, M. 1996. Chinese Enterprise Reform, Human Resources and the 1994 Labour Law, *International Journal of Human Resource Management*, 7(4) December, 779–96, London: Routledge.

Warner, M. 2008. Reassessing Human Resource Management with Chinese Characteristics, *International Journal of Human Resource Management*, 19(5), May, 771–801.

Wei, T. 2007. Flying the Busy Skies, *Beijing Review*.

Williams, A. 2006. *Developing Strategies for the Modern International Airport: East Asia and Beyond*, Aldershot: Ashgate.

Williams, A. 2007. Low Cost Carriers and the Need for Consolidation: A Speculative Overview, *Journal of Aviation Management*, Singapore, SAA-CAAS, 67–74.

Williams, A and Williams, B.A. 2008. *Labour Contract Reform under the Fourth Generation, some Emergent Problematics in China's Labour Market*, Fifth Bi-annual Conference of the New Zealand Development Network – DEVNET, Victoria University of Wellington, 3–5 December, 1–15.

Williams, D. 2004. Chinese Airline Industry's Indigenous Transformation, *Asian Aviation*, 5(8), 22.

Wilkinson, F. (ed.) 1981. *The Dynamics of Labour Market Segmentation*, London: Academic Press.

Wong, J. and Ding, L. 2002. *China's Economy in the New Century: Structural Issues and Problems*, London for Singapore University Press: World Scientific.

Wragg, D. 2007. *The World's Major Airlines*, Chalford, Gloucester: Sutton Publishing, MPI Media Group Ltd.

Xiaoping, Deng. 1985. *Building Socialism with Chinese Characteristics*, Beijing: Foreign Languages Press.

Xie, R., Chen, H. and Nash, C. 2000. *The Migration of Railway Freight Transport from Command Economy to Market Economy: The Case of China*, Institute of Transport Studies, University of Leeds, Working paper 554, ITS White Rose Consortium.

Xiehong, Fan. 2004. Grasp the Core of Informization, Jiefangjun Bao in FBIS, 8.

Yang, D.L. 1996. Governing China's Transition to the Market International Political Choices and Unintended Outcomes, *World Politics*, 48(3) April, 422–57.

Yang, D.L. 2004. *Remaking the Chinese Leviathan, Market Transition and the Politics of Governance in China*, Paulo Alto: Stanford University Press.

Yang, J. and Gakenheimer, J. 2007. Assessing the Transportation Consequences of Land Use Transformation in Urban China., *Habitat International*, 31(3–4), September–December, 345–53.

Yueng, C. 1998. *Hong Kong, China the Red Dawn*, Sydney: Prentice Hall.

Yom, S.L. 2002. Power Politics in Central Asia, *Harvard's Asia Quarterly*, 6(4) Autumn, 1–7.

Zhang, A, 1997. *Industrial Reform and Aviation Transport Development in China*, University of British Columbia Business School Occasional Paper No. 17.

Zhang, Y and Round, D.K. 2008. China's Airline Deregulation Since 1997 and the Driving Forces behind the 2002 Consolidation, *Journal of Air Transport Management*, 14(3), 1–48.

Zhao, S.X., Tong, C.S. and Qiao, J. 2002. China's WTO Accession, State Enterprise Reform and Spatial Economic Restructuring, *Journal of International Development*, 14(3), 413–33.

Zheng, L. and Ong, A. 2008. *Privatizing China: Socialism from Afar*, Ithaca, London: Cornell University Press.

Zhou, W. and Szyliowicz, S. 2004. The Development and Current Status of China's Transportation System, *World Transport Policy and Practice*, 12(4), London, Lancaster: Eco-Logica Ltd.

Index